Improving Reading Instruction

DONALD D. DURRELL

Professor of Education, Boston University

Improving
Reading Instruction

HARCOURT, BRACE & WORLD, INC.
NEW YORK, CHICAGO, SAN FRANCISCO, ATLANTA

PREFACE

THE QUALITY OF reading instruction depends primarily upon one person: the classroom teacher. Basal readers, supplementary materials, supervisory assistance, and professional books are intended to help the teacher serve pupils better; but all of these are futile unless they are used with imagination and good judgment. The remarkable challenge of teaching every child to read, instead of dropping half of the children from school by the end of the sixth grade as we did prior to 1920, has been met in a most commendable manner. Yet teachers are not content with their present achievement. No subject in the elementary school curriculum attracts more teachers in university courses and in professional meetings.

In the sixteen years since the appearance of *Improvement of Basic Reading Abilities,* the author and his associates have shared the reading instruction problems of more than twelve thousand teachers through extension courses. Each group of teachers begins with a self-survey of the reading needs and instructional problems of children in classrooms. This analysis is followed immediately by a host of questions which must be met in a specific and practical fashion, usually accompanied by demonstrations with children from local classrooms. This book contains our present answers to the questions which most commonly arise.

The emphasis in reading instruction is rapidly changing from remedial to *developmental.* We are more concerned about prevention of difficulties through excellent classroom teaching. The reading consultant who helps the teacher with slow learners is rapidly replacing the remedial teacher who works with children who have already failed. It is most encouraging to find many school systems in which reading disability is exceedingly rare. While the need for remedial instruction continues, the more successful methods of the remedial teacher are the same as those used in the more effective classrooms. The problems of children in our Educational Clinic are almost exactly the same as those found by the classroom analyses made by teachers. Remedial, clinical, and classroom instruction are very similar and no separate treatment of them is presented.

Our aim is to present a practical handbook, not a research report. While it is tempting to support the recommended practices by detailed summaries of pertinent findings from the five hundred master's and doctor's studies which have been conducted at Boston University, space does not permit their addition. The research background for this volume will appear in an accompanying monograph, *Reading Research: Problems, Techniques, and Findings.*

The reading service and research program at Boston University is shared by many highly competent people: Helen B. Sullivan, Helen A. Murphy, B. Alice Crossley, Olive S. Niles, Thomas H. Eames, Lorraine E. Tolman. I am grateful to them for assistance in the preparation of this volume and for the zest which they bring to the search for ways of improving services to teachers and children.

DONALD D. DURRELL
Boston University

CONTENTS

CHAPTER 1 **Effective Reading Instruction**

THERE ARE MANY ways to teach reading well. There are also many ways to teach it badly. Despite the large number of publications on the teaching of reading—professional books, teachers' manuals, national committee reports, magazine articles, and research studies— we have not yet discovered a definite series of steps which a teacher may follow with the assurance that all pupils will grow in reading in the most efficient manner. No basal system of reading has been produced which makes automatic adjustments to the instructional needs of the pupils. Even with the best of currently used materials, the effectiveness of learning depends far more upon the activities of the teacher than upon the basal-reading system being used.

There is little hope of discovering a "one best way" that will fit all pupils, all local situations, and all teachers. What is required for a small group of pupils of high intelligence in an economically favored community may be very different from the requirements of a large class of pupils of marked differences in mental ability in an impoverished community. A fine school library, a highly cooperative public library, a rich supply of magazines in homes and schools, a public ready to cooperate with services of all types, and a high interest in the education of children, offer teaching opportunities not found in situations where the reverse is true.

What is needed in the content of reading for schools of a densely populated industrial city may be quite different from the needs of a sparsely populated farming community. One must admit, also, that there are marked differences in the ability and interests of teachers. Thus, a teacher with little training and low ability may do better with a system in which every step is given in detail. A teacher with better training and experience will give much superior service to pupils by providing her own variations from any system.

Need for enterprise in teaching

Reading instruction is not a well-established field in which all knowledge has been revealed, all steps to building skills known, and all methods of developing a rich variety of tastes and interests well understood. While research and intelligent observation have provided us with many helps to understanding the problems and methods of teaching reading, there are still large areas for exploration and discovery. We still produce large numbers of "reading disabilities" of different degrees and are more apt in finding plausible excuses for our failure than in searching for ways to prevent the failures. We are still searching for better methods of analysis of weaknesses in learning, better ways of providing for differences in reading level and learning rate, more successful ways of giving intensive instruction for children's particular needs, and more effective motivation of learning.

No one can claim a highly successful program in the development of initiative in a variety of tastes, interests, and uses of reading. We still produce some permanent aversions to poetry, drama, fiction, biography, history, science, and reading in general. And in the field of the development of personal and social qualities through our methods and materials of instruction, teachers produce marked differences in results without knowing why.

We are not alone in imperfection of our activities. This rather embryonic state of knowledge is to be found in all areas of human endeavor. A state of perfect knowledge and practice is not to be found in medicine, engineering, law, government, industry, business, banking, or religion. We still have diseases of which we do not know the cause or cure, and medical service varies greatly in its competence and availability. Constant improvements in automobiles, electric appliances, and machines suggest far greater future improvements. Everyone is aware of traffic injuries and fatalities, and city dwellers are unhappy about parking problems.

We still have labor strife, farm problems, tax problems, delinquency and crime problems, and we are never free from the threat of war. The huge flow of prospective laws and regulations in our state and national legislatures, the large industrial research laboratories, the great foundation grants, and the tremendous number of research studies in universities provide evidence of the vigorous search for improvement in all sorts of human endeavor.

This state of relative imperfection is not to be deplored. Actually it provides the main incentives for mankind and the chief defense of the democratic way of life. The search for the laws of matter and man and for ways of using and conforming to these laws is the basic activity of all professions. Democracy is the best instrument thus far discovered for encouraging enterprise in the solution of these problems.

When there is so much to be learned, every individual must be free to pursue promising paths to better living. The greater the variety of approaches, the greater the possibility of making advances in knowledge of better ways to serve society. Regimentation and standardization of current ignorance are characteristic of controlled societies, and although democracy occasionally produces regulations and laws which at least temporarily standardize current ignorance, it does provide a ready avenue for change. The encouragement of differences, of change, and of progress is fundamental in a developing society.

The urgency and scope of public education are so great that we must enlist all of the wisdom and imagination of the profession to find better ways of serving children. No other national activity is so intimate in its relationship to the development of personal qualities and achievements. No other is so universal or requires so much time of every individual. No other takes a larger share of local tax support or has the compelling force of legislation to require its use. It is therefore highly important that every teacher share the responsibility of the search for improved service to children.

Fortunately the teacher is relatively free to take part in this search. Federal control of education is universally opposed as unwise, and the more enlightened states have resisted the imposition of regimentation on the local school boards. Even when the teacher has no part in the selection of the textbooks she uses, and when curricula are standardized by state law, the areas of individual freedom are greater than the areas of control. In view of the wide opportunities for variation and of the obvious imperfections in our achievements, it is somewhat surprising that there is such great uniformity in American schools. The best school systems are doing a great deal to encourage individual teachers to follow promising paths to more effective education. These systems take pride in the vigor that teachers show in finding different ways to enrich education, and they benefit from the exchange of successful practices by their teachers.

The teacher should not be afraid of being different. Differences are the springs of progress. Every forward step has required an individual who has differed from his fellows in some way. Differences in background, in points of view, in interests and tastes, and in methods are to be encouraged. They increase the likelihood that knowledge will move forward and that the future will be better than the past.

However, differences are not encouraged merely for the sake of difference. Where experience has clearly demonstrated the values of certain methods and content, a teacher will do well to utilize these gains. New ventures in education should show real promise of greater effectiveness. There must be constant evaluation of the ventures, and there should be provision for exchange of effective practice.

Of course, not all uniformity is undesirable. There must be overall plans, agreement on areas of responsibility, limits set upon the individual for the greater good of all individuals. Schools would be chaotic if every teacher decided what subjects should be taught, what should be included in each subject, the length of the school day, the time of recess periods, the use of various school services, and so on. Service to pupils requires over-all planning and the cooperation of teachers in those plans. Many of the objectives of education require team programs and planning, with every teacher joining whole-heartedly in the group venture. But there are so many areas of freedom within any group program that the individual teacher will usually find room for all of the imaginative planning of which she is capable.

Providing for individual differences: The new task in education

The chief problem in teaching is providing for individual differences. This problem is so new to education that we have made only a beginning in solving it. Before 1920 there was little concern about individual differences in the classroom. All children started in the same books, and the instruction progressed at the same rate for all pupils. Those who failed to make adequate progress were simply "held back" and given another try the next year. It was common to hold back about 30 per cent of first-grade pupils. The child guilty of failure was usually given a maximum sentence of three years in first grade and two years in each of the following grades if the offense was repeated. By the time he reached fourth or fifth grade, he was old enough to leave school, much to the relief of both pupil and teacher. In 1920, only one half of the entering pupils remained in school after the sixth grade.

This practice worked so well that one seldom heard of "reading difficulties." There were no remedial-reading classes, reading clinics, reading consultants or supervisors of reading. Children with reading difficulties were no longer around school after grade six. They were forgotten by the teacher, and the parent was resigned to the fact that his child was not capable of schooling.

High-school teachers were relatively happy with the children they received in 1920. They should have been. Less than 30 per cent of the pupils who started first grade survived to enter high school. This skimming the "cream off the cream" left only one half of the starting pupils in school after the sixth grade. These were the "good old days" when "standards were maintained"; perhaps not as "good" as thirty years earlier when the system was more effective and only 10 per cent arrived at high school. At the present time, over 70 per cent of all children enter high school, with 50 per cent of the pupils finishing tenth grade.

In the day of uniform instruction for all, the teacher's task was merely to offer the opportunity for learning. Those children who failed to keep up with the class were not her responsibility. Poor reading was merely an evidence of dullness or lack of application; it was considered good policy to get these laggards out of school as quickly as possible. The teacher recognized the inevitability of having a collection of this "human debris" in the primary grades, and thus these children were stored in classrooms until they reached working age.

With the long depression of the 1930's, there was little opportunity for children in the labor market, and working certificates were hard to obtain. At the same time, the wider use of intelligence tests in schools showed that at least 25 per cent of the failing children had normal or superior intelligence. The education of teachers improved greatly, since the school administrators no longer needed to employ the high-school graduate with six weeks of technical training. There was a greater desire on the part of the public for longer education of children. These causes and others accounted for a change of interest in the slow learner. Special classes were established for atypical children. Few children were held back in any grade; at the present time many school systems have less than 2 per cent retardation. It is now generally accepted that every child has a right to at least twelve years of schooling at public expense, and that it is the responsibility of the school to provide effective education for all.

This change in attitude makes providing for individual differences the main problem in skills instruction. In the "good old days" of elimination of slow pupils, a teacher of fourth-grade pupils needed only a fourth-grade reader, a fourth-grade social studies book, a fourth-grade arithmetic, a fourth-grade speller. The pupils were responsible for bringing fourth-grade achievement to the classroom, and finishing with skills adequate to meet fifth-grade standards. At present, the teacher of fourth-grade pupils expects to have a range of abilities about the same as she would find in all grades of a one-room rural school. And she is expected to provide teaching which will enable each child to make progress. This requires a high order of teaching ability. However, we have made such progress that any comparison of current elementary school achievement to that of the "good old days" shows that children make far greater progress under present instruction. We hope that in the future the child in the elementary schools who cannot read will be as rare as the child who cannot speak.

Opportunity for pioneering in the teaching of reading

Since most schools use basal-reading systems, it is sometimes believed that the teacher is relieved of the responsibility for individual decision; that the task of teaching is largely standardized. Actually the basal-reading system can provide only a fraction of the reading program. Most of the important decisions that affect the progress of the pupils remain in the hands of the teacher. Adjustments to differences in level of ability and learning rate, supplementary practice for slow learners, the challenging of rapid learners, the use of supplementary materials for practice and independent reading, the use of activities related to the reading program, the interrelationships between reading and the other language arts and other subjects—these decisions and others may be suggested by the manuals of the various basal-reading systems, but their selection, their development, and their use must rest upon the initiative of the classroom teacher.

It is the purpose of this textbook to suggest and illustrate many ways in which the teacher may supplement the basal reader to the advantage of her pupils. The chief difference between good and poor teaching of reading is found in the intelligence and initiative of the teacher in doing the following things:

1. Providing for individual differences in skills learning.
2. Providing for pupil initiative in a great variety of uses of reading.
3. Providing instruction which improves personal and social qualities of pupils.

Effective instruction in reading skills

Every teacher must be competent in skills instruction. While pupils may profit by differences in teacher emphasis on the literary and practical uses of reading, the teacher who claims professional competence must know how to analyze and improve the reading skills of her pupils. Freedom to try enriched instructional activities is based on an excellent skills program. Parents are not interested in activities to reach the broader objectives of education when it is evident that skills instruction is neglected. No amount of praise of the improvement in personal qualities and interests of the pupil, of his social and citizenship qualities, will satisfy the parent of the child who is not making progress in reading skills.

The first essential of skills instruction is the teacher's faith that every child can make progress. Regardless of the mental ability of the child, there is a level of learning suitable for him. If the teacher makes use of this level of learning, gives special practice to overcome special weaknesses, and assures a high level of motivation, every child can make progress in reading. There will be no progress where the teacher feels that the "child's mind is like a sieve" and that there is nothing to be done about it; nor will the teacher make much effort when she is immersed in theories of psychological and neurological quirks which are supposed to impede progress. Our current research shows that every child can make progress when suitable instruction is provided. Research shows us also that growth in reading ability depends on a great many factors other than intelligence, and that we have no ways of predicting clearly the rate of progress of any child.

The task of adapting instruction to various levels and types of pupil abilities in reading is done by skilled teachers in many ways. The following list of the activities of the superior skills teacher is a composite picture of the practices observed in the classrooms of many different teachers. No teacher need feel inferior because her classroom does not contain all of the elements in the program. A teacher may work effectively by combining only a few of these recommended practices. She should estimate which of these practices she does well and which might be added to her teaching repertory.

1. Providing for flexible grouping

The teacher has flexible grouping for reading instruction. The children are placed into reading groups on the basis of the most effective use of the pupils' and teacher's time. In basic-reading skills they are grouped for reading level and are provided with suitable materials. Sometimes the groups are large, and sometimes the pupils work independently or in pairs. In dramatic reading and various class projects the groups include children of various reading levels but these children are kept from having pride or social stigma attached to them. When it is advantageous, pupils are used as teachers.

2. Analyzing instructional needs of pupils

The teacher analyzes the instructional needs of the pupils. Informal measures and observations show each child's needs in vocabulary abilities, oral and silent reading, comprehension and recall, study abilities, and motivation needs. The observations are supported by definite check lists of the essential abilities. Instruction is then provided to help each child or group of children in the weaknesses discovered. Standard tests are used to evaluate growth in reading.

3. Providing for vocabulary growth

There is full attention to growth in vocabulary. The effective reading program always provides for three phases of vocabulary growth— meaning, recognition, and analysis. New materials are skimmed for unknown words, and their meanings taught in a variety of ways. Explanation is given through oral or pictured illustration, dramatization, or even field trips when the content presents a new experience. Children are taught to identify unknown words, to use context clues, and to use the dictionary. When materials are much too difficult for the child's reading vocabulary, but when learning of the ideas is essential, the materials are presented orally by the teacher. Recognition of new words is established by a variety of exercises and many types of presentation. Usually there is an emphasis on the meaning of the word rather than on its name. Growth in word recognition is measured by review tests in which the words are presented in new context.

Word-analysis abilities that improve learning rate in sight vocabulary and also enable the child to solve new words independently are built through carefully graded instruction. They include auditory and visual discrimination of words and elements, instruction in applied phonics, syllable analysis, and word building. The word-analysis exercises are often attached to the spelling lesson rather than to the reading lesson, and there is a unification of the vocabulary work in reading, spelling, handwriting, and composition. Children reading on a preprimer level who have difficulty in remembering words are given special perceptual training.

4. Providing effective oral-reading instruction

Oral-reading instruction is used effectively. When oral reading is used primarily for practice in reading, small groups or pupil pairs are used so that each child's turn comes often. The questions and comments of the pupils are related to the meaning of the story being read, and help is given quickly on difficult words to aid the flow of ideas. In oral-reading instruction, the material used contains not more than one difficult word in twenty running words. Instruction in oral reading has already been preceded by silent-reading preparation.

Skills of expression in oral reading are built through extensive reading of plays, choral reading, and the reading of especially interesting parts of stories, anecdotes, jokes, or new information useful to children. Audience interest is maintained through comments and questions, even in oral-reading practice. There is little "looking on the book and keeping the place" while other children are reading. Special help is given to pupils who have difficulty in phrase reading, voice, enunciation, or expression.

5. Assuring security and comprehension in silent reading

Security and comprehension are assured in silent reading. The child is helped to maintain his attention through the use of pre-reading discussion which makes the reading important, through the use of pre-reading study of essential words, through the use of study guides of various levels of details, and through the use of discussion after reading. Imagery in fiction is kept alive by children's reports of the different pictures of characters and situations in their minds. Speed of reading is encouraged by simple narrative reading, aided by occasional speed tests with records of improvement. However, speed is not gained at the expense of comprehension.

There is extensive use of supplementary readers, individual library reading, and reading of special topics related to content subjects. Children with faulty habits, such as lip movements and whispering in silent reading, are helped to overcome these difficulties. In all silent-reading instruction, the teacher helps the child find materials of a suitable level which are of interest to the child and to the class.

6. Giving specific help in study skills

Specific help is given in various types of study skills. The ability to remember what is read, to find applications and relationships with the points made, to read critically, and to adapt the rate of reading to the task, are considered of equal importance to the simple intake of ideas through reading. Children who have difficulty in giving an oral account of what they read are aided by graded exercises in paired practice in recall. Oral and written recall are given importance through reports of pupils on individual topics. Organization of ideas is taught through various steps to outlining and through the identification of major and minor ideas, and through paragraph patterns.

Adjusting reading rate to the task is taught through demonstrating differences in the requirements of various types of detailed reading as contrasted to skimming and locating relevant information. Specific instruction is given in applying knowledge acquired through reading, in finding relationships between such knowledge and current living, in many types of critical reading. In addition, children are given practice in the use of reference materials, card catalogues, indexes, tables of contents, and other sources of information.

7. Making the skills program a zestful experience

The skills program is made a zestful experience. Under superior teachers, there is a team spirit in the attack on skills. Children recognize differences in ease of learning and they help each other to make progress. Pride and shame are not attached to achievement when equal effort is made, and the children are ready to give or receive help in learning. Progress is observed in small units and in various parts of the reading program. This is aided by analyses of difficulties and the charting of specific items learned as steps along the way. Thus the child knows his difficulties and enlists the help of others to overcome them. At the same time, there are constant experiences in using reading for enjoyment and for many practical purposes. Abilities learned in one language-arts area are transferred to various other areas so that each unit of learning is made more important.

Monotony is avoided and interest increased through presenting the skills practice in many different ways. Instructional material may be presented on lantern slides, through opaque projectors, on cards or charts, through adaptations of many kinds of games, through various types of gadgets for sorting, classifying or matching. Many kinds of content materials are collected which provide practice in the use of skills at different levels.

Job sheets, workbooks, and special units of instruction are used to assist the child to master particular abilities. Variety is provided through different groupings of pupils, through changing partners in pairing, through locating the reading class in different areas, and through other methods of avoiding monotony.

Effective instruction in the uses of reading

As the chief objective in education is the intelligent self-direction of living, the chief objective of reading instruction is a mastery of the art of its many uses. Reading skills are tools. These tools may be used well or badly, and it is their use rather than their acquisition that provides the true measure of the success of reading instruction.

The skilled teacher excels in establishing a variety of reading interests, and she provides experiences which stimulate the child to continued use of reading. An effective reading program includes much more than the exposure to children's literature and the presentation of the materials in the textbooks of school subjects. If the child is to have initiative in using reading as an essential service to the many activities of vigorous living, the activities of the classroom must provide experiences which further that objective. The essential activities of vigorous living may require storybooks, poetry, and plays. Equally often they require catalogues, handbooks, guidebooks, travel books, manuals, brochures, maps, timetables, directions, encyclopedias, "do-it-yourself" books, magazines, newspapers, pamphlets, advertising folders, letters, essays, hobby books, and publications of various organizations.

Superior teaching of the use of reading requires alertness to children's questions, comments, purposes, desires, ambitions, and interests, with equal alertness to how these needs may be served by particular reading sources. While incidental suggestions to individual children are helpful, it is desirable to follow a planned program to demonstrate the many ways that reading may serve the individual child.

Not all uses of reading are to be taught by every teacher every year. An effective program requires planning throughout the school, with different aspects of the use of reading being emphasized according to the age of the child, the curricular materials of different grades, the differences in the special abilities and interests of the teacher.

1. Resources for reading made available to children

The superior teacher always finds ways to increase reading resources. Library cooperation is usually available and utilized fully; if the school has a library, children investigate its possibilities. Classroom materials are provided in variety and abundance. Often great ingenuity is shown in the acquirement and use of materials. Free materials are obtained from industries, government agencies, travel bureaus, and organizations. Handbooks, cookbooks, sports books, crafts books, bird books, flower books, animal books, as well as encyclopedias are obtained. Garden catalogues, crafts catalogues, specialized catalogues, and general catalogues are part of the instructional equipment. Newspapers and magazines are available.

Files are made containing stories, anecdotes, pictures, and illustrative materials for many subjects and occasions. Reading lists are drawn up for summer reading, for home purchase, or as suggested gifts for the school. Letters are exchanged with children in various parts of the world.

2. Pupil initiative encouraged through individualized reading

Children follow individual responsibilities in units of content subjects. The answers to questions which arise in discussion are looked up by individuals and reported to the class. Reading specialties may be allied to many topics which are useful for classroom enrichment. Children may plan summer or supplementary reading on various areas. A child who is to move to a different part of the country or who is to travel with his parents may read about where he is going. Children with particular hobbies or interests may plan their reading in relation to them. Narrowness of interest is guarded against by an enriched school program. Individual ventures in reading are recognized in the evaluation of reading achievement, and time is provided for such reading.

3. Pupils' interests stimulated in literary and imaginative reading

At appropriate times, children are introduced to the universally known stories of children. They read stories of adventure and exploration, of romance and mystery, of early times and other lands. They become acquainted with the sources of traditions and myths. Reading of plays is frequent, and all take part. The reading of many plays is preferred to the staging of a few. The pleasures and uses of poetry are taught through choral reading, and children are encouraged to memorize those poems that appeal to them. Humor has a definite place, both in incidental and planned instruction. The literature program is often a whole-class experience, with oral presentations helping to establish the delights and values. Television, radio, and commercial motion pictures may supplement the literature program. Tape and disc recordings, lantern slides, and a school film library are freely used.

4. Experiences provided in use of reading in history, travel, and current affairs

Elementary-school children rate social studies among the less interesting subjects because of remoteness from them in time, space, and responsibility. Superior teachers bring these areas to life by demonstrating their use. Thus, reading before traveling is taught by instructional units that include field trips. Reading of distant countries is accompanied by letters written and received from those lands. The use of reading in conversation is taught by having frequent classroom visitors who know the country or problem being studied. Discussion of current problems is accompanied by suitable reading. The American heritage is taught through biography, through historical fiction, and through dramatization that is related to holidays, birthdays, local history, and relationships. Exhibits, displays, and special events are also a part of this program. The teacher makes constant use of pictures, motion pictures, museum visits, and all kinds of objects and articles that can be related to the time and places studied.

5. Reading related to interests in child's immediate world

It is in the area of the child's world that much reading is stimulated by children's questions, comments, desires, interests, and ambitions. Curiosity about various aspects of science leads to reading about stars, weather, geology, trees, ferns, flowers, frogs, snakes, insects, shells, animal pets, farming, planets, telescopes, photography, electric motors, atomic energy, and television. Boys' and girls' club activities offer many opportunities for reading. Boys especially will welcome books which help to improve their abilities in camping, swimming, sailing, baseball, football, skiing and other sports. Books on cooking, dressmaking, costume design, decoration, and household arts will interest girls. Collecting and constructing hobbies are aided by suitable books. Fine arts, practical arts and crafts, music, and dancing all are enhanced by books and articles. Children's early vocational interests are open invitations to reading. Curiosity about religions, causes, purposes, social relationships, personal problems, and all other interests within the child's immediate world may be satisfied through reading.

Superior teachers use this area of reading to establish the American tradition of resourcefulness and versatility and to demonstrate values to the group of differences in interests and knowledge. They use it to teach the broad cultural concept that excellence can be found in many areas, and they use it to teach the social equality of all useful labor.

Effective instruction in personal and social values

Educational thinking has been constantly concerned for many decades about personal and social values as opposed to skills and knowledge objectives of education. It is universally acknowledged that character values are more important than possession of facts and skills. This emphasis has produced many courses of instruction in schools of education: Character Education, Education for Citizenship, Mental Hygiene of the Classroom, Guidance in the Elementary School, Child Psychology, Foundations of Method, The Activity Curriculum, Child Development. Others will be establshed in the future by zealous persons who feel that they stand alone for the child as opposed to grim "subject specialists." Actually, this point of view is shared by all who think about values in education. It stems from the beliefs and traditions of western religions.

This does not mean, however, that the highest standards of personal and social values are attained automatically and equally well by every teacher. Although every person is reached through schools, we still find in our society some remaining elements of crime, delinquency, corruption, special privilege, deceit, dishonesty, greed, vindictiveness, laziness, irresponsibility, narrowness, unfair competition, injustice, unhappiness, and low achievements in relation to ability.

Fortunately, the majority of our citizens value honesty, generosity, responsibility, sympathy, justice, maintenance of equal opportunity for all, and other precepts which make a desirable society. Schools contribute greatly to the maintenance of social and personal values, but this area of character values is an area for improvement through more effective methods.

The teaching of separate subjects and skills does not exclude the teaching of personal values, as is sometimes implied in fuzzy terms such as "We teach children, not subjects," and "Teach the whole child." Although some "child development" zealots have advocated the abolition of the teaching of separate subjects in favor of activity programs in which skills are taught incidentally, there is no evidence that personal and social values are reached more effectively through such programs. Actually, such activity programs are seldom found in schools, with the exception of the demonstration classes of certain schools of education, and this usually in the summer session only. Apparently separate subject teaching is relatively universal, and it may be the most effective way to reach the personal values, as it has been found the most effective way to teach skills and knowledges.

The single aim which should guide the teacher in the program for developing personal and social values is best expressed by William James in his *Talks to Teachers on Psychology*.[1] In his chapter on *habits,* James states that the object in education is to "fund and capitalize desirable habits so that one can live at ease on the interest of that fund." Habits that tend to lower the child's future achievement and worth to society are discouraged; habits that seem advantageous to the child's future are encouraged. Teachers will differ as to what habits are advantageous and on how best to encourage good ones and discourage poor ones. However, the descriptions of superior teaching of skills and of the uses of reading have already suggested many ways to help the child to acquire good personal habits.

There are so many personal and social objectives, expressed so often in general terms, that it is difficult to focus attention on a specific program to be emphasized in teaching. Many values are inherent in the general methods used by the teacher. Other values and habits must be taught incidentally as individual and group needs arise. A classification of the basic elements of this program of developing personal values through the teaching of reading is given below.

1. Building standards of good workmanship

Security and confidence are built through many methods suggested in the skills program. The level of learning is suited to the child's achievement. His difficulties are made clear, and he overcomes them. Plenty of specific practice is given at points of weakness, and his progress is made evident to him. He works in a situation free from pressures of unfair competition and undesirable comparisons. There is a spirit of mutual helpfulness among his fellow pupils, and he is assured of the interest of the teacher in his progress.

While security is important, it is not the end of living. It is merely the basis upon which a life of service and enterprise may be built. Good workmanship, which makes the child valuable to society, consists of many habits that the child may be helped to develop. Some of these habits are persistence in the face of difficulty, promptness

[1] William James, *Talks to Teachers on Psychology*, New Edition (New York: Henry Holt and Company, Inc., 1939).

and dependability, neatness and order in work, self-criticism, willingness to give and to receive help and to try new approaches, ready cooperation, delight in the achievement of others, and the essential virtues of honesty, self-reliance, and generosity.

2. Building initiative in a variety of desirable interests

The child with limited interests is a danger to himself and to society. He finds life dull and is easily tempted to laziness and undesirable behavior. The program suggested in the use of reading offers unlimited opportunities to open desirable fields of interest which may serve the child well throughout his life.

Independent initiative in the pursuit of interests, not classroom-centered motivation, is the final test of the program. The individual must eventually direct his own life. Interests are well established only when they stimulate independent observation, inquiry, planning, and action.

3. Establishing habits of social responsibility

The superior teacher sets the stage for habits of social responsibility by creating a sense of adventure in group learning. She does this by planning with her pupils the possibilities of the year and also the various activities of each week. She establishes a spirit of mutual helpfulness so that the children are ready to give and to accept assistance. She recognizes individual differences frankly and openly and treats them as opportunities for group achievement. The teacher is the senior helper, rather than the taskmaster. Grouping for instruction in skills carries no implication of individual worth, and the grouping changes constantly in many types of activities.

Opportunities for personal responsibility for group welfare are recognized by children in many ways and are accepted as the normal actions of any person. The children become responsible for picking up around the wastebasket, in the halls, or on the playground, for seeing that each child has equal opportunity for pleasure in work and play, for recognizing work well done by other pupils, for avoiding undesirable criticism and comparisons. They learn courtesy in conversation and generosity in precedence. Group failures in social responsibility are discussed with the group while individual failures are usually talked over privately.

Individual acceptance of social responsibility depends on many things. It depends on a feeling of personal worth, often based upon the assurance of achievement, on the recognition that each person increases or diminishes the store of general welfare, and on a sense of participating in an important social adventure. Social responsibility is difficult to attain in unfair competition in learning unimportant skills and knowledges.

Through reading about children in other less fortunate areas and through group projects to help such children, the reading program may help extend social responsibility beyond the immediate environment. Many books help establish the great heritage of work and sacrifice for the advancement of the cause of freedom.

SUGGESTIONS FOR FURTHER READING

Bond, Guy L., and Wagner, Eva B. *Teaching the Child to Read,* Revised Edition. New York: The Macmillan Company, 1950. Chapter 3.

Betts, Emmett A. *Foundations of Reading Instruction.* New York: The American Book Company, 1946. Chapter 7.

Russell, David H. *Children Learn to Read.* Boston: Ginn and Company, 1949. Chapters 1, 4, and 12.

Whipple, Gertrude. "Characteristics of a Sound Reading Program," in *Reading in the Elementary School,* The Forty-Eighth Yearbook of the National Society for the Study of Education. Chicago: University of Chicago Press, 1949. Chapter 3.

Yoakam, Gerald A. *Basal Reading Instruction.* New York: McGraw-Hill Book Company, 1955. Chapters 2 and 3.

CHAPTER 2 The Reading Program

THE READING PROGRAM in the various grades of American schools is not standardized in procedure and content. Every child in a third grade does not read the same book and follow the same lessons at the same rate as other children in third grades. There are many reasons why reading programs should not be standardized. The first reason is that children are not standardized. Children come to first grade with marked differences in learning rate and instructional needs, and these differences widen each year under good instruction. The second reason is that we lack the knowledge to prepare a "perfect" reading system. The best system we now have in our elementary schools is probably very poor compared to those systems of the future.

A third reason why reading programs should not be standardized is that opinions differ about the value of the content of reading material for children. Possibly we will always need much variation of content if we are to have a strong society. A fourth reason is the differences in competence and interests of teachers. Some teachers of reading will need very detailed assistance most of the time, while others will serve the children better when they are free to make suitable variations.

Use of basal-reading systems

The advantages of orderly procedures in reading instruction are such that few, if any, teachers can serve all pupils well by incidental or improvised reading methods. This is particularly true with slow or average pupils in primary grades. Such children need the assurance of carefully balanced and graded lessons, worked out in step-by-step detail.

The well-planned basal-reading systems presented by experienced textbook publishers have many advantages. They provide the orderly practice required for the development of a sight vocabulary and the perceptual abilities to assure future growth. They save the teacher countless hours of preparation of materials, although she will still have plenty to do if slow learners are to be served well. The manuals accompanying such systems give advice for the motivation of instruction, for adapting to individual differences, and for observation of pupil needs. They are particularly helpful for the beginning teacher. A detailed study of the manuals of basal-reading systems is the first step to learning how to teach reading.

Basal-reading systems for intermediate grades are somewhat less helpful than those for primary grades. The chief reasons for this are the increased complexity of the task and the lack of knowledge of the essential skills and the learning sequences necessary to build them. The broadened vocabulary is full of meaning and word-perception problems. The sentences become more complex and the ideas more abstract. The tasks set for lessons in content subjects require a variety of study and thinking abilities, and the growing reading powers provide a greater choice of the content of reading.

The basal readers are no longer the "reading lesson." Most of the reading is done outside of the reading period and, as a result, reading-skills instruction becomes largely the teaching of "transfer abilities" about which professional knowledge is less secure. At the same time, differences among pupils have grown wider, due both to the nature of intelligence growth and to differences in voluntary reading and in response to classroom instruction. The basal-reading systems have not yet discovered how to meet this complex task and consequently they serve less effectively than the primary-grade basal readers.

The reading service offered in the future for intermediate grades may be very different from the present approach. Word-analysis abilities may be included in the spelling period. Word meaning and vocabulary growth may be allied more closely to composition and other subjects. Study skills may be taught through graded lessons related to social studies or science, or they may be developed through independent workbook methods. The teaching of literature may be separated from reading-skills instruction. Meanwhile, the teacher will select those basal readers which seem to offer the most help in solving this complex task, and at the same time will recognize the need for supplementing the program in many ways.

Developmental levels in reading

Manuals of basal-reading systems are the best source for discovering the professional recommendations for the skills to be taught in each grade. Such manuals include a list of new words to be taught at each level of instruction in primary grades; the word elements to be presented in the word-analysis program; the silent- and oral-reading abilities to be taught; the comprehension and recall levels to be expected. Basal readers become, in most schools, the course of study in reading skills for most grades—*but for the average pupil only.* Slower learners and faster learners must be provided with separate reading programs if they are to develop their reading powers effectively.

For the purposes of this chapter, the reading program is divided into three stages of development: reading readiness, primary-grade skills, and intermediate-grade skills. However, the use of a reading program is a process of continuous growth and is not susceptible of even these broad divisions. Each teacher will find that her pupils are at several stages of development and that a single program will not suffice for all children in any grade.

The reading-readiness level

The reading-readiness period is one in which children are given the backgrounds for beginning reading: perceiving sounds in spoken words, learning letter names and forms, acquiring the beginnings of a sight vocabulary. Some children will acquire these abilities adequately for first-grade reading before coming to school. Others will learn them in kindergarten if the program includes ear training and the ability to read and write letters and a few words. The main responsibility rests upon the first-grade teacher in the first two months of school. If she cannot do the job, teachers of later grades or remedial teachers must provide the instruction. Detailed suggestions for reading-readiness evaluation and instruction are found in Chapters 3 and 4.

The activities of the teacher at the reading-readiness period are the following: fitting instruction to learning rate for words, teaching the forms and names of letters, and teaching the child to hear the sound structure of words. These activities are described below and on page 25.

1. Fitting instruction to learning rate for words

A test for learning rate will show that some pupils are ready to start reading immediately, others will need to proceed slowly, while still others are not ready to begin to learn words. Children high in learning rate and background skills may start at once with the pre-primer. Slower pupils may start with a small sight vocabulary, but the rate of introduction of new words must be watched by the teacher very carefully.

2. Teaching the forms and names of letters

Preliminary testing will discover which pupils know letter names, which can only match letter forms, and which cannot do even that. Inventory tests for different levels of mastery of letter and word forms are presented in Chapter 3. They indicate the proper place to start instruction.

3. Teaching the child to hear the sound structure of words

Tests of the need for ear training will enable the teacher to provide advanced instruction for the faster learners, the essential background abilities for the average learner, and the beginning skills for pupils who have no ear for sounds in words. Without this ability, the child will be unable to progress far in acquiring a sight vocabulary.

Common weaknesses in reading-readiness programs

Common weaknesses in reading-readiness programs may be due in part to inadequacies in basal-reading materials, in part to teacher misinformation, and in part to special learning problems of pupils. Those most frequently observed are the following:

1. *Failure to observe differences in the specific abilities mentioned above.* Uniform reading-readiness instruction which ignores differences in abilities brought to first grade is wasteful and ineffective.

2. *Failure to start reading instruction immediately for rapid learners.* When the preliminary testing shows a high learning rate and good letter-and-sound background abilities, there is no need to put children who are rapid learners through a "reading-readiness" program.

3. *Failure to provide instruction adequate for mastery of reading-readiness skills.* It is not enough to "offer the opportunity" for learning letter names, sounds in words, and a small sight vocabulary; there must be sufficient amount and variety of practice for a high degree of mastery. Informal tests and observations will show the teacher when the child is ready to move on to new skills.

4. *Following an over-complex program with too many nonessential abilities.* While reading-readiness programs which emphasize motor skills, language skills, thinking skills, nonverbal, visual, auditory, and visual-perception skills, and also social skills, may be useful

in the child's general development, they often mislead the teacher and the child as to the importance of the specific auditory and visual abilities related to reading.

5. *Attempting to build a sight vocabulary before teaching letters and sounds in words.* One of the older standard recommendations was to teach a sight vocabulary of seventy-five words before beginning phonics. While there might be some justification for delay of phonics instruction, this does not apply to letter forms and names, or to ear training. See Chapters 3 and 4.

6. *Evading responsibility for reading-readiness instruction.* Some teachers are still under the odd impression that their main task is to "wait until the child is ready" to read; that nature will provide reading readiness for each child. Others are too concerned about "immaturity," children's personality or emotional problems, or difficulties in the home to give the child the much-needed reading-readiness help. Other evasions are based on the assumption that a mental age of six is the magic formula for reading readiness. Actually reading readiness rests upon specific perceptual abilities which are fairly independent of mental age.

The primary-grade reading level

The main tasks of reading instruction at the primary-grade reading levels are the following: developing a constantly growing sight vocabulary; developing an effective word-analysis attack; building skills of oral reading; developing security and understanding in silent reading, and acquiring initiative and independence in the use of reading.

1. Developing a constantly growing sight vocabulary

Since the primary-grade child has an oral vocabulary of several thousand words, the reading task is to develop a reading vocabulary based on these words and to retain and expand the meanings of the words.

Chapter 10 presents ways to introduce new words with samples of word-recognition drills and devices, methods for getting children to respond to word meaning rather than to the "name" of the word, and many methods for providing both practice and review.

2. Developing an effective word-analysis attack

Developing a word-analysis attack consists of ear training to sharpen perception of sounds in words, visual-discrimination practice to enable quick and accurate perception of word structure, phonics to assist the child to solve unknown words, and the use of context clues to assist in word recognition and word meaning. Ear training and visual-discrimination exercises are found in Chapter 4. Further development of these abilities, steps in word-analysis learning, applied phonics, and supplementary helps for word analysis are presented in Chapter 11.

3. Building skills of oral reading

Through oral reading, the child's growth in sight vocabulary is observed, his ability to read in phrases developed, and skills of expression and understanding improved. In addition, oral reading has many values of its own. Chapter 8 presents ways of motivating oral reading, techniques for improving phrase reading, helps for common difficulties, and ways of improving voice and expression. Choral reading and the reading of plays and poetry are found in Chapter 14.

4. Developing security and understanding in silent reading

The transfer from oral to silent reading is an important step in which the child needs specific help. At all stages of silent reading, comprehension requires constant encouragement through many teacher and pupil activities. The beginnings of study skills are also presented. Suggestions for insuring meaningful silent reading, methods of improving attention and recall, and ways to overcome faulty habits in silent reading may be found in Chapter 9. Some of the study skills described in Chapter 13 are applicable to the primary grades.

5. Acquiring initiative and independence in the use of reading

Even before the child learns to read, listening to reading shows him the wealth of pleasure and information to be found in books. As soon as silent-reading skills are established, he will begin his own ventures in stories. Later he will use reference materials and follow longer reading and study projects. The foundation for independent reading is laid in primary grades.

In Chapter 14 the teacher will find helps for broadening the reading interests of children and for stimulating the many practical uses of reading.

Materials of primary reading

A single basal-reading system is not an adequate reading program for primary grades. The teacher will find need for any additional materials she can find to assure progress for her pupils; some of these materials she must build for herself, others may be provided by the school or library.

1. Need for several basal-reading systems in beginning reading

There are many reasons that a teacher be provided with several basal systems for classroom use. Since children progress at different rates, the use of different basal readers in different groups gives each group a feeling of freshness in reading. The slower groups, then, are not merely treading on ground already familiar to more rapid learners. The recommended construction- and play-activities are suited to particular stories, and these will come at different times for various groups if the same readers are used. Since such activities are more useful in language and social development than in building reading skills, all children may join in the activities of any group.

The basal readers of one group may be used as supplementary readers for other groups, and the word-recognition and analysis materials of all readers will serve to give supplementary practice for slow learners.

2. Preprimers and beginning reading materials

Most of the basal-reading systems offer a variety of materials for establishing sight vocabulary and for continuing word-perception practice of the reading-readiness period. At this level it is well to hold closely to the vocabulary of the preprimer of the basal-reading system being used, since preprimer vocabularies differ and the child needs the security of a restricted vocabulary. Extra materials are needed to establish word-analysis abilities and for meaningful review on new words presented in the lessons.

3. A variety of practice materials to help build particular skills

No basal reader can provide enough material to assure every child mastery of each phase of reading instruction. Extra practice material may be built by the teacher from suggestions offered by the various chapters in this book, and also by the teachers' manuals of basal-reading systems. Workbooks, commercial materials, games, and materials from other basal-reading systems may be selected and used to reinforce instruction. Provision must be made for saving and storing materials which are most commonly needed. With each year of experience, the teacher adds to her supply of suitable supplementary aids.

4. Supplementary materials and library resources

A child does not learn to read by the use of the basal reader alone. Supplementary readers are needed for class instruction, and library resources are needed for encouraging independent reading. Every classroom needs a "library corner," and each pupil should have access to a good supply of books in a school or a town library. Home libraries provide reading adventures for many pupils. State and town libraries often aid the classroom teacher through loans of sets of books and through regular visits of the "bookmobile."

Common weaknesses in primary-reading instruction

Some of the more frequent faults in primary-grade reading instruction are the following:

1. *Failure to allow rapid learners to progress as rapidly as effective instruction requires.* Most studies of achievement in relation to ability reveal that bright children achieve less in relation to capacity than do average or dull children. Rapid learners need not be held to the slow pace of basal-reading systems. They will profit little by much of the workbook exercises which accompany reading lessons. Their ventures into independent reading will often require the word-analysis skills of higher grades, and practice in word analysis should be given. The use of readers of future grades is to be avoided, however, since the teachers of those grades should have the right to initial presentation of such materials.

2. *Failure to adjust to the level and learning rates of slower learners.* Children do not make progress in reading that is largely word struggling and confusion. Both the level of material and the rate of introduction of new vocabulary and word-analysis skills need to be fitted to the pupils. The informal tests in Chapter 5 will be of great help to the teacher in determining the instructional needs of children.

3. *Failure to provide extra practice at points of weakness.* Children's learning is uneven. They will show progress in one ability and not in another. Special practice must be provided for the weaknesses which appear. A large share of the chapters in this book deal with materials and methods for providing such extra practice for these weaknesses.

4. *Over-emphasis on mechanics rather than meaning.* In the urgent desire to help pupils to learn, some teachers stress exercises which

emphasize word names rather than meanings (Chapter 10) , phonetic analysis not safeguarded with meaning (Chapter 11) , and also oral and silent reading which is largely the saying of words (Chapters 8 and 9) . These four chapters emphasize the importance of word meanings and give suggestions for word-recognition exercises, drills and devices.

5. *Using instructional materials on which the child has previously failed.*   Although a child should not be pushed through a reader without mastery, occasionally he is expected to start over. In such case, he deserves a fresh start on a new basal reader. He will find discouraging the use of the same materials that he already associates with a feeling of failure or frustration, and it is likely that he will become inattentive.

6. *Failure to provide adequate motivation for reading activities.* The need for knowledge of progress, for a variety in reading lessons, and for confidence in ultimate success in acquiring reading skills is discussed in Chapter 7, while all chapters offer specific motivation suggestions. Occasionally the child will be discouraged through practices that he considers unfair, or by a feeling that he is unimportant in the classroom. This feeling of discouragement may be avoided by following the suggestions for variations in grouping suggested in Chapter 6.

The intermediate-grade reading level

Although many children in intermediate grades will require instruction on the primary-grade reading levels, the average and superior children will need instruction on more advanced skills. While many of the reading abilities in intermediate-grade reading are merely extensions of primary-grade reading, there are some significant differences.

The reading material is full of word meanings outside the child's oral vocabulary. Word-analysis abilities take a much more significant place, since the vocabulary is far less controlled than in primary grades. Much of the silent reading is expository and informative rather than simple narrative. Reading rate must be adapted to a variety of tasks and more accurate and complete recall is required. Elaborative and critical thinking in relation to reading are expected of the child. Greater independence in outside reading and study becomes necessary, and opportunities for varied uses of reading are richer.

The reading program in intermediate grades cannot be considered in relation to the basal reader only. Such a program involves social studies and science, spelling and composition, and independent uses of reading. See Chapter 14 for suggestions for encouraging the independent uses of reading.

Some of the essential factors in intermediate-grade reading instruction are described below.

1. Providing experiences and skill for growth in word meanings

Each content subject has its specialized vocabulary, and there must be growth in general vocabulary which is allied to all reading. While word meanings may be taught in various ways in connection with the daily lessons, there are many transfer abilities which are essential to independent growth of meaning vocabulary. Instruction in various uses of the dictionary is essential.

See Chapter 12 for suggestions in improving word meanings. Other chapters suggest methods of adjusting to word difficulties in silent reading and study.

2. Building advanced word-analysis skills

The simple phonics instruction of the primary grades is replaced with syllable and word-part analysis. A high degree of fluency and accuracy is required since the reading contains so many new words and since the greater amount of independent reading does not permit classroom instruction in advance of the reading. Word-analysis abilities are closely related to spelling, and their combination with spelling is recommended.

Chapter 12 suggests some of the techniques of building word-analysis and spelling abilities.

3. Improving comprehension and recall

With the increased difficulty in reading materials, comprehension and recall become harder. Methods of aiding comprehension in silent reading are illustrated in Chapter 9. Systematic instruction to improve oral and written recall through the use of graded study guides and small-group instruction is described in Chapter 13. Marked improvement in children's comprehension and recall results from the teacher's use of these graded study guides with teams of two or three pupils.

4. Adjusting reading speeds to different reading tasks

Techniques for improving speed of narrative reading are found in Chapter 9. Various levels of skimming and other speeded reading techniques appear in Chapter 13. The use of different kinds of speeded reading exercises will enable the pupil to adjust his reading rate to different comprehension tasks. Suggestions are given for assuring the child's comprehension in the various types of speeded reading such as skimming to locate specific information and rapid reading to classify materials.

5. Developing thinking skills in relation to reading

Intermediate-grade study tasks and the application and evaluation of reading require the pupil to apply several types of thinking abilities to the results of his study. Organizational, elaborative, and critical thinking techniques in relation to reading are suggested in Chapter 13.

Many of the techniques in improving recall are based upon attending to the organization and relationships of ideas in the material studied. Elaborative thinking, in which the pupil associates new material with other ideas and experiences, provides the significance and usefulness of facts learned. Critical thinking evaluates ideas in relation to standards or purposes, and it is always essential to intelligent action.

6. Developing initiative in independent use of reading

The increasing maturity of the child, his broadening experiences and interests, and his greater reading ability, all combine to increase the importance in the intermediate grades of providing specific experiences in independent reading. This program should include the many types of imaginative reading, history and travel reading, reading in relation to activities, objects, and purposes in the immediate world, and reading for satisfying attitudes, ideals, and personal growth.

Methods of planning an effective use of such a reading program will be found in Chapter 14.

7. Maintaining and improving skills in oral reading

While improving skills in oral reading is usually not a major objective in intermediate-grade reading, it should not be neglected in the intermediate-grade reading program. There are many occasions in which the child, as well as the adult, needs to read well orally; the brighter the pupil, the greater his likelihood for a need for oral reading.

Chapter 8 deals with basic skills in oral reading, while Chapter 14 suggests practice in dramatic and choral reading.

8. Developing skill in library and reference usage

Although these skills are not treated in detail in this volume, unit assignments and independent study are greatly aided by specific instruction in them. Each subject and each special field of interest has its own specific reference task. Individual research assignments and the following of personal specialties introduce the pupil to resources for expanding his knowledge. Librarians are most helpful in introducing children to the rich resources available in a library and also in teaching children how to use reference books, how to use a card catalogue, and how to make effective use of all library skills.

Chapter 14 provides suggestions for supplementary materials and bibliographies in many areas of children's interests.

Instructional materials in intermediate-grade reading

It is difficult to serve the many needs of intermediate-grade reading through basal readers alone. Too much of the reading program is found in social studies, science, and independent reading. Some of the instructional materials necessary for an effective intermediate-grade reading program are discussed below. They include basal readers, library and reference materials, and materials to fit special instructional needs.

1. Several different basal readers

From different series of basal readers, stories may be selected which illustrate different possibilities of the uses of reading, word-analysis and word-meaning development lessons, special types of reading, and study practice. Certainly there is no need in the intermediate grades to purchase more than five or six copies of any basal reader, since individual-skills needs are served through small-group instruction. Superior pupils in intermediate grades will seldom be served well by basal readers. Their need is for a much broader literature and study program than any basal reader can provide.

2. Library and reference materials related to the instructional program

The classroom will need to have encyclopedias and supplementary history and science textbooks. It would be highly desirable to have different levels of history and science materials based upon similar organization. Independent reading, small-group and individual projects in content subjects, and the use of a reading program call for a school or town library, with some separate volumes immediately available in the classroom. The teacher should have collections of plays, poems for choral reading, biographies, travel books, craft books, catalogues, monographs, magazines, newspapers, and specialty collections available for illustration and for teaching the uses of reading. Libraries of films and recordings will also enrich the instructional program.

Chapter 14 contains many suggestions for library materials that will help in the uses of reading. At the end of the chapter is a list of useful books that will help the teacher obtain and evaluate instructional reading materials.

3. Collections of reading-skills materials to fit special instructional needs

Reading-skills materials to fit special needs may be commercial, such as workbooks; dictionaries and dictionary-skills materials; developmental lessons on a particular needed ability; word-analysis lessons, especially in connection with spelling; study guides and workbooks which accompany social-studies and science books; and various other materials that fit instructional needs and assist in building essential skills.

A great deal of the intermediate-grade skills program will need to be provided by materials built by the teacher. After she has built these intermediate-grade materials she should file them for use in the future. Such materials are suggested in the various chapters in this book.

Common weaknesses in intermediate-grade instruction

Most of the weaknesses in intermediate-grade instruction are related to the following: failure to provide for individual differences in level of pupil ability; failure to provide sufficient amounts and types of instruction to establish needed reading skills; and failure to provide a specific program of teaching initiative and providing motivation techniques in the uses of reading.

Some of the more commonly observed faults and weaknesses are the following:

1. *Failure to analyze the differences in the reading needs of pupils.* Because of the wide differences in the reading development of pupils in the intermediate grades, early analysis of the skills of pupils is essential to the planning of an effective reading program. Suggestions for informal analysis of essential intermediate-grade skills are found in Chapter 5 under "Analysis of Reading Needs in Intermediate Grades." More detailed methods of observation of particular skills are found in other chapters.

2. *Failure to provide instruction at primary levels for slower pupils.* The attempt to shift to primary teachers the blame for poor preparation of pupils does not serve the pupils in any way. Slow learners cannot complete primary-grade reading skills in three years. If the promotional policies of the school system move these slow learners to intermediate grades, the children must be given instruction which will permit them to improve their primary-grade reading skills.

3. *Failure to adjust to the reading needs of superior readers.* The usual basal-reading instruction is much below the instructional needs of superior readers. They will profit more by independent reading in relation to content subjects, through reading related to personal specialties, and through cooperation in helping with teaching slower learners. If these superior readers *must* be given daily instruction in reading, the materials that are available to them should be in larger units of suitable literature, with the entire volume on a single subject or theme.

These pupils may be superior silent readers, but they may still need special instruction in oral reading, in preparing and giving reports, in written and oral summaries of the material they have read. These superior readers need special instruction to improve these abilities.

4. *Following a basal-reading system in detail, regardless of special instructional needs of pupils.* Children may make progress in reading simply through reading practice in basal-reading systems. Special weaknesses of pupils are hardly likely to be overcome, however, by the very few practices on various skills which can be provided in a

basal reader. If the teacher has no concept of essential skills to be established and no plans or techniques for teaching them, it probably is better to follow a basal-reading system than to have no program at all.

5. *Assuming that word-analysis abilities belong only in primary grades.* The intermediate grades have a particular need for word-analysis skills. If a child is not quick and accurate in syllable and word-part analysis, the teacher should see that he is given daily instruction in such analysis until he has a reasonable security with new words.

6. *Failure to provide intensive instruction at points of weakness.* The many different abilities which make up intermediate-grade reading will require different amounts of practice for different pupils. Such instruction should be specific and intensive. Particular attention is called to the improvement of recall through graded study guides in small-group instruction illustrated in Chapter 13. Speeded reading and thinking skills also presented in this chapter can be of help to teachers.

7. *Failure to adjust to reading levels in the content subjects.* Sometimes teachers are aware of the need to fit reading instruction to pupil levels in the reading period, but they use a single level of textbook for all pupils in social studies and science. If a single level of textbook cannot be avoided, methods of adjusting pupils to the situation are suggested in Chapters 13 and 14.

In Chapter 13 the teacher will find samples of detailed-question study guides for social studies and also helpful suggestions for using the guides.

8. *Failure to plan an effective program in teaching initiative in the uses of reading.* The child cannot acquire initiative in the many uses of reading through following the classroom activities of a basal-reading system or the textbooks in content subjects. Classroom activities which provide practice in the many uses of reading, materials of instruction in great variety, and independent ventures for class or individual purposes are essential in teaching initiative in the use of reading.

Teachers will find help in Chapter 14 which gives suggestions for teaching the uses of reading.

9. *Failure to provide motivation techniques to keep interest high and to establish group morale and a spirit of mutual helpfulness.* The intermediate-grade curriculum should be a zestful experience, filled with evidence of growth in reading skill, wide opportunities for exploration in interesting knowledge and skills, and a delight in being a part of a learning team. All chapters in this book are intended to suggest ways to keep motivation high, to keep meaning foremost, to establish and maintain group morale. Chapter 7 and Chapter 14 deal especially with motivation methods.

SUGGESTIONS FOR FURTHER READING

Gates, Arthur I. *The Improvement of Reading*. Third Edition. New York: The Macmillan Company, 1947. Chapter 2.

Hildreth, Gertrude. "Reading Programs in the Early Primary Period," and "Reading Programs in Grades II and III," in *Reading in the Elementary School*. The Forty-Eighth Yearbook of the National Society for the Study of Education. Chicago: University of Chicago Press, 1949. Chapters 4 and 5.

McKim, Margaret G. *Guiding Growth in Reading in the Modern Elementary School*. New York: The Macmillan Company, 1955. Chapter 2.

Russell, David H. *Children Learn to Read*. Boston: Ginn and Company, 1949. Chapters 5, 7, and 8.

Yoakam, Gerald A. *Basal Reading Instruction*. New York: McGraw-Hill Book Company, 1955. Chapter 15.

Teacher's manuals for series of readers also provide specific recommendations for materials and methods in each grade. Some of the recent basal readers are listed here:

Betts, Emmett A., and Welch, Carolyn. *Betts Basic Readers*. New York: American Book Company.

Bond, Guy L., and Others. *The Developmental Reading Series*. Chicago: Lyons and Carnahan.

Durrell, Donald D., Sullivan, Helen B., and Others. *Basic Reading Abilities Series*. Yonkers, New York: World Book Company.

Gates, Arthur I., and Others. *The Macmillan Readers*. New York: The Macmillan Company.

Gray, William S., and Others. *The New Basic Readers: Curriculum Foundation Series*. Scott, Foresman and Company.

Hildreth, Gertrude, and Others. *Easy Growth in Reading*. Philadelphia: The John C. Winston Company.

McKee, Paul, and Others. *Reading for Meaning*. Boston: Houghton Mifflin Company.

O'Donnell, Mabel. *The New Alice and Jerry Basic Reading Program*. Evanston, Illinois: Row, Peterson and Company.

Russell, David H., and Others. *The Ginn Basic Readers*. Boston: Ginn and Company.

Witty, Paul A., and Others. *Reading for Interest*. Boston: D. C. Heath and Company.

Yoakam, Gerald A., and Others. *The Laidlaw Basic Readers*. Chicago: Laidlaw Brothers.

CHAPTER 3 Reading Readiness: Nature and Analysis

THE FIRST APPEARANCE of reading difficulty is in the first weeks in the first grade. What happens to the child's reading in these weeks determines to a large extent his later success or failure in reading. It is here where the child's reading difficulties begin and where he meets confusion and frustration in learning to read words. It is here where emotional problems arise in relation to reading. If the reading-readiness program is adequate, reading difficulties are avoided and the need for remedial classes largely eliminated.

Background abilities for beginning reading

Much research has been done in relation to the background abilities of children who learn to read readily as compared to those who have difficulty. It is now clear that differences in success in beginning reading depend upon a variety of pre-reading abilities that the child acquires through specific experiences at home or in school. A bright child who lacks certain of these abilities will not learn to read; a dull child who has them will make progress.

Certain of these background abilities have been clearly established as essential to reading success. We know how to observe and measure them and how to teach them effectively. We also know that the ability to read improves markedly when they are taught. Other background abilities appear important, and they are included in the reading-readiness program despite the lack of research evidence of their value.

Two background abilities known to be important to beginning reading are visual- and auditory-discrimination of word elements. The minimum requirement in the first background ability, that of visual discrimination of word elements, appears to be the ability to match letters. If the child cannot tell letters apart, it is futile for the teacher to attempt to teach him words. He cannot attach meaning and name to a word that he cannot recognize when he sees it a few seconds later.

Children come to school with very different stages of development in visual discrimination of letters and words. How to observe and measure these levels, and how to help the child to higher levels of ability will be discussed later in this chapter.

The second background ability, that of auditory perception of word elements, is equally important to reading success but somewhat harder to observe and measure. It consists in being able to notice the separate sounds in spoken words—in the ability to identify the *m-m-m* sound in *mother, most, magic, machine,* for example. Unless the child notices the separate sounds in spoken words, there is no sense for him in the way words are spelled. While he may acquire a small sight vocabulary without this ability, he quickly runs into confusion with words which look very much alike. He has no system that will relieve this confusion.

Phonetic writing is an excellent invention, as compared to non-phonetic systems, but it depends upon the reader's ability to hear the sounds in the words he speaks. Many children come to first grade deficient in this ability. On the best group measures we have been able to design, 30 per cent of the children get zero scores. We do not yet know how to measure early stages of the ability to hear sounds in words. Fortunately we know how to teach it to most children, and we know that rate of learning to read improves greatly when it is taught. The ability is not assured by direct teaching of phonics. Many children who come to reading clinics after several years of phonics instruction are surprised to learn that the words they speak "have sounds in them." It is not assured by an excellent vocabulary and clear pronunciation.

There are no more speech defects among children who need this type of ear training than among those who are high in the ability, nor are there more monotones in singing or hearing defects among them. The child who lacks the ability can copy a teacher's pronunciation of new strange words as well as can children high in the ability. The key is the ability to identify separate sounds at the beginning, ending, or middle of words.

Girls generally have acquired abilities in visual and auditory discrimination of words better than have boys, despite equal intelligence of the boys. In a large measure this accounts for the greater amount of reading difficulty among boys than among girls. When boys are given six weeks of eye and ear training on word elements, their rate of learning to read equals that of girls.

Just why boys are slower in developing these abilities in preschool experience is not known. The best guess seems to be that the girls spend more time in many types of quiet play in which the auditory and visual perceptions of words are developed.

Two other factors appear to be of importance to success in first-grade reading: interest in printed words and in books, and the ability to maintain attention in the reading task. While we have no standard measures of either of these factors, both may be observed during the first few days of school, and either may be a serious handicap to the child's progress in any phase of the beginning reading program. Both of these factors are the result of pre-reading experiences, and will, if weak or absent, be improved by an instructional program in the first grade.

Some children are eager to learn to read and write long before coming to school. They bring books to parents or older brothers and sisters to read, and occasionally ask, "What word says that?" They spend hours in coloring books and ask what the big print at the bottom of the page says. They race to a parent with the comic section of the Sunday paper. They learn the station and network symbols on the television screen. They learn highway route numbers and signs.

Some children have spent hours in various writing activities and can write both capital and lower-case letters, make lists of words they can spell, and laboriously write letters to grandparents, asking help on the spelling of each word. The desire to write seems to appear before the desire to read, and many children have developed considerable writing skill before they arrive at school. Other children have shown no interest in symbols, and although they are willing to make an unenergetic effort to learn words they find other activities much more exciting.

The ability to maintain attention to the reading task is a highly complex factor. The child may do well one day, poorly the next. He may be highly attentive in the story hour, but distractible in the reading period. He may work well in group activity, but be apathetic in self-directed work. He may respond to individual teaching, but refuse to try in the competitive situation of the group. He may be challenged by a new task, or he may be comfortable only in familiar activities. He may have faith that he can learn through persistence, or he may give up if he can't be successful on the first try.

It is easy to blame the home or the kindergarten teacher for the difficulty. However, when inattention gets in the way of learning to read, the only person who can provide the experiences to help the child in persistence of attention is the teacher.

It may be well at this point to discuss the home environment in relation to reading readiness. Some teachers and parents are so frightened at the prospect of reading difficulty that they believe that the home should scrupulously avoid any work with letters, words, and books. Few, if any, reading difficulties arise from home reading and writing activities. About the only things that a parent can do in the preschool period to make it difficult for the teacher are these: to cure the child of the desire to read, through forced instruction; and to use the school primers and first readers as a basis for teaching.

If the child initiates the reading-related activity, the parent is safe in giving any help as long as the child returns for more. It is difficult to imagine any "wrong system" when the child enjoys the activity.

Almost every "system" provides the child with good background. Sounding letters, spelling words, printing or writing, copying, using a typewriter, and even "memorizing" instead of true reading—all these can be turned to good account as reading-readiness background. Suppose cursive writing is used instead of manuscript writing, or suppose that manuscript letters don't follow the pattern set by the school. At least the child has acquired an interest in written language, has learned to persist in it, and is familiar with the school task.

One obvious strand in the development of reading-readiness background is that of oral language. However, the child usually has a much richer oral vocabulary than that required for reading first-grade material. The relatively few words outside the child's experience may be taught when the words are presented in reading.

Lack of oral-language background is almost never found as a cause of reading difficulty except, of course, with children who are unfamiliar with English or are feeble-minded. Oral-language activities always have a place in reading-readiness programs, despite the lack of evidence that they enhance the child's success in learning to read. They have value in social, personality, and language development generally, and they may help in the improvement of attention and interest in written symbols.

Speech defects may give some infrequent or minor trouble in reading. Stuttering or stammering may block the child's pleasure in oral reading, while articulatory defects may cause some difficulty in ear training or phonics instruction. Usually these may be corrected during the ear-training period, or they may require remedial speech training. Speech defects are rarely the cause of slow learning in reading, although such defects may present serious oral-language problems.

Motor skills of all sorts are highly useful to the child's development, but except for the ability to write letters, none seems to have an important relationship to success in beginning reading. However, readiness programs themselves use a number of workbook skills which demand coloring, drawing, tracing, making circles, folding, pasting, and so on, and experience in these skills will assist the child in adjusting to reading activities which require them.

Erroneous concepts of reading readiness

Several false concepts of reading readiness have been responsible for a large number of reading failures. Here are three of these false concepts:

The "mysterious appearance" concept. The first, and most dangerous concept, is the "mysterious appearance" theory which says simply that "A child will learn to read when he is ready." The thinking of people who follow this erroneous concept apparently goes something like this: "A child will learn to read when he is ready. He develops inside something like a cabbage. When the little leaves are formed, he will read. It is dangerous to force this process by teaching him before he is ready. Beware of teaching words, letters, sounds, and especially phonics. Forced teaching will lead to emotional maladjustments. You will know when he is ready to read. He will simply read as an indication that he is ready. The teacher should do nothing about lack of readiness but *wait* with patience and understanding. He may not be ready in first grade, nor may readiness appear in second or third grades. Just wait until he is ready."

There are several erroneous assumptions about this theory of readiness. The first is that emotional maladjustments can be avoided by the waiting process. Actually, of course, there is no way to *wait* without the child's knowing that he is falling behind. If other children in the room are reading, or even if his cousins of the same age in other towns are reading, the child cannot help comparing his reading ability with theirs, with the resulting disappointment at the comparison.

It is futile to speculate on the possibility of withholding reading from all primary-grade children until the mysterious mantle of reading readiness descends upon the slower pupils. Too many children want to and do learn to read before they come to school. The first grade seems to be the time that a child requires the ability as a part of his maturing equipment.

Another false element in this "mysterious appearance" concept is that reading readiness is a mysterious force that suddenly appears. This is entirely opposed to the nature of development of almost every other ability. Each has its early stages, and each depends upon gradual development of these early stages. A child does not suddenly become a good baseball player. He first has experience in walking and running, in catching, in hitting, in reaching, in throwing—all in early and easy stages.

Still another weakness is found in the belief that specific teaching of beginning elements of reading should be avoided. What is unique about reading that exempts it from specific teaching of background abilities? In almost every other phase of development children are encouraged through selection of toys, use of various tools, drawing and coloring, throwing and catching, playing many kinds of games. The key to the objection is apparently in the word "forced," and to this any teacher would agree. But there is no need for the teacher to force the child to learn the background abilities in reading when these abilities are presented with imagination and at a level which assures success.

The emotional and personality-adjustment concept. A second "mystery" concept is that success in reading rests primarily upon emotional and personality adjustment. It apparently assumes that all the background skills are present, but that the child is prevented from learning because of emotional or personality difficulties. Only when these difficulties are corrected may one expect the child to read. Followers of this theory find emotional maladjustment in all reading failures, and they delight in an earnest inquiry about the home life of the child. This explanation concerning personality adjustment is widely used to account for reading difficulties at all levels and is discussed in detail in Chapter 16.

At this point, it is sufficient to advise the teacher to be very slow to assign the failure to an emotional or a personality cause. The first task of the teacher is to see if the child has background abilities necessary for reading and, if these are lacking, to provide the specific experiences to build them.

The mental-age concept. Despite lack of research support, many people believe that a mental age of six or more assures success in reading. Mental age, as determined by most tests of intelligence, bears a very low relationship to the rate of learning to read in first grade. Correlations between the two abilities run from zero to as high as .60, much too low to assure success in individual cases. Many children with severe reading difficulties had mental ages of eight or more when they started first grade. It has been demonstrated that reading can be taught to pupils with mental ages of four.

While the mental age of six or more may be a useful guide for general adjustment to first-grade work, it is somewhat irrelevant in regard to predicting success in primary-grade reading. Rate of learning to read seems to depend more upon auditory and visual perception of word elements and other developmental factors than upon scores on intelligence tests.

Informal observation of reading readiness

There are many standard tests of reading readiness, some of which are listed at the end of this chapter. Most of them are rather general measures of various background skills, and they are designed more for prediction of success than for indicating a specific instructional program.

Through informal tests which the teacher may easily build, she can discover more exactly the strengths and weaknesses in various elements of background abilities. For example, a standard reading-readiness test may indicate that the child is weak in visual perception of words; the informal test will show exactly what letters he knows and his level of mastery of them. Informal tests can be adjusted to different levels of ability and may inventory more accurately the instructional needs.

The first week of school is not too early to discover background abilities in the first grade. As we progress in knowledge of early stages of reading readiness, we shall probably find many ways of observing these abilities and providing encouragement for them in kindergarten or preschool. Many of the tests may be presented as short and simple matching games, used casually as a part of the day's activities. Generally it is best to keep any primary-grade testing on a "game" level, making sure that the tests are short enough to hold attention and easy enough for every child to meet with some success.

The earnest, silent, strained atmosphere in which some tests are given should be avoided. With very young children, testing must be done with small groups so that every child is within reach of the teacher. It is better if the groups are not larger than six or eight pupils. At this age each pupil needs to feel that his activity is important, and he likes personal recognition of each achievement if his attention is to be maintained.

Of course, all of the elements in good testing should prevail. The light should be adequate on the child's paper and on the testing materials. The testing should be done early in the day before fatigue sets in. The materials for testing should be neat and orderly and should look important to the child. The atmosphere of testing should be alert but free from strain, and the teacher must radiate interest and be quick to help the child who loses his place or shifts his attention to irrelevant ideas or situations. Children who are fatigued or temporarily not at their best will need retesting.

Some essential tests that the teacher should make during the first week of school, if possible, are tests for learning rate, visual perception, and auditory perception. She should also observe carefully other reading-readiness abilities such as interest in words, persistence and attention in learning, and oral-language ability.

Testing learning rate in reading

The first and most obvious test to be made is that of learning rate in reading. The best way to see if a child can remember words taught is to teach him some words and see if he can remember them. This is much more direct than measuring his mental ability or computing his score on reading-readiness tests and then trying to predict his reading readiness from them. The surest way to discover the answer to the question "Is this child ready to read?" is to teach him some words and see if he can remember them.

The learning-rate test is also the best way to divide children into groups for reading instruction. While a single learning-rate test may not always be relied upon, the results of several such tests are better as a basic for grouping for reading instruction than any combination of standard-test results.

Learning-rate tests may be given in several ways, and the inventive teacher will modify the suggested tests to suit her desires. These are the steps in the process:

1. The teacher prepares flash cards with words to be taught.
2. She teaches the words to the children.
3. After an hour, she tests each child apart from the others to see how many words are remembered.

1. Preparing the learning-rate test

In preparing the learning-rate test five or six words are best for the average first grade. If the children are known to be a superior group, eight or ten words may be presented; if they are known to be slow, three or four words may be enough. The number of words retained may depend upon the number taught. A child may retain all words when only three are taught, but remember none when ten words are taught. The size of the task may confuse or frighten children who would be secure with a smaller number.

When all children in a class are to be compared, the same number of words should be presented to all. After the first test shows superior and slower learners, the subsequent learning tests may be lengthened or shortened to fit the group being tested.

The learning rate will depend also upon the nature of the words selected and upon the similarity or differences among the words grouped together. The meanings of the words must be known to the child, and they should be reasonably colorful so that many illustrations may be given in the teaching. For example, *funny, baby, catch, letter,* and *tree* would be better than *both, for, away, them,* and *when.* The teacher may wish to choose words that can be pictured, and present the pictures as a part of the teaching. The words may be below the pictures on the cards, or they may be on separate cards but combined in the teaching.

The general length and formation of the words will make a difference in the learning rate. A combination of long and short words will be easier learned than all words of the same length. For example, a combination of *sandwiches, milk, dog, pencil,* and *horse* would be easier than *fast, tree, rain, door,* and *flag.* Words that look alike will present a harder learning situation than those that contain different letters or different shapes. These would be difficult to learn in combination: *fast, first, fine, last, five; work, want, went, sent, wish;* and especially the words containing the letters b, d, p, q which are commonly confused in early reading—*dog, big, pig, bed, buy.* With these suggestions in mind, the teacher may choose words which will appear in primers or first readers used by the class.

The words selected are printed on flash cards, with the print large enough to be readily seen by every child in the group. Printing or manuscript writing should be used in place of cursive writing, since most of the reading instruction will be in printed materials. The printing should be carefully done, and a felt pen or lettering pen used to make the letters very distinct. All cards should be of the same material, the same size and shape, and should contain no smudges or other means for the child to identify the word by some characteristic of the card.

Despite the differences in learning rate which will result from the number, selection, and combination of words tested, the results in a single classroom will be valid if all pupils are taught the same words in the same way. However, if three or four groups are to be tested at different times, it is important that the later groups tested not see the words at the time they are taught to other groups. If three groups of children are taught and tested separately, the teacher should use a different set of words for each group. Then she should change the sets on the following days so that each child will have been taught all of the words.

2. Teaching the words to the children

The teacher may follow any method of teaching she commonly uses in teaching reading, but it is important that the same methods be used with the same words for all groups being tested. Thus comparisons can be made on the basis of equal teaching. While some variations will always appear, it is well to hold closely to the same number of practices, the same or similar illustrations, the same amount and type of pupil response, and the same length of time in teaching.

Suppose the words to be taught are *green, baby, catch, letter,* and *tree.* The teacher shows the word *green,* and directs the children as follows:

This word is *green.* What things are green? Can you see something green? [Give a few illustrations through discussion or pointing.] Now what is this word? That's right. *Green.* Say it again. Look at it carefully to see if you can remember it.

[Then present the word *baby.*] This word is *baby.* Do you know any babies? [Let the pupils make a few statements about babies they know.] Now what is this word? *Baby.* That's right. Say it again. Now try to remember it.

[Present the word *green* again.] What is this word? *Green.* That's right. Say it again.

The remainder of the words are presented in the same way, with questions appropriate to bring out the meanings. Review previous words after each new teaching. After all words have been taught, show the words again two or three times, giving help where necessary, and asking each child to say the words. Change the sequence of the words so that the child will not try to memorize the order.

This suggested program may be changed or supplemented as the teacher wishes. Pictures may be used to help with the words, children may be asked to find the words on the board or on individual mimeographed copies of the words, a pack of flash cards may be shown with the words repeated several times, and so on.

3. Testing the children to see how many words are remembered

After an interval of at least an hour, test each child separately on all of the words taught. Show each word to the child and ask him what it is. If he does not know, tell him what it is. (While this may help him to eliminate errors on later words, its value in assurance to the child outweighs that of keeping the test a "pure" measure of learning.) Record the number of words known. If desired, give a child a second chance on the list; but be sure to record the words known on the child's first try.

4. Variations in learning-rate tests

Some teachers present a word a day to the entire class. After ten days, individual testing shows the differences in learning rate even though the children may receive help at home in different amounts. One teacher regularly teaches the names of colors in this manner, with the name of a new color each day. Other teachers make a game of reading various kinds of signs. Some teachers post pictures of objects or animals with the names written below, and thus a longer time is devoted to learning. Others present words of the preprimer, according to the methods suggested in the manual. After ten of these preprimer words are taught, the teacher checks the number each child has learned.

The learning rate obtained at the first of the year is not permanent. It changes as the child acquires better perceptual background, gets more adjusted to the classroom and its activities, improves in interest, attention, and persistence. Reading groups based on learning rate will need constant adjustment, but they are generally more satisfactory than groups formed by other methods.

The learning-rate testing identifies the "nonreaders" in the first month of school. It enables the teacher to begin an effective reading-readiness program at once. The first step with these pupils is to measure their ability in visual and auditory perception of word elements in order to discover the need for building these word-background skills.

Testing visual perception of words and letters

Since words and letters look so much alike to the child, a familiarity with the differences in the forms of letters is essential to success in first-grade reading. Some children come to first grade with considerable experience with letters and words. They know the names of both capital and lower-case letters, can write all of them without copy, and may be able to read primers and write several words. Other children have had no interest or experience in these things and are unable even to match letters correctly.

Tests of visual discrimination will aid the teacher in discovering the level at which to begin reading readiness with pupils, and will serve also to indicate what letters need to be taught. There are many ways to test visual discrimination of letters and words. Certain tests are provided on pages 55–56, but suggestions are given for testing other levels and types of ability.

The two sample tests may be duplicated and used by the teacher. The first test measures the child's ability to identify capital letters shown on a flash card; the second test measures the same ability with lower-case letters. Fresh copies of the same record blanks may be used for measuring children's ability to identify letters named by the teacher.

Materials for the testing are mimeographed forms for pupil use and flash cards for the letters to be tested. The mimeographed forms are prepared as follows: The stencil is divided into 26 boxes by drawing a vertical line in the middle of the page and horizontal lines to make the boxes. If every third horizontal line on the mimeographed form is drawn heavier, it will be easier for the child to keep the place and easier also for the teacher to check to see if the child is following the test.

Letters are printed or typed in the boxes in the order shown in the sample blank. A primer typewriter may be used but, if none is available, a regular typewriter may be used or the letters may be printed by hand. If manuscript writing is to be used for most of the teaching, the letters may be printed in manuscript.

Flash cards are printed in black letters about two inches high. The form of the letters should be the same used in the pupils' tests, although there would be some justification for having the flash cards in manuscript and the pupils' forms in type if both are to be used in teaching reading.

Cursive writing of letters should not be used in either pupils' forms or flash cards. The child has enough trouble with variations between

IDENTIFYING CAPITAL LETTERS

Pupil's Name _____   Shown   Named

D	H	O	T		E	K	O	M
R	X	J	F		V	H	L	B
L	Y	A	E		T	G	C	D
D	C	S	B		E	W	T	M
T	V	P	W		K	B	V	L
C	Z	S	U		F	N	G	Z
F	L	H	I		X	J	P	U
P	E	X	R		T	C	Y	A
L	Y	I	F		N	F	W	L
O	S	N	E		G	Y	D	O
P	O	B	U		C	Q	X	T
B	Z	I	N		G	U	M	J
A	F	R	B		V	T	K	Y

IDENTIFYING LOWER-CASE LETTERS

Pupil's Name _____   Shown   Named

h	v	o	m	q	j	e	b
y	x	j	t	y	x	v	a
s	w	p	a	t	k	f	o
l	r	n	c	l	m	g	n
u	i	s	b	e	a	f	s
d	x	p	f	h	r	j	n
t	i	o	m	w	h	v	b
m	f	u	h	u	y	n	c
h	k	n	r	p	f	l	b
p	u	z	y	o	b	g	d
c	m	t	e	f	t	l	i
v	g	z	w	m	g	a	p
n	i	r	d	q	o	h	d

print and manuscript without adding the quite different forms of cursive writing to his problem.

When the flash cards have been printed, they should be placed in the following order:

Capitals—O X A B T C L R I S P N F E H D
M K Z J Y W G Q U V.

Lower case—o x s c i p t m k z e w r j y f n a
h v u b d l g q.

The order of the letters as shown above is the approximate order of difficulty when beginning first graders are asked to tell the names of letters.

Directions for giving the tests

Each pupil is given a test form and a pencil. If he cannot write his name, the teacher will write it. Then the teacher will direct as follows:

I am going to show you some letters. I will show you the first one, and you are to find it in the first box right below your name. It will be right in that first row of letters. Here is the first one. [Show *O*.] See if you can find this one. Put your finger on it. [Check to see that each child has found the right letter.] Now draw a little circle around it. [Have them keep the circles small. If you wish, illustrate by having the first two boxes of letters drawn on the board, showing the child what is to be done. Check to see if each child has circled the *O*.]

Now move down to the next row. See if you can find this letter and draw a circle around it. [Check the papers again, helping each child to circle the right letter.]

Then present each of the other letters, always watching to see that the children are at the right place on their blanks. Since this is an "identification from memory" test, turn the card down after the pupils begin to hunt for the letter. Do not allow a second look. If children have difficulty in keeping the place, markers may be used by each pupil. Some teachers like to make drawings of small objects to identify each row for the pupils.

If the test is being used on older pupils, each row may be numbered, and the teacher may say, "In row 5, find this letter." If small groups are tested and markers are used, there is little trouble in the child keeping the right place. While inability to follow directions given to a group is a handicap in learning to read, it is not the function being tested.

The test for identifying lower-case letters is given in a similar manner. When each test has been given, the papers are scored. Examination of the results will enable the teacher to find answers to the following questions:

1. Which pupils have high discrimination of letters?
2. Which pupils have marked confusion in letters?
3. Which pupils are secure on capital letters, but weak on lower-case letters?
4. Which capital and lower-case letters need to be taught to each group of children?

Testing the ability to identify letters named

Fresh copies of the same pupils' forms used in the previous test may be used in identifying letters named by the teacher. While accurate letter perception is possible without knowing the names of letters, recognition of letters by name indicates a higher degree of maturity. Since children must very soon use letter names in various aspects of reading, writing, and spelling, it is desirable to test this ability.

Since pupils will remember some of the letters circled in each group in the previous test, it is well to use a different order of letters. The test blank was designed with this in mind. The order of letters for this test of identifying names is as follows:

Capitals—T R L C P S I X F O B N A M H G E K Z U Y W D Q J V.

Lower case—m t s r u x o h k p c z i e v f n a j w y b d l g q.

In giving this test, proceed in this way:

I want to see if you can find the letter I name in each row. In the first row, find *T* and draw a circle around it.

Check to see that the pupils understand the directions. If necessary, put the first two rows of letters on the blackboard to show what is to be done. Proceed with the remainder of the capital letters, then test the lower-case letters.

Be clear in enunciation of letters which sound like other letters. Allow time enough for the pupils to find the letters, but move the group along rather rapidly. If some children stay too long on one letter, direct as follows:

Never mind that one. Just skip it. Now try this one in the next row [Give the name of the letter].

Using the test results, the teacher can answer these questions:

1. Which pupils can identify letters named?

2. Which pupils need instruction on letter names, capital or lower case?

3. Which capital and lower-case letters need to be taught to each group of children?

Testing the ability to give the names of letters

The ability to give the names of letters is not assured by a high score on the previous test. Some children can identify letters when the teacher gives their names but are not sure of many names of letters when they have to give them themselves. All that is needed to test the child's ability to name letters is a list of printed letters in random order. The cards used in the identification-of-letters test will serve, or the letters may be printed on a single card for the child to read to the teacher.

The same lists of letters can be used if the teacher wishes to know which of the pupils can give the sounds of letters. Few pupils have this ability at the beginning of first grade so that its use is limited to the pupils who are superior in knowing the names of letters.

Variations of the tests in visual perception

The tests in the visual perception of letters may be varied at the pleasure of the teacher:

1. For pupils who cannot identify letters from memory, a lower level may be tested by various types of matching tests. Many of these

are found in reading-readiness workbooks for children. Matching ability only is too low a level of perception as a basis for establishing a sight vocabulary. The child must remember how the word looks if he is to give its name.

2. If pupils are high in letter perception, it is well to know their background in sounds of letters. Fresh copies of the pupils' test sheets used in the identification-of-letters tests may be used to check the child's ability to identify the sounds of letters. The teacher gives the sound, and the child circles the appropriate letter.

3. Tests may be made harder or easier by combining in the pupils' sheets the letters that are easily confused or letters that are very dissimilar.

4. The relationships between capital and lower-case letters may be tested by using the pupils' test sheets for lower-case letters, then showing the capital letters on the cards, and saying, "See if you can find the little letter which goes with this one."

5. Tests may be given in shorter units as a series of games on different days. If six or fewer letters are tested at once, each pupil may be given cards with the letters, and the "game" for the pupil is for him to select and hold up the letter that is shown or named by the teacher.

6. Many of the suggestions for teaching identification and names of letters may be used as tests.

7. Visual perception of whole words may be tested by using the tests for this purpose suggested in the chapter on analysis of pupil needs in primary grades.

Testing auditory perception of sounds in words

The ability to hear separate sounds in spoken words is easy to test if the child knows the names of letters or can match them accurately from memory. Such tests are illustrated in the following chapter. However, it is rather difficult to build auditory-perception tests of word elements when the child does not know his letters. We have not yet developed tests to measure the early stages of this ability. We know much more about auditory-perception tests which seem to bear little or no relationship to the ability to identify sounds in spoken words.

Some of the tests which have *little or no relationship to auditory perception of word elements* are the following:

1. The ability to identify different sounds of objects being struck or sounded, such as bells, boxes, cans, and the like; of the voices of different children; of bird or animal sounds.

2. The ability to pronounce words spoken by the teacher, even words of four or five syllables.

3. The ability to tell whether words pronounced by the teacher are the same or different.

4. Tests of clarity of enunciation, or tests of hearing acuity.

All of these abilities are valuable abilities, and they may represent early stages of development of auditory perception, but high ability in them does not indicate that the child has the background of noticing the separate sounds in words that is required by reading.

The simplest way to test this ability is to teach it to groups of children and observe the differences in their responses. The following test for the ability to hear certain initial sounds is taken from *Building Word Power*,[1] where it appears as Lesson 1. The fact that a child can identify the sounds in this lesson does not mean that he knows all of the other initial sounds. It does indicate, however, that the child will have difficulty in learning them if he does not know them already.

Testing similar sounds at the beginning of words

(Lesson 1—*Building Word Power*)

In giving directions such as in the first sentence on the next page, say the sound of the letter and not the name.

[1] Donald D. Durrell, Helen B. Sullivan, and Helen A. Murphy, *Building Word Power* (Yonkers, New York: World Book Company, 1945).

I am going to say some words that begin with *s*, like *seven*. Listen and see if you can hear the *s*. [Dictate these words.]

said   see   sent   set   say   sand   sister

Did you hear the *s* at the beginning of each word? Who can tell me a word that begins with *s*? [Let individual children try to give words beginning with *s*.]

Now I'll say some words that begin with *r*, like *room*.

rabbit   robin   rolls   run

Did you hear *r* in all the words? [Let the children add other words they know.]

Listen carefully now. These words begin with *f* like *father*.

feet   fall   fit   fairy   funny

Who can think of another word that begins with *f*?

Let's play a game. Close your eyes and listen. I'll say some words that begin with *f*, like *for*. When you hear a word that doesn't begin with *f*, clap your hands. Listen carefully for *f* in each word. [In dictating the words, be careful not to indicate by dropping your voice the word that does not begin with *f*.]

face   fairy   fall   *room*   family   farm   fat

[Notice each child's reaction. Watch carefully to see which children get the difference first, and which ones just follow the leader.]

Close your eyes. Listen again. Be sure to clap your hands when you hear a word that doesn't begin with *f*. Ready.

first   finger   fish   fit   fix   far   *box*   feed   find

Listen now to these words. Keep your eyes closed. They begin with *g*, like *girl*.

gun   give   got   girl   gate

Did you hear *g* in each word? Keep your eyes closed. If you hear a word that doesn't begin with *g*, clap your hands. Ready.

gas   go   gold   game   gets   garden   gift   girl   gum   *fun*   goods
going   golf

Good. Listen again for the words that begin with *g*. Clap your hands when you hear one that doesn't begin with *g*. Ready.

gallop   gasoline   give   goes   Goldilocks   gone   guess   game   got
right   goose   gate

Now shut your eyes and listen carefully. This time I'll say some words that begin with *m*, like *Mary*. Listen.

man   match   mail   many   move   meat   Monday

Did you hear *m* in each word? Now listen again. This time stand when you hear a word that does not begin with *m*. Ready.

man   made   mail   make   me   meadow   mother   mouse   movies
music   *name*   my   mark   market

Good. Now listen again for words beginning with *m*. Stand when you hear a word that does not begin with *m*.

minute   mamma   many   march   may   milk   meet   Monday   mind
kind   monkey   morning   most

This time I'll says words that begin with a different letter. These words begin with *h* like *hat*. If you hear a word that doesn't begin with *h*, stand up. Listen carefully and see who will be the first one to hear a word that doesn't start with *h*.

had   hall   hand   handkerchief   have   heavy   help   horse   hurry
hot   hammer   hair   *boy*   head   heel

Now, are you ready? Listen for the words that begin with *h*. Remember to stand when you hear a word that doesn't start with *h*. Close your eyes everyone. Listen.

half   hard   hatchet   horn   house   hill   home   hose   hope   hunt
hungry   hit   *sing*   hello   him   herself

If the teacher is unable to observe which children are responding accurately when this lesson is taught, and which children are merely quick to follow the lead of other children, she may have the children raise their hands quietly instead of clapping or standing. The teacher may make up similar lessons, or she may modify this one by the more frequent addition of words that do not begin with the sound indicated.

A more complete inventory of the ability to hear sounds in words is presented in the *Murphy-Durrell Diagnostic Reading Readiness Test* [2] in which the sounds are checked by having the child mark pictures of objects with names beginning with certain sounds. This reading-readiness analysis also has a test of visual discrimination of letters and words and a test of learning rate. Norms are provided for all tests.

Another way to test the child's ability to notice beginning sounds is to prepare a large chart on which is painted or drawn pictures of

[2] Helen A. Murphy and Donald D. Durrell. Published by World Book Company.

objects representing different initial sounds. Suppose the chart is designed to test initial *c*. Pictures scattered on the chart are as follows:

corn   rooster   coat   cow   cup   car   cake

cookies   carrots   fish   gun   house   rabbit

table   gate   fence

Children are told the names of all of the things in the pictures, just to be sure that *rooster* will not be called *chicken,* and *car* named as *automobile,* and other similar changes. Direct in this way:

Here are some words that begin with *c*. Listen carefully to see if you can hear the *c* at the beginning of the word.

can   call   cook   catch   curtain   cut

Say them after me, *can   call   cook   catch   curtain   cut.* They all begin alike. Now you look at the pictures and see if you can find a picture of something that begins with *c* like *call* and *cut*. [Have different children in the group try to pick out the objects.]

Other letters can be tested by preparing suitable charts. These charts make excellent teaching devices, and they may be prepared for a number of different purposes. Lantern slides for testing and teaching initial and final sounds are found in *Phonics on Film.*[3]

Observing other reading-readiness abilities

Some reading-readiness abilities that cannot be measured satisfactorily are interest in words and persistence and attention in learning. They must be estimated from children's reactions to certain questions and situations. The oral-language ability of some children can be evaluated, if the teacher thinks it necessary.

Interest in words

We have no standard way of measuring the child's interest in printed words. It can be observed informally during the tests of learning rate and perception of letters and sounds. At the time children

[3] A series of film slides for developing auditory and visual discrimination of word elements, by B. Alice Crossley and Donald D. Durrell.

are tested individually on learning rate, the child may be asked if he can read any other words, such as road signs, names of other children or of other members of his family, names of newspapers or magazines, names of different kinds of breakfast foods or other foods, names of television programs, or other words that come to the attention of young children. If the child has learned none of these, it indicates a low interest in symbols. Such children will need dramatized activities in which words become important. A numerical rating may be used to record the estimated level of interest in words:

> High interest in words—1
> Average interest in words—2
> Low interest in words—3

Persistence and attention in learning

Determination of persistence and attention also requires informal observation since we have no satisfactory way of measuring them. Again, they may be estimated from the children's reactions during the giving of the earlier tests. Children who are always alert to the task at hand may be given a rating of 1. Children who are usually holding their attention on the task may be rated as 2. Children who are easily distracted from the task are given a rating of 3. Low attention and easy distractibility indicate a need for instruction in very small groups and lessons which require frequent individual response.

Oral-language ability

Oral-language ability is highly important to the child in most phases of learning, but almost all children have an adequate oral vocabulary for first-grade reading. Most have better oral vocabularies than are required for second-grade reading. If there are doubts about the oral-language background of children, the teacher may follow these procedures:

1. Read stories from the first or second reader and ask children questions about the stories afterwards.

2. Show pictures from readers or from other sources and ask the children about situations and objects in the pictures.

3. Talk with the children about their families, their play activities, or other interests.

If the children are reluctant to talk, are unfamiliar with essential words in stories, or seem handicapped in English, help in oral-language background is indicated.

Picture-vocabulary tests and intelligence tests in which the children follow oral directions are helpful in evaluating growth in vocabulary and language abilities. However, these tests do not relate directly to the vocabulary need for reading, and a more valid measure is to test the child's ability to handle the language of the stories in the readers.

Use of check list of instructional needs in reading readiness

When the tests have been completed, it is useful to make a chart of the attainments and instructural needs of the pupils. A suitable check list is shown on the following page. Children are grouped by their scores on the learning-rate test, and their attainments are to be indicated. The number of letters or sounds known should be indicated in the columns. If instructional needs only are to be noted, a check √ is placed in the column to indicate that instruction is needed at the level or in the ability checked.

REPRESENTATIVE STANDARD TESTS OF READING READINESS

American School Achievement Tests: Readiness. Young, Robert, and Others. Bloomington, Illinois: Public School Publishing Company, 1941.

Gates Reading Readiness Tests. Gates, Arthur I. New York: Bureau of Publications, Teachers College, Columbia University, 1939.

Harrison-Stroud Reading Readiness Tests. Harrison, M. Lucile, and Stroud, James B. Boston: Houghton Mifflin Company, 1950.

Lee-Clark Reading Readiness Tests. Lee, J. Murray, and Clark, W. W. Los Angeles: California Test Bureau, 1931.

Metropolitan Readiness Tests. Hildreth, Gertrude, and Griffiths, Nellie L. Yonkers, New York: World Book Company, 1949.

Monroe Reading Aptitude Tests. Monroe, Marion. Boston: Houghton Mifflin Company, 1935.

CHECK LIST OF INSTRUCTIONAL NEEDS IN READING READINESS

	Learning Rate (Number Known)	Visual Discrimination of Letters				Matching	Sounds in Words	Interest in Words	Attention-Persistence	Oral Language	
		Names of		Identifying Letters							
School _____		Caps.	L.C.	Named	Shown						
Grade _____				Caps. L.C.	Caps. L.C.						
Date _____											
Teacher _____											
High Learning-Rate Group											
Average Learning-Rate Group											
Slow Learning-Rate Group											

Murphy-Durrell Diagnostic Reading Readiness Test. Murphy, Helen A., and Durrell, Donald D. Yonkers, New York: World Book Company, 1949.

SUGGESTIONS FOR FURTHER READING

Adams, Fay, Gray, Lillian, and Reese, Dora. *Teaching Children to Read.* New York: The Ronald Press, 1949. Chapter 4.

Anderson, Irving H., and Dearborn, Walter F. *The Psychology of Teaching Reading.* New York: The Ronald Press Company, 1952. Chapter 2.

Artley, A. Sterl. *Your Child Learns to Read.* Chicago: Scott, Foresman and Co., 1953. Chapter 2.

Betts, Emmett A. *Foundations of Reading Instruction.* New York: The American Book Company, 1946. Chapters 8 and 13.

Bond, Guy L., and Wagner, Eva B. *Teaching the Child to Read,* Revised Edition. New York: The Macmillan Company, 1950. Chapters 5 and 6.

Dolch, Edward W. *Teaching Primary Reading,* Second Edition. Champaign, Illinois: Garrard Press, 1950. Chapter 4.

Gates, Arthur I. *The Improvement of Reading,* Third Edition. New York: The Macmillan Company, 1947. Chapter 6.

Harris, Albert J. *How to Increase Reading Ability,* Third Edition. New York: Longmans, Green and Company, Inc., 1956. Chapter 2.

Hildreth, Gertrude. *Learning the Three R's,* Second Edition. Minneapolis: Educational Publishers, Inc., 1936. Chapter 7.

McKim, Margaret G. *Guiding Growth in Reading in the Modern Elementary School.* New York: The Macmillan Company, 1955. Chapters 3 and 4.

Yoakam, Gerald A. *Basal Reading Instruction.* New York: McGraw-Hill Book Company, 1955. Chapter 7.

CHAPTER 4 The Reading-Readiness Program

THE CHART of instructional needs of pupils presented in Chapter 3 will enable the teacher to place children into groups for teaching. While the results of the learning-rate tests provide the best basis for grouping, the strengths and weaknesses shown on other tests and observations will also be helpful in grouping. A child high in learning rate may need extra help on lower-case letters. Several of the high learning group may need extra practice in noticing sounds in words. These children may join those in lower learning-rate groups when the lessons are suited to them.

Some of the children in low groups may have special strengths in letter names, and they may be added to the high learning-rate groups who are working at writing letters or learning the sounds of letters. There will be many shifts of pupils from group to group during the early stages of first-grade work. Grouping should not be considered permanent, and the combining of groups frequently will make the changes easier. In many of the exercises, children may work together in pairs or groups of three. Some children who have difficulty in paying attention in larger groups work well with pupil teachers who are superior learners.

Children high in learning rate and reading-readiness abilities

Some children will be ready for preprimers without needing to go through the reading-readiness preparatory period. However, they will enjoy doing the lessons in the early reading-readiness books, and th re is probably little harm in letting them have the added practice even though it is not necessary. The materials should be presented at a faster pace, and much of the instruction requiring the teacher's direction may be omitted for them. Items clearly below their level of maturity may be omitted, or the child may be allowed to complete several days' work in a single day. It must be remembered that unnecessary practice in skills is one of the main sources of time-wasting for the rapid learner.

The rapid learners who show weaknesses in letter names, either in lower case or capitals, may begin games and practices to master those that they do not know. Some children will want to learn to write letters and words and will be ready for learning correct forms of manuscript writing. All of the children will want to build their own lists of words, and they will refer to these lists in writing notes and letters.

Most children in the high learning-rate group will need practice in ear training to become more secure in noticing sounds at the beginning, middle, and end of words. Those children who know the names of letters and are quick at noticing the sounds in spoken words may begin to learn phonics—to associate sounds with letters.

These children should join the slower learners in many of the reading-readiness exercises. They may be paired with other children or serve as pupil teachers or leaders for groups of two or three children. It is here that the group responsibility for giving and receiving help is begun, and a cooperative spirit is allied to the mutual task of seeing that everyone in the room makes progress. It is important to remember, however, that these rapid learners are ready for progress in the preprimer. They need to feel the pleasure of acquiring new words and of moving through the stories at a stimulating pace.

Children of average learning rate and reading-readiness abilities

Children of average reading-readiness abilities will be ready for the activities provided by the reading-readiness materials in regular basal-reading systems. Usually they will find enough practice material to learn to match letters and to identify letters, but there will need to be extra practice in learning letter names. Almost all will need supplementary help in ear training. But they will need this ear training at the level of identifying sounds in words, not at the lower level of auditory-attention drills for miscellaneous sounds and noises. Children in this average learning-rate and reading-readiness group who have high skills with letters or with sounds in words may join the rapid learners who are practicing higher levels of these reading-readiness abilities.

Children low in learning rate and reading-readiness abilities

An examination of the chart of instructional needs may show that these children require subdivision into two groups: those who are ready to work with letters, and those who need practice in highly motivated "attention training." The children who have some success with identifying the letters shown and who were rated fair in attention and persistence may begin with letter matching and the other materials of the reading-readiness books, with provision for extra practice.

Children who are very weak on identifying the letters shown, who have difficulty in matching letters, who are unable to understand what is wanted in the tests of identifying sounds in words; and children who are rated low in interest in words, in attention and persistence, and in oral language, will need much attention training before they can start on the reading-readiness materials provided by the reading system.

Readiness materials in visual discrimination of letters

Children in average classrooms will be able to learn the names of capital and lower-case letters at the following rates: high learning-rate group, approximately two weeks; average learning-rate group, one month; slow learning-rate groups, six weeks to two months. Instruction in sight vocabulary need not be delayed until children know the names of all letters. However, children should be able to identify letters from memory and should be able to match words accurately. If the child does not see differences in letters, he will constantly stumble in his sight vocabulary.

The introduction of new words before accurate visual discrimination of letters and words is established must be very slow. The child could easily become confused and discouraged by the "different names" of words which look the same to him.

Suggestions are made below for teaching the visual discrimination of letters. They are presented in the following order:

1. Learning the names of letters.
2. Meaningful practice with capital letters.
3. Matching capital and lower-case letters.
4. Learning to match letters and words.
5. Visual-attention exercises—non-letter forms.

The first three abilities are suitable for high learning-rate groups and for pupils in average learning-rate groups who were able to identify several of the letters shown. Children who were very poor in the test of ability to identify letters shown will start with the fourth level. The very slowest learners will need the visual-attention exercises.

As in the teaching of all skills, slow learners will need to go step-by-step, with only a few letters introduced at a time, with plenty of practice and review, and with a fair mastery of each group of letters before new ones are introduced. Little transfer of learning may be expected, each letter and each stage of visual discrimination being a separate unit of learning. Rapid learners may take larger groups of letters, may combine several stages of discrimination at once, and will need only small amounts of practice and review. However, progress for all pupils should be as fast as security in learning allows. Even the slowest pupils should know the names of both lower case letters and capital letters at the end of eight weeks of instruction.

Learning the names of letters

Learning letter names is not an "isolated meaningless drill" to the child. He enjoys it heartily. He is quick to show off his knowledge at home by pointing out letters he knows, and he uses it in shouting to parents, "What is this word—h-u-r-r-y?" He asks, "How do you spell *thank?*" and he receives the answer in letters. He finds a knowledge of letter names a valuable tool—one of the mysteries possessed by adults and older children.

Although the abilities in naming letters and in identifying letters named were tested separately in the informal analysis, actually the two abilities are so close that they may be taught at the same time. The order of learning the names of capital letters is approximately as follows, from easiest to hardest: O X A B T C L R I S P N F E H D M K Z J Y W G Q U V. The order for lower-case letters is as follows: o x s c i p t m k z e w r j y f n a h v u b d l g q.

In planning games for learning letter names, groups of letters easiest to learn may be presented first, with harder groups coming later. Children should master one group of letters before going on to another group as they may be confused by too many letters being introduced at once. Provision should be made for frequent review of letters previously taught.

It has not been established whether it is better to teach both capital and lower-case forms of each letter at the same time, although many teachers prefer this method. Others may wish to teach all of the capitals, then give the matching games to associate capital letters with small letters, then teach the names of small letters. Still others may wish to teach the names of both forms at the same time and to provide exercises for matching capital and small letters as a part of the same learning situation.

Here are some games for teaching letters:

1. Each child is given sets of cards bearing the same five letters. The teacher or pupil leader shows each letter in turn, giving its name. The children select the same letter, hold it up, and say its name. After the children are fairly sure of the names of letters, the teacher calls the name of a letter without showing it and asks the children to show it to her. Then the letter is shown so that the pupils may check their selection.

2. Multiple-choice sheets similar to those used in the testing may be made for the pupils, but with only a few letters being tested at a time. The teacher shows the letter, gives its name, and the child repeats the name of the letter. The teacher turns the letter down, and the child circles it on his sheet. These multiple-choice exercises should be made very easy at first by using letters of very dissimilar appearance in each box. Later they may be made harder by combining letters which are commonly confused.

3. After a letter is shown, or after several letters have been presented, children are asked to find the letter in words printed on the blackboard, on a picture chart with names below the pictures, from pages in a book, or on sheets containing words.

4. A child may serve as "postman," carrying a box for "mailing" letters. Each child may read his pack of letters, dropping them into the box if he says them correctly.

5. A set of pockets may be sewn on a large piece of cloth, with each pocket labeled with a letter of the alphabet in order. The child takes his pack of cards, gives the name of each one and places it in the right pocket. Another child who is "postmaster" or "librarian" checks the names of letters given.

6. Letters may be written on the blackboard in random order. As a child says the name of a letter, he erases it.

7. Children have letters pinned on their blouses. The teacher spells a word and children arrange themselves to make the word.

8. Various games may be made up similar to Lotto and Authors and used for learning letter names.

Meaningful practices with capital letters

Some of the meaningful uses of capital letters which interest children are the following:

1. Initials of children in the class
2. Names and abbreviations on automobile license plates
3. Radio and television call letters
4. Traffic signs
5. Compass points—N   E   S   W
6. Names and abbreviations of street signs
7. Letters on high-school athletic sweaters
8. Names of brands of foods, of newspapers and magazines
9. A.M., P.M., R.R., R.F.D., P.O., Y.M.C.A., A & P, and similar use of letters

As it is difficult to control the order of practice or to provide intensive instruction at points of need while using these sources of letters, the games suggested below should be interspersed with the lessons suggested in the foregoing section.

Some of the games for meaningful use of letters are the following:

1. Children may wear their initials, or the initials may be placed on their desks. Children may in turn ask "Who is E. R.?" "Who is J. D.?" and so on, with other children in the group giving the names of the child.

2. A pack of cards may be made with children's initials, and the "postman" may read them aloud and deliver them to the right children. When a mistake is made, another child becomes "postman," or they may take turns, each delivering three "letters."

3. Children may read the initials on cards and sort them by boys and girls.

4. A map may be drawn showing where different children live, their homes being indicated by their initials. A game of "deliveryman" may be played, with the child showing where he would go to deliver three parcels to A. H., R. D., and M. M., and so on. As each parcel is delivered to the child to whom it is addressed, the deliveryman tells who the child is.

5. Children may "choose up" for games, calling others by their initials.

6. Cards with children's initials may be dealt to members of the group, with each child telling "Who is coming to my party," or "I have letters to mail to these people," reading the initials and telling their names.

7. The letters N E S W are shown and the pupils point the direction indicated.

8. "Going on an automobile ride" may utilize various kinds of signs, license plates, traffic signs, store signs, and railroad signs. Questions are asked or directions are given which call for the use of the signs.

9. Children may tell things that happen in the A.M. or P.M.

10. A game of "radio station" may use call letters of local stations read by "announcers" who tell items of news or weather.

11. Rows of chairs may be arranged as theater seats, with each row indicated by letters. Children tell the "usher" the row indicated on their tickets, and the usher checks the ticket and seats them in the right row.

12. "Going shopping" may be played with charts on which are pasted names and pictures of foods or brand names the children know. The children may then make shopping lists by copying the letters.

Various meaningful situations which use writing or copying of letters may be built by the imaginative teacher. The desire to write seems to appear before the desire to read, with many children of four insisting on "writing" and sending letters to relatives and friends. This early desire to write may well be utilized in the reading-readiness activities of learning letters and words. It is, in part, the basis of reading systems which follow a "written language" approach to reading.

If writing is used in the reading-readiness period, it must be printing or manuscript writing. It would add to the children's confusion if a new set of cursive forms of letters needed to be learned at the same time.

Matching capital letters and small letters

Since it is difficult to make meaningful games with small letters, it is well for the child to be able to learn the names of small letters by matching them with capital letters. Only a few letters have exactly the same shape as capitals and lower-case letters, and it cannot be assumed that the child knows the names of lower-case letters because he knows the capitals. When children are able to match capital and small letters accurately, and when they know the names of capital letters, the names of lower-case letters are easily learned through games such as those suggested on page 74.

Most reading-readiness workbooks contain exercises in matching capital and lower-case letters. If additional practice is needed, a chart with capital letters above and small letters below may be placed on the blackboard or bulletin board. The child may refer to this chart for help in matching letters.

Other supplementary materials for practice in matching capital letters and small letters are suggested below:

1. Worksheets of various sorts may be made, in which the child draws a line from capitals to small letters or circles the small letters which match the capital letters at the side.

2. Pockets in a large card or on a cloth are labeled with capital letters. The child sorts small-letter cards into the correct pockets. Another child checks the accuracy, either at the time of placing cards in pockets, or afterwards.

3. Word wheels may be made with capitals on the outside wheel, small letters on the inside in random order. Two children see how quickly they can go around the wheel matching the capital and the small letters. A third child checks to see that pairs of letters are correctly made.

4. Two children may have sets of several letters, one with capitals, one with small. One child holds up the capital letter, the other finds the small letter.

5. Various modifications of standard gains may be played in which capital and small letters are matched.

6. A typewriter is very useful for learning the association between capitals and small letters. When the capital letter is struck, the small letter is produced.

Learning to match letters and words

It is much easier to match individual letters than it is to match words. Letters should be presented individually in matching exercises before they are shown in words.

Children need not stay on the letter-matching level more than a few days, nor must they establish complete accuracy before going on to the stage of learning the names of letters. Most of the games for teaching letter names also help children to establish the skill of matching.

Word matching will also improve as letter names are learned. The lower-case forms of *b   d   p* and *q*, of *m* and *n*, of *f* and *t*, and other combinations may show confusions which will remain for some time, even after letter names are learned. If these are seriously confused, it is often best to avoid intensive drill on them and assure the child that he will learn them later.

Matching exercises are often dull, even when games are devised for making them palatable. Errors often appear because of low motivation rather than lack of perceptual ability. Learning letter names is more satisfying and more meaningful to the child. He can use this skill immediately, and it allows him to use his voice as well as his eyes. Prolonged presentation of matching is to be avoided. It is probably better to intersperse practice in matching with learning the names of letters after each group of letters has already been matched accurately.

Matching exercises may be made easy by exercises which contain letters or words that are very different. These exercises may be made hard by combining letters or words much alike and commonly confused. Group activities are more fun for the children but occasionally take more time for "activity" than for discrimination. Individual worksheets require more attention and persistence and are duller for children. The teacher will do well to use both group and individual exercises.

Some of the common types of matching activities are as follows:

1. Various types of work-sheet activity in which one letter or word is indicated at the side of a row, the child drawing a circle around or marking other letters or words that are the same.

Letters: t—m   t   f   r   t   h
             m—w   n   m   r   m   m

a) Words that begin with the letter:
    h—hunt   hot   bell   help   cool   last
    n—best   nice   live   next   nose   milk

b) Words that *contain* the letter:
    t—take   went   walk   fast   winter
    r—way   ride   can   mark   car

c) Words that *begin with the same letter as the word at the side:*
    most—more   many   table   mark   listen
    came—cross   count   grow   ever   cake

d) Words that have the *same first and last letter* as the word at the side: (Difficult)
    want—walk   went   glad   won   waist
    good—gone   gold   tied   glad   ground

2. Letters or words in parallel columns. The child draws between letters or words that are alike, have the same first letter, the same first and last letters, and so on.

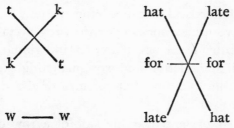

3. Games and devices which are variations of (1) and (2) above:

a) Each child has a set of cards containing letters or words. The same letters or words appear on a chart or on the blackboard. Each child in turn finds his letters or words on the chart.

b) Each child has two sets of cards containing the same letters or words. He matches the letters or words, combines words beginning with the same letter, and so on. This is more fun when two children work together.

c) Letter or word wheels which have the same letters on the inside and outside wheels, in different order. Children find the words which go together.

d) One child is provided with a chart containing several letters; another child has a pack of cards on which the letters are printed. One child shows a card, the other finds the letter on the chart. Words may be used instead of letters. This game may be varied so that several children have copies of the same chart of letters. Then one child acts as leader, showing the letters and checking on the others who find the letter.

Visual-attention exercises—non-letter forms

Visual-attention exercises on non-letter forms are for the children who are very low in attention, have difficulty in following directions, and have shown little interest in words. We have no evidence that they bear any relationship to visual perception of letters and words. They may be considered "reading-readiness" exercises in the sense that they give the child background in following directions, in maintaining attention, and in practice in some of the activities that will soon be used with letters and words. As soon as the child shows good skill in matching pictures, objects, and forms, he should begin at once matching letters and learning letter names.

The reading-readiness books contain many visual-attention exercises, and these provide the best source for individual seat work. They are very much like the letter- and word-matching exercises described in the section above, except that pictures or drawings are used in place of letters or words.

1. A picture is presented at the side of a row of pictures. The child marks the same picture when it is repeated in the row, or the child marks the pictures that are different. (This exercise may be hard or easy, depending upon the closeness of the pictures or drawings to be matched. It can be made difficult if the teacher uses a row of pictures the same as the stimulus picture, but with some minor detail changed on one or more.)

2. A large picture or chart contains several objects which are shown separately on cards. The child points to them in the picture.

3. Various games of "find the missing part" may be played. A drawing of a man's face may leave out an eye; a cow may have no front legs; a wagon, no wheels, and so on. The child tells what is missing.

4. Jigsaw puzzles, with only two or three parts, may be combined. These may be pictures pasted on cards, then cut apart for the child to assemble.

5. Picture puzzles may be made, using duplicate pictures. One is cut into four to six sections, and the child reassembles it by placing the parts on or beside the whole picture.

6. Cardboard objects may be cut into different shapes—circles, squares, diamonds, triangles—which are then traced on a larger cardboard. The child places the forms in the correct places on the larger cardboard.

7. Simple adaptations of Lotto may be made, with six or eight squares on each card containing drawings or pictures. One child shows cards containing the pictures, and the others cover on their cards the one shown.

There are endless variations of visual-discrimination games. Electrical matching boards may be made or purchased, and various games may be adapted to chart or blackboard presentation. Children may work in pairs, groups, or individually. The important thing to remember is to move to letter perception and learning letter names as quickly as possible. Even the rapid-learning groups enjoy these games, but such practice is largely time wasting for them in relation to improving their reading readiness.

Instruction in auditory discrimination of word elements

Since the ability to notice sounds in spoken words is essential to learning to read a phonetic language, it is highly desirable to give the child this ability as soon as he encounters systematic teaching of reading. Almost all children will need some help in noticing the sounds in words.

Children in high learning-rate groups may identify initial consonant sounds but will need help on blends, final consonants, and larger word parts. Average learning-rate groups will need a fairly complete program in ear training for sounds in words. Slow learning-rate groups will need much extra help, often including lessons in showing how sounds are produced, similar to the instruction given deaf children. The very slowest of the children may require auditory-attention games before they can be introduced to sounds in words.

Auditory discrimination of sounds in words provides the basis for effective use of phonics. Unless the child has heard the sounds in words, it is futile to teach the sounds of letters, blends, or phonograms. The chief weakness of the phonic systems of earlier date was the inability of the child to combine the sounds after "sounding out" the word. Reading clinics of the 1920's and 1930's were full of children who were fluent in "sounding out" printed words, but after such sounding made random guesses at the word. They were completely unable to identify sounds in spoken words. After a period of ear training in identifying sounds in words, their phonics became effective. More than a hundred years ago Horace Mann noted that "It is futile to teach phonics unless the child notices these sounds in the words he speaks."

Since instruction in ear training as reading readiness is of relatively recent origin, most basal-reading systems fail to provide adequate instruction to establish the ability. The teacher will usually need to provide large amounts of supplementary practice for most pupils. But, here again, complete mastery of all sounds is not essential before beginning the sight vocabulary. After the child has a fair ability with identifying the main consonant sounds, he should begin expanding his sight vocabulary. A more complete equipment in ear training may be acquired during the teaching of reading.

Because of the need for large amounts of supplementary practice in ear training, it is desirable to purchase materials designed for the purpose. Many types of supplementary lessons are available: lessons to be used by the teacher such as *Building Word Power;* [1] film slides, such as *Phonics on Film;* [2] and various phonograph recordings. A list of materials which may be purchased is provided at the end of this chapter.

It is not difficult to build ear-training materials that are highly interesting to children. The children who are advanced in the ability may help build such materials for use by slower learners. As effective charts and games are made, the teacher should save them for use in the future, since it is in the *use,* not in the construction of such charts, that the children learn more effectively.

We do not have the clear knowledge in regard to the order of the teaching of auditory discrimination of word elements that we have of the order of teaching letters. *Building Word Power,* which has the widest use of any of the supplementary materials for the training of auditory-discrimination, presents the sounds in the following order:

Initial sounds—f b h g c l m d j n k p r w s t y v th wh ch sh dr tr gr br fr cl fl pl

Words that rhyme with—fall men play will run pig bell in out look fill

Final sounds—f g b l m d p r k n s t y

Listening for vowel sounds is not taught at this stage of learning, primarily because of the frequent variation in vowel sounds. When a consonant represents more than one sound, the most frequently used sound is taught; *g* as in *game, c* as in *cake, s* as in *sing.* Children are told that these letters sometimes indicate other sounds, but that they can generally depend on the one taught.

There are several other problems in the teaching of auditory discrimination that have not yet been solved by research. Is it more effective to teach the child to listen for initial sounds, and then to teach listening for final sounds later? Or should the sound be studied in both initial and final positions at the same time? Probably it makes little difference which way the sounds are taught, and the teacher may choose which she prefers.

[1] Donald D. Durrell and Others. Published by World Book Company.
[2] A series developed by B. Alice Crossley and Donald D. Durrell.

Should one listen for the *m* (letter name) in *make,* or should one listen for the *m-m-m* (sound of *m*) in *make?* Here again, it probably makes little difference, since children are successful either way. The child will have to learn both the name and the sound eventually. Thus a safe rule is to listen for the *m* sound when the task is identifying sounds in words, and to use letter names in all visual presentations of letters. Until clear answers are provided by research in regard to these problems, the teacher should follow whatever practice seems most effective with her pupils.

Methods for teaching discrimination of word elements

Some of the methods that may be used for teaching auditory discrimination of word elements are the following which use pictures and questions:

1. Picture charts which illustrate beginning sounds, described on pages 63–64 in the previous chapter and used in the manner suggested there, are excellent for teaching. Some charts may teach a single initial or final sound; others may combine two or more sounds for teaching or for review lessons.

2. Children may be asked to look through old magazines to collect pictures that illustrate the initial sounds being taught. These pictures may be used in making charts or games for use with small groups of pairs of children.

3. The teacher can proceed in this way:

There are many things to eat which begin with the same sound as these words—*came   card   cut* [Emphasize the initial *c* sound.] Can you think of things to eat which begin like *came   card   cut?* What are some of them?

Children should think of such things as cake, candy, cookies, carrots, corn, cabbage. Other questions may be about things to wear, names of animals, names of children, street names, names of flowers or birds, or other classifications known to children. Similar questions may deal with things to take on a picnic or a vacation, presents to give for birthdays, things one would like for Christmas, things in this room, things in a grocery store, things on a farm, things to pack in mother's trunk, and the like.

4. Pictures indicating sounds to be taught are placed on a tack board or in the chalk trough. For example, there may be pictures of a fence, a house, ball, and a girl. The children say the names of the pictured objects to make sure they have the right words with each picture. Then the teacher directs the children in the following way:

I am going to say some words that begin the same as these words. *Hand.* You say it. Which one of the pictures does it belong with?

The child points to *house* and repeats the two words, *hand—house.* If, instead of having the pictures posted, each child has copies of the pictures on cards, he may select the right picture and hold it up, repeating the words, *hand—house.*

5. Although the suggestions should indicate initial consonants, similar methods may be used with final consonants, initial or final blends, or rhymes.

6. Rhyming words are often taught by making up rhyming riddles, with children supplying the appropriate words. Silly jingles will allow children to suggest last rhyming words.

Games for teaching and testing discrimination of sounds

When children know the names of letters, there are many ways to teach and test the discrimination of sounds. If, for example, the names of the letters *s, p, t, m* are known to the children, the following games are possible.

1. Children have sets of cards containing the letters. The teacher proceeds in this way:

Here are some words which begin with *s* [use the name, not the sound, when letters are used at this time]—*sand   soft   sister   suds.* You say them. [Repeat the words.] Show me the letter these words begin with. [Then do the same with the letter *p,* using such words as *paste   push   point   paint.*]

Now I'm going to say some words, and you are to show me which letter they begin with—*sand.* That's right, now show me the first letter in this word—*south.*

The same words used in the illustrations may be repeated, but new ones should be added. As two sounds have been mastered, other sounds may be taught and reviewed.

2. A practice sheet may be made with pictures in boxes with letters beneath. Here is an example:

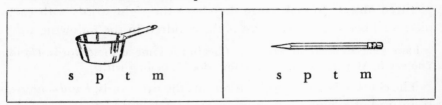

| s   p   t   m | s   p   t   m |

The teacher says, "The first picture is a pan. What letter does it begin with? Draw a circle around it." Then go on to the next picture. The teacher will need to name the pictures, since the child may easily use another name, even when the picture is well drawn.

3. Variations of a "ladder game" may be made, with letters or pictures on or between the rungs of the ladder. The teacher says a word beginning with the letter or else names the picture, and each child says a word which begins with the same sound as the word given. The child may keep on up the ladder until he makes a mistake. Then another child tries to climb the ladder, giving words not used before.

Variations on this are "climbing the hill to the castle," "seeing how high I can fly my kite," "see if I can go all around the bases," "fishing" —with strings tied to letters or pictures in a box, and so on. Such games are good for review or for additional practice after sounds have been taught other ways.

Devices that call attention to the speech structure of words

Devices that call attention to the speech structure of words are useful. They help children who are not successful in noticing the separate sounds in words through the methods described above. Books of speech correction or on teaching speech to the deaf contain many helps of this type.

1. The explosive sound *p* is illustrated by putting a small flag or a piece of thin paper in front of the lips, then saying *put paste*

pin paper penny. Attention is called to the movement of the paper whenever the word begins with *p*. The child may try this himself, repeating words given by the teacher. He then tells when words begin with *p*. This may be done with small groups of children who should be able to see at once which of these words begin with *p*: *point page roll mail push pie noise pay*.

2. The child watches the teacher's lips while she says *fast fire farm fine*. He may observe his own lips in a mirror. Then he is asked to notice the lips when the following words are said: *house hurt heavy hand*. Lists of words are given which begin with the two sounds, and the child is asked to tell which begin with *f* and which begin with *h*.

Care should be taken to use sounds which are formed very differently and can be clearly told apart by looking at the lips. For example, *m, p,* and *b* begin with the lips closed. Only a few sounds need be taught in this manner for the child to see that words are formed differently.

Auditory-attention exercises

It is doubtful if auditory-attention exercises are helpful in reading readiness except as training in paying attention to directions given by the teacher. They may be used for a few days with children who are very retarded in attention and persistence, or may be interspersed as variety in the learning of sounds of words. Some of the suggestions for auditory-attention training are the following:

1. *Location of sounds.*   Children sit in circle with eyes closed; other children are placed in different corners behind the group. The teacher says, "Where is the kitty?" and points to one child in the corner, who says "Meow." The children with eyes closed point to the source of the sound.

2. *Identification of voices.*   Children sit in circle with eyes closed; the teacher touches one child, who says, "Who am I?" Others guess who he is.

3. *Identifying sounds of objects struck.*   Children are shown several objects which produce different sounds when struck—bell, glass,

box, bottle. The children close their eyes. The teacher strikes the different objects, and the children identify the object struck.

4. *Number of sounds heard.* The teacher stands behind the children and taps one, two, or three times. The children repeat the number of taps heard. This may be varied with sounds in different cadences.

5. A poem is read which contains refrains at the ends of stanzas or lines. The children repeat the refrains at appropriate times.

Teaching other reading-readiness abilities

Although visual and auditory discrimination of word elements are the main factors in reading readiness, attention to other abilities is often desirable. The following suggestions will provide variety in the daily lessons, will stimulate interest in reading, and will help the child to improve his attention.

Improving interest in learning printed words

Children who have not shown previous interest in learning to read words will need various activities in which printed words are important to them—activities involving immediate response to words associated with action or pictures. Even though the child does not have to read the words, he will get the idea of the value of reading from some of the following activities:

1. Children's names are guessed from their initials, as suggested on pages 75–76.

2. Objects in the room are labeled. Children are given cards containing the names of these objects, then find the object indicated on the card by matching with the label. Then the child says the word.

3. Various simple direction cards are made with pictures with words printed below. The cards may contain the drawings of parts of the face. The teacher then says, "Show me your _____." (showing card with drawing of nose, with the word below). Each child points to his nose. Then the next card is shown.

After two or three cards are shown, the teacher covers the picture, leaving the word exposed. Then she says, "Now see if you can show me this." After the children try, she may expose the picture as check.

4. The same type of game may be played with the word "GO" underneath a green traffic sign, the word "STOP" under a red circle. The children walk slowly across the room, following the *stop* and *go* signs. Then the colors are covered, with the children following the printed directions.

5. Children can play store, with the names of food attached to pictures on a chart which is the store. Or a more elaborate "store" can be set up with packages which show pictures and names of the things they contain. Each child is given a set of cards on which names of food appear. At the store, he matches the words, then tells what he has bought.

6. The teacher may read stories for which she has key words prepared on cards. These key words should be strongly indicated by context. When she comes to an important word as she reads or tells the story, she holds up the card and waits for children to tell what it is. She should not wait more than two or three seconds, so that the story will not be interrupted, nor should the key words appear too frequently in the story.

7. The teacher and the children can make "experience charts," with the children telling what should go in the "newspaper." The teacher writes on the board. After each child has made a contribution, the group should read what he said. Children may be asked to point to the word which says "cold," "mother," and so on.

Improving ability in maintaining attention

Ability in maintaining attention is largely a matter of motivation of learning on a level which assures success. Such lessons should require immediate action of each child, without prolonged waiting for his turn to come. Lessons which help children who are low in attention have been described in "Visual-Attention Exercises" on pages 80–81, in "Auditory-Attention Exercises" on pages 87–88, and in

"Improving Interest in Learning Printed Words" on pages 88–89. Additional helps will be found in the following sections on "Improving Motor Abilities" and "Improving Oral-Language Abilities." Children who are low in attention and persistence will require continued use of activities which demand immediate response to meaning during the early stages of developing a sight vocabulary.

Improving motor abilities useful in activities related to reading

The only motor abilities that have a demonstrated relationship to learning to read are the writing and copying of letters. Since it is generally observed that the desire to write comes long before the desire to read, the writing of letters and words will probably eventually become an important part of reading-readiness activities, despite the present professional bias against it. Many children can write all of the letters before coming to school. Some have even corresponded with friends, with the help of parents on many words. A few reading systems have been developed in which writing precedes reading. The "kinesthetic" method is based upon tracing of letter forms as an aid to word analysis.

The teacher who wishes to make writing a part of reading-readiness instruction may be aided by the following suggestions:

1. The manuscript form of letters should be taught, since they are close to the printed form and do not confuse the child as do cursive forms.

2. The suggestions for beginning writing presented by established writing systems will be helpful in regard to size and shape of letters. Simple drill on letter forms, however, will not hold the attention of the child.

3. The child should do "purposive writing" in which the words written are important to something immediately ahead:

a) Making "shopping lists," in the *playing store* game on page 89.

b) Making word cards for use in games, by copying words written below objects and pictures.

c) Copying invitations to P.T.A. meetings, or other notes to parents.

d) Copying his contributions to the "newspaper" suggested on page 89.

Motor abilities often required by workbooks in reading are coloring, cutting with scissors, drawing lines and circles, tracing, pasting, folding, drawing lines between objects, turning pages, handling cards, and so on. However, few of these abilities require special training and are best developed by using them as they are required in lessons. Some pupils will be awkward and will need to be helped with the correct way of using scissors, holding a pencil, and other motor abilities. Help may usually be given individually and incidentally rather than through a planned program. The development of motor abilities is of high importance in education and will be given a higher place in the elementary curriculum, but it does not appear to be important to success in beginning reading.

Improving oral-language abilities

If children are unable to understand the words and ideas presented in the readers, it will be necessary to provide oral work with pictures, discussion, dramatization, construction projects, and play activities related to the vocabulary of the reading. Except for children from non-English speaking homes, most children will be found to have an oral-language ability far beyond that presented in beginning reading material. However, ease in oral expression, in listening, in asking questions, in taking part in discussion, and general participation in verbal activities of all kinds is a most important ability in all learning.

Some of the ways that children can be helped in oral-language abilities are the following:

1. Taking part in conversations stimulated through pictures, questions about home activities, radio and television programs, play activities, birthday parties, summer activities, families, and other interests.

2. Making plans for construction projects, conversations before and after field trips, planning exhibits, planning dramatizations.

3. Dramatizations of activities: playing house (with suggested themes such as "getting ready for school in the morning," "getting ready for a birthday party," "getting ready for a visit to grandmother," and so on), playing store, building a house, dramatizing stories or events known to children, dramatizing a story stimulated by a picture series, creating activities for familiar television characters.

4. Telling about objects brought from home, telling events which interest others, showing picture books and telling about them, telling about favorite activities, making up stories.

SUGGESTIONS FOR FURTHER READING

Betts, Emmett A. *Foundations of Reading Instruction.* New York: The American Book Company, 1946. Chapters 14 and 18.

Bond, Guy L., and Wagner, Eva B. *Teaching the Child to Read.* New York: The Macmillan Company, 1950. Chapter 7.

Broom, M. E., Duncan, Mary A., Emig, Dorothy, and Steuber, Josephine.

Effective Reading Instruction in the Elementary School. New York: McGraw-Hill Book Company, 1942. Chapter 4.

McKee, Paul. *The Teaching of Reading in the Elementary School.* Boston: Houghton Mifflin Company, 1948. Chapter 7.

Most beginning reading systems contain instructional materials suitable for building auditory and visual discrimination of word elements. Some additional materials developed at Boston University are the following:

Bresnahan, M. M., and Pronovost, W. L. *Let's Listen.* Boston: Ginn and Company, 1955. Phonograph records for ear training for reading readiness and speech development.

Durrell, Donald D., Sullivan, Helen B., and Junkins, Kathryn. *Ready to Read.* Yonkers, New York: World Book Company, 1941. Pupil's workbook for developing visual discrimination of word elements and other reading-readiness abilities.

Durrell, Donald D., Sullivan, Helen B., and Murphy, Helen A. *Building Word Power.* Yonkers, New York: World Book Company, 1945. A teacher's manual containing forty exercises in ear training.

5 Classroom Analysis of Reading Needs

INFORMAL TESTS based upon the reading materials used in the classroom and observation of faulty habits and weaknesses in regular reading tasks provide the best basis for planning classroom instruction. Children learn to read at unequal rates and develop unequally in the various habits and skills of reading.

At least once or twice a year, the teacher should take an inventory of the various needs for special instruction, and she should make a chart of those needs. Day-by-day casual observation may result in constant postponement of the intensive practice needed to overcome particular weaknesses. The classroom analysis enables the teacher to group children for special help, to plan methods and materials to overcome difficulties, and to observe progress in the various aspects of reading.

A standard test is a helpful way of "keeping score" on children's progress in reading over a year's time. Such tests are useful at the beginning and end of the year to observe the general effectiveness of the skills program in reading. While some standard tests give useful information about growth in different reading skills, they are not designed to evaluate many of the essential reading abilities.

Standard-test results provide a useful evaluation of the reading status of the pupils in the class, and the use of such tests is recommended in connection with the informal analysis. However, if standard-test scores are not available, the informal analysis of instructional needs is not greatly handicapped.

Intelligence tests are helpful supplements to the "score keeping" aspects of standard reading tests, and aid in administrative decisions about the grouping of pupils. However, they offer little assistance to the teacher who is seeking to help her children in reading. After the children have been assigned to a particular classroom, there is seldom any course of action in reading to be altered by mental-test results. A mental age is nothing more than the child's *average achievement* in the abilities measured by the test. Half of such abilities are above his mental age, half below. The mental age or the I.Q. is merely an indication of the child's general capacity in relation to other children, and it sets no strict limits on learning. Fifteen per cent of all children read a year or more above mental age, while four per cent read two or more years above.

The teacher should not press or relax her effort in helping children to achieve in reading because of any relationship between reading and mental age. Every child is entitled to the best efforts of the teacher to improve his reading progress. One special warning about mental tests is desirable here. If the mental test has a high reading content, it provides an erroneous evaluation of the mental age of the child who is low in reading ability.

General suggestions for reading analysis

Informal analysis of reading does not represent a loss in the time devoted to reading instruction, since it is really supplementary practice. Many of the tests suggested in this chapter are suitable for use as regular practice exercises. Many of the observations may be made in the regular reading lessons and do not require special materials.

The teacher need not use all of the tests suggested for each of the various abilities, nor need every item be included on the check lists for observation of faulty habits. There are often several different suggestions for observing instructional needs, and the teacher should choose those which she feels best suit her purpose. It is not necessary to fill out the entire observation chart in a single week, since it may seem best to make a careful evaluation of the different reading skills at the time a period of intensive instruction is planned in those skills.

Group testing, or group observation, is recommended wherever it can be done effectively. Individual testing is usually more accurate, but it requires much more time. Oral reading and oral recall must be observed individually, and if the same materials are to be used with several different children, the tests should be given apart from the class so that children to be tested later will not become acquainted with the materials.

The informal analysis to be made depends upon the reading level of the child, not upon the grade in which he is enrolled. If a child is a nonreader or a preprimer reader, he should be given the reading-readiness tests described in Chapter 3, regardless of whether he is in the third or fifth grade. The primary-grade tests should be given to intermediate-grade readers who are reading at primary level. Children who are reading above grade level will occasionally need help in some of the skills in the higher grades, but for these pupils it is better to emphasize the *use of reading* rather than the skills program.

Analysis of reading needs in primary grades

Analysis of reading needs in the primary grades consists of finding answers to the following questions:

1. Does the child have adequate oral background for reading?
2. Is the child making a vigorous attack on learning to read?
3. Is his reading material of the right level for effective learning?
4. What faults and difficulties appear in his oral reading?
5. Is the rate of presentation of words faster than the child's learning rate?
6. Are his word-analysis skills adequate?

7. Is his silent reading effective?
8. Is he making good progress in comprehension and recall?

Oral-language background

Most children have a much richer oral-language background than is necessary for understanding primary-grade material. The pre-school years have given the child the oral background to take care of most of his needs. He can follow directions, relate his experiences, ask questions, and express his desires. He has listened to stories by his elders, often has spent countless hours before the television set, and has played imaginative games with his friends. This has given him an oral-language background of several thousand words, while the demands of reading will require only a few hundred words in the first year, and less than two thousand in the first three grades.

If it is felt that the child is deficient in oral language, however, the best way to discover such lack is to measure his oral language in relation to his requirements for reading. This may be done informally by reading stories from the basal reader and asking the child questions about the story. Sample questions are "Where was Bobby going?" "What did he want to buy?" "Who went with him?" "What did he see at the store?" "What did he buy?"

Another way of checking oral background is to make a series of questions about the child's experience, forming these questions from the vocabulary usually found in the back of the basal reader. "What is your name?" "Do you have a baby brother or sister?" "How many dogs do you know?" "When is your birthday?" "What do you like to eat?" "Can you jump rope?" By checking off words used in such questions, it is not difficult to build a series of questions which use a large share of the vocabulary in the primer and first reader.

Occasionally the stories will call for information outside the child's experience. If there is a farm unit, a transportation unit, or a city unit in the readers, it is well to find out if the child has had the experiences which will make the reading real to him. This may be done by asking such questions as the following: "Have you ever been to a farm?" "Have you ever seen a cow?" "Have you seen corn grow-ing?" Similar questions may be asked about transportation and city experiences.

If a rating scale is desired, "1" indicates a rich language back-ground, "2," a superior language background, "3," a background ade-quate for reading, and "4," a lack of knowledge of words in reading. A more analytical observation would include separate ratings for un-derstanding spoken language and for freedom of expression in con-versation.

Vigor of attack in reading

The child who delights in reading, and is attentive and eager when new skills are being learned, has much greater chances of success than the child who is listless and inattentive, and who avoids the use of vol-untary reading. In order to observe and record the motivation needs of children in reading, the teacher requires only a simple scale of attitude and interest.

"1"—Delights in voluntary reading; eager to learn new skills.

"2"—Reads with enjoyment; attentive in class and all group ac-tivities.

"3"—Reads assigned work; average attention and effort.

"4"—No voluntary reading; has difficulty in both attention and effort.

"5"—Avoids reading; little persistence and attention.

Separate scales may be used for amount of voluntary reading and for attention and effort in class work.

Oral-reading level and instructional needs

The oral-reading tests discussed below and on the pages that fol-low are suitable for pupils in primary grades and for the slow learn-ers in intermediate grades. The tests cover oral-reading level, the suitability of the materials used, and faulty habits and confusions in oral reading.

In a series of well-prepared basal readers, select short stories of two or three pages from each book from primer through fourth reader. From each book, choose two stories, one in the first part of the book and one in the last part, since materials at the beginning and end of such books usually differ in difficulty. Some care will be needed to choose stories typical of the section of the book. Occasionally stories in the latter part of the book may be easier than earlier stories. While the selections need not be more than one hundred words in length, it is often difficult to find such short units for third- and fourth-grade books. In this case, use part of a story. The longer the selection, the greater will be the time that the teacher must use for testing, and it is especially important that the individual testing be made as brief as possible.

Some readers, especially basal readers, have review stories at intervals; these are particularly well suited for testing oral-reading level. It is desirable, too, to use selections not already read. A child with a good memory for stories can often give the appearance of reading while merely telling the story from memory.

For each selection that the teacher chooses from these basal readers, she should prepare five or six questions on cards. She should avoid questions which the children could answer by a "Yes" or a "No."

Example of selections chosen from basal readers for informal tests

O'Donnell, Mabel. THE ALICE AND JERRY BASIC READERS. Reading Foundation Program. Row, Peterson and Company, Evanston, Illinois, 1954 Edition.

THE NEW DAY IN AND DAY OUT
pages 6 through 9 (Low Primer)
pages 156 and 157 (High Primer)

THE NEW FRIENDLY VILLAGE
pages 16 through 18 (Low Second)
pages 234 and 235 (High Second)

THE NEW ROUND ABOUT
pages 16 through 18 (Low First)
pages 203 through 205 (High First)

THE NEW IF I WERE GOING
pages 22 and 23 (Low Third)
pages 330 and 331 (High Third)

Hildreth, Gertrude, Felton, Allie Lou, Henderson, Mabel J., and Meighen, Alice. EASY GROWTH IN READING. The John C. Winston Company, Philadelphia, 1951.

AT PLAY
pages 38 and 39 (Low Primer)

ALONG THE WAY
pages 38 and 39 (Low Second)

FUN IN STORY
pages 146 and 147 (High Primer)

THE STORY ROAD
pages 114 and 115 (High Second)

I KNOW A SECRET
pages 21 and 22 (Low First)

FARAWAY PORTS
pages 10 and 11 (Low Third)

GOOD STORIES
pages 92 and 93 (High First)

ENCHANTING STORIES
pages 178 and 179 (High Third)

McKee, Paul, Harrison, M. Lucile, McCowen, Annie, and Lehr, Elizabeth. READING FOR MEANING. Houghton Mifflin Company, Boston, 1951.

WITH JACK AND JANET
pages 17 and 18 (Low Primer)
pages 182 and 183 (High Primer)

ON WE GO
pages 232 and 233 (High Second)

LOOKING AHEAD
pages 47 and 48 (Low Third)

UP AND AWAY
pages 11 through 13 (Low First)
pages 168 and 169 (High First)

CLIMBING HIGHER
pages 309 and 310 (High Third)

COME ALONG
pages 7 and 8 (Low Second)

Russell, David H., and Others. THE GINN BASIC READERS. Ginn and Company, Boston, 1948.

THE LITTLE WHITE HOUSE
pages 17 through 19 (Low Primer)
pages 146 and 147 (High Primer)

AROUND THE CORNER
pages 212 and 213 (High Second)

FINDING NEW NEIGHBORS
pages 22 and 23 (Low Third)

ON CHERRY STREET
pages 15 through 18 (Low First)
pages 190 and 191 (High First)

FRIENDS FAR AND NEAR
pages 299 and 300 (High Third)

WE ARE NEIGHBORS
pages 24 and 25 (Low Second)

Have the child read apart from the group in a book suited to his grade level. If the selection is too difficult, try one from the next lower level. If this also is too difficult, try a still easier one. A selection is considered too difficult if the child has difficulty with more than one word in twenty, or if he reads in a slow, labored manner. When a fairly satisfactory level is found, have him read the story and ask him the questions on the card. Help him on words on which he hesitates five seconds or more and correct his errors at once.

As the child proceeds in oral reading, several reading characteristics should be noted. Use a check list of errors and record those on which the child needs help. Ignore occasional mistakes, as they may be only temporary. The following should ordinarily be noticed, either during the testing or during the regular classroom reading:

1. Phrase reading
   Word-by-word reading
   Inadequate phrasing
   Incorrect phrasing
   Eye-voice span too narrow
2. Voice
   Strained, high-pitched
   Monotonous tone
   Too loud, too soft voice
3. Enunciation
   Poor enunciation in all reading
   Poor enunciation of difficult words
4. Expression
   Ignores punctuation
   Habitual repetition of words
   Habitual addition of words
   Omission of words
   Marked insecurity evident
5. Word skills in oral reading
   Makes errors on easy words
   Ignores his mistakes
   Will not try hard words
   Use of context clues
6. Comprehension
   In easy material
   In hard material

The eye-voice span is the distance the eyes are ahead of the voice in oral reading. Children who read word by word have almost no eye-voice span, while those who read by phrases have an eye-voice span of several words. Although it is not essential to informal analysis in primary grades, the eye-voice span test is easily made. Have the child read a relatively easy paragraph. After a line or two, slide a card over the page and tell the child to continue to read all of the words he has seen. The page should ordinarily be covered at the beginning of a new line, preferably at the beginning of a phrase or normal grouping of words. Give several trials, and be sure the child knows what he is expected to do. The eye-voice span is the average number of words read after the page is covered.

A sheet for recording oral-reading abilities should contain a check list of the instructional needs observed. The list may serve as a class-record blank, with the child's name at the side and the items at the top. A sample record sheet may be found on page 110.

Learning rate

It is important to know how many words the child can learn and retain, since this indicates the number of new words which may be safely presented each day. The learning-rate test is described in Chapter 3, pages 50–51. Select ten words which are within the children's speaking vocabulary, but not in their reading vocabulary, such as *radiator, decorate, engine, perfume, wreck, typewriter, tunnel, damage, audience,* and *electricity.* Or select words which are new to them from stories not yet read. Teach the words by presenting them in different ways as you would in your regular teaching, allowing about ten minutes for initial presentation of the words and five minutes more for practice.

After an hour has elapsed, test the children separately on a list of the words, telling the child the words he misses. Then, at the end of the day, test the child on the words again, recording the number remembered as his learning rate.

Another way to estimate learning rate in the regular classroom work is to make a list of the twenty words taught most recently in the regular lessons. This list may be put into a story to be read orally. If a few words will not go into the story, simply list them at the end of the selection. Test each child on the words, recording the number of words read. The results will indicate whether or not the rate of presentation of words is faster than the child's learning rate.

Abilities in word analysis

There are three essential abilities in word analysis: (1) the clarity of seeing the forms of words and of noticing their visual similarities and differences; (2) the ability to notice the separate sound elements in spoken words; (3) phonics—the ability to give sounds for letters and letter combinations and the ability to use this skill in solving new words. Ways to test these word-analysis abilities are given on this page and the pages that follow.

Test for visual discrimination of words

The test of visual discrimination requires the child to look at a word on a flash card and then find it in a group of words which look very much like it. The teacher will need to prepare a set of flash cards with the test words and to duplicate enough test blanks for the pupils.

Flash cards are printed in black letters about two inches high. The form of the letters should be manuscript or approximately the same as the letters in the test. Capital letters should not be used, nor should cursive writing. It helps to keep the flash cards in order if they are numbered on the back. The pupil's test forms may be duplicated from a typewritten stencil. Although typewriting is smaller than the print in primary-grade books, it will be satisfactory for this visual-discrimination test.

The teacher should prepare a set of flash cards with the following words on them:

1. f	11. first	21. different
2. h	12. some	22. mountain
3. in	13. last	23. practice
4. go	14. just	24. weather
5. was	15. drop	25. advance
6. top	16. clean	26. secure
7. dog	17. part	27. probable
8. now	18. ought	28. contract
9. end	19. quiet	29. meditate
10. black	20. station	30. regulation

In giving the test, the child is told, "Look at this letter. You are to find it in the first box on your sheet and draw a circle around it." Children may use markers under the boxes on the sheet, moving to the next box after each word is marked. Or the teacher may call the

Test for VISUAL DISCRIMINATION OF WORDS

Name_____

1 y b d g f	**16** clear clean close climb lean
2 m h n r t	**17** par park trap party quart dark part
3 no on imp in nip	**18** eight sought rough ought taught aught tough
4 goes do go ago dog	**19** quite quick quack point quiet question quit
5 saw war as was waste	**20** state elation tasted station stationed started skating
6 pot tab tap top pat	**21** dinner differ difference deferent deferent different deference
7 girl dog boy dig day	**22** nomination notion mention mountain mountains motion mentioned
8 won no now mow was	**23** quarter portion bracelet particle practice practical poultice
9 and tend on ended end	**24** other the weather wealth whether whither wealthier
10 lack clock clack black dark	**25** obscure advice above advise advances dance advance
11 frost first fast firm trust	**26** sure obscure scare secure second server cure
12 same came name some somebody	**27** portable possible probably probable problem practical desirable
13 slat last lost lot blast	**28** contact contain contract contracts contacts capital convict
14 jump jest just jot must	**29** immediate meditates mediate mistake meditate material meditative
15 drip prop drops rap drop	**30** regular regulate regulation registration negotiation radiation recognition

number of the word, saying, " Here is number six. Find it and draw a circle around it." The word should be exposed for about three seconds, then turned down when the children start to look on their blanks. A second look is not permitted, nor should either teacher or children pronounce the word.

Norms: The following scores are typical of middle-of-the-year achievements in the primary grades: Grade 1—18; Grade 2—25; Grade 3—30.

Test for hearing sounds in words

The purpose of the hearing test is to discover how well a child can identify sounds in spoken words. If a child is unable to identify sounds in spoken words, instruction in phonics or word recognition will make little progress. The test is suitable only for those children who know the names or forms of letters. If a child does not know his letters, the teacher should use the auditory-perception tests in Chapter 3.

The teacher will need to type and duplicate copies of the "Test for Hearing Sounds in Words." The method of giving the test is as follows:

Give each child a marker of colored paper to use under each line. This will not only help to keep the child's attention on the correct line but will also help the teacher to observe that each child has the correct place.

DIRECTIONS: PART A

Print on the board the letters *p b t n a,* just as they appear on line 1 of the child's paper. Direct the children in the following way:

Today we are going to use our eyes and ears to see if we can find the right letters in words. You will need to listen and look carefully. Put your marker on the first line under the big letter A. [Check to see that each child has the right place.]

I'll say a word and you are to listen to see if you can find the letter the word begins with. Listen—*top.* What is the first letter in *top?* Yes, *t*—so you draw a circle around *t* on your paper. [Draw a circle around *t* on the board. Then check to see that each child has circled the correct letter.]

Test for HEARING SOUNDS IN WORDS — GRADES 1–3

Boston University 1955

Name _____ Grade _____ School _____

City _____ Teacher _____

A

1.	p	b	t	n	a
2.	e	p	c	d	t
3.	d	f	g	v	h
4.	g	k	v	l	i
5.	k	r	b	d	s
6.	o	s	n	b	t
7.	y	l	d	f	g
8.	f	t	j	r	b
9.	c	d	k	m	i
10.	f	v	p	h	o
11.	l	v	n	t	u
12.	s	q	r	z	p
13.	c	m	a	b	o
14.	h	m	s	e	w
15.	m	v	e	r	a
16.	n	e	h	a	o
17.	w	q	j	n	e
18.	j	l	s	t	y

B

1.	garrulous	pertain	warrant
2.	milligram	sweltering	shrapnel
3.	chemist	stereogram	hydrocarbon
4.	ponderous	spectacular	military
5.	finesse	intended	rebuff
6.	linoleum	periwinkle	cacophony
7.	brethren	noblemen	burlesque
8.	premium	gypsyism	glaucoma
9.	hexameter	generation	hydrogen
10.	proficient	presumptive	dominant
11.	cavalry	martinet	castinet
12.	filiform	felonious	deciduous
13.	meander	monotony	rancour
14.	sheathing	shameful	collateral
15.	bronchitis	platonic	breechblock
16.	theorem	reckon	thermion
17.	drammock	druidism	pyrogenic
18.	eroded	chiseled	charbon

C

1. ind r bl x t ing	7. tion ex pl f h an
2. a m sp f d ng	8. ure g d sm k in
3. ar k st w ight p	9. op r en a l v
4. ous b sh th f con	10. o b sp el er ist
5. n ck for cl w ate	11. ent a be c n v
6. in ep ow tw a fl	12. d un gr b qu l

Score

A _____
B _____
C _____
Total _____

Now move your marker to the next line below. Now I will not help any more. Be sure you look and listen carefully. Ready. Draw a circle around the first letter in *cup*. [Repeat the word, if necessary. Wait until the children have finished making a circle around the letter. This usually takes not more than five seconds. Count five slowly on all later words in this test.]

[Direct in this way for the rest of the words.] Move your marker to number 3. Find the first letter in *dog*.

4.	garden	9.	machine	14.	handle
5.	recess	10.	fountain	15.	every
6.	noise	11.	vacation	16.	olive
7.	lemon	12.	polish	17.	waste
8.	bacon	13.	absent	18.	supper

DIRECTIONS: PART B

Direct as follows:

Now move your markers up to number 1 under the big letter B. [Write on the board the words *garrulous   pertain   warrant*.]

Now this time you are to listen for the *last* sound in the word. Listen to this word—*spoon*. Which word on the board has the same *last* sound as *spoon*? Yes, the middle one has the same last sound as *spoon*. So we draw a circle around it like this. Now draw a circle around the same word on your paper.

Now move your marker down to number 2. Listen for the *last* sound in this word—*until*. Find the word that has the same sound at the end as *until*. Draw a circle around it.

[Direct in this way for the next four words.] Move your marker to number 3. Which word has the same *last* sound as *visit*? Draw a circle around it.

3. visit   4. wonder   5. railroad   6. company

On number 7 and following, the child listens for the first and last sounds. Direct as follows:

Now on number 7, you are to listen for *both the beginning and ending sounds*. [Write on the board the following words: *brethren   noblemen   burlesque*.]

Which of these words has the same beginning and ending sounds as *between*? [Wait for answers]. Yes, the first one begins and ends like *between*. So we draw a circle around it. You draw a circle around the word on your paper.

[Direct in this way for the remainder of the words in PART B.] Move your marker to number 8. Find the word that begins and ends like *geranium*.

9. happen	14. shovel
10. present	15. break
11. cabinet	16. thicken
12. famous	17. drink
13. motor	18. child

DIRECTIONS: PART C

Write these letters on the board: *ind r bl x t ing*. Then direct as follows:

Now move your marker down to number 1 under C. Listen to this word *blinding*. Draw circles around all of the sounds you hear in *blinding*. [Circle *ind bl ing* on the board.] How many of you circled these sounds?

[Write on the board *a m sp f d ng*.] Now find all of the sounds you can in this word—*sporadic*. Which did you circle? Yes, *sp, a* and *d*. The other sounds are not on your paper.

[Direct in this way for the rest of the words.] On number 3, circle the letters you hear in this word—*starlight*.

3. starlight	8. indenture
4. continuous	9. envelopment
5. fortunate	10. elocutionist
6. twinflower	11. benevolent
7. exemplify	12. unqualified

How to score: PART A—Count the number correct. Maximum score—17.

PART B—Count the number correct. Maximum score—16.

PART C—Count the number of parts of words circled correctly. Maximum score—33.

Tentative middle-of-year norms: Grade I—20, Grade II—42, Grade III—48.

Ability to use phonics

The teacher's manuals in most basal-reading series will indicate word-analysis skills which should have been acquired at different stages of learning. To test ability in using phonics to solve new words, prepare a list of ten to twenty words that are not in the child's reading vocabulary, but in his speaking vocabulary. These words should be made up of phonetic elements that have been previously taught. If we assume that all of the more common consonants have been taught in first grade, in addition to several of the consonant blends and various word endings, then the following words would be suitable for the analysis:

hook, lake, wall, sound, tight, fold, rest, bring, shop, spun, stick, small, blink, clock, skate, tray, flag, swell, twin, snip

Other elements which should be used in composing word-analysis tests in the primary grades are the following:

1. The ability to read compound words when both words are known.

2. The ability to use common suffixes like the following: *s ed ing er est*.

3. The ability to use certain rules which are sufficiently stable to be of use.

The knowledge of the sounds of individual letters, blends, or phonograms may be best tested by using the phonics test above. However, a child may be asked to give the sounds of lists of these word elements. It is often the case that the child knows the sounds of individual word elements but is unable to use them in reading new words. For this reason, both sounding word elements and the ability to use sounding successfully should be noted.

Since spelling and writing are closely related to word analysis, a test of spelling may be added to the informal analysis. Any difficulty that the child has in letter formation or persistent errors in writing should also be noted.

Silent reading

Many facets of silent-reading ability may be observed in the regular classroom work. The most important factor is the level at which the child can read with attention and persistence. This may be from one half to a full grade below his oral-reading ability, or it may be on the same level. Some children have great difficulty in making the transfer from oral to silent reading and will need special help in attentive silent reading. The level of independent silent reading should be noted on the analysis chart.

Occasionally it may be well to test individual children in silent reading in the same manner as was suggested in the oral-reading tests. In this case the child is asked to read the selection to himself, to ask for help on difficult words, and to answer questions about what he has read. If a child needs help on more than one word in twenty, he will be unlikely to understand the story, and a lower level should be used.

Attention and persistence should be rated. If a child is always caught by the story and can continue reading without being distracted, he should be rated "1"; if he is usually attentive and persistent, he may be rated "2." Other ratings may run to "5," which would indicate little attention and persistence in silent reading. A similar rating might be made of speed of work in silent-reading tasks, including response to workbook activities and games which require silent reading.

Lip movements or whispering in silent reading indicate that the child has not made a complete transfer from oral reading. Most children in primary grades will resort to lip movement if the material is hard or the situation tense, but some children will move their lips or whisper in all silent reading. If a child needs help to avoid lip movements or whispering, the item should be checked on the analysis chart.

The child's degree of comprehension in silent reading should be noted, both in his ability to answer questions and to give a coherent oral account of what he has read.

Analysis chart for primary grades

The analysis chart on page 110 is presented as a method of recording the findings of the various tests, observations, and ratings. It need not be copied and duplicated exactly as it appears there. A teacher,

CHECK LIST OF INSTRUCTIONAL NEEDS (Primary Reading Level)

School _____
Grade _____
Teacher _____
Date _____
(Instructional Group)

(Instructional Group)	Age	M.A. or Listening Comprehension	Reading Age	Reading Interest	Oral Reading: Level	Comprehension	Phrasing	Ignores Errors	Repetition	Adds or Omits Words	Errors on Easy Words	Expression	Voice: Enunciation	Word Attack	Use of Context Clues	Word Abilities: Learning Rate	Visual Analysis of Words	Hearing Sounds in Words	Sounding Elements	Solving New Words	Spelling	Writing	Silent Reading: Level	Attention and Persistence	Lip Movements	Speed of Work	Recall: Questions	Unaided Oral

or a group of primary teachers, may prefer to change some of the items or to add or omit items. While rating scales have been suggested for certain of the observations, the teacher may indicate instructional needs by using any marks she wishes. Some may wish to use a single check to indicate a need for some help, and a double check for serious difficulty. Others may wish to rate every pupil, with a plus which indicates superior ability, a check for average ability, and a minus for low ability. Some may prefer an A–B–C–D–E–F scale on rated items.

It is better to group the pupils on the chart by instructional groups rather than alphabetically through the class. This makes it easier to observe the group needs and to plan instruction.

Analysis of reading needs in intermediate grades

Pupils in intermediate grades who have a reading ability of third grade or below should be observed through the use of the primary-reading analysis. Any who read on primer level or below will need the tests described in the reading-readiness chapter.

Analysis of reading needs in the intermediate grades can be somewhat easier than in the primary grades since many of the abilities may be observed through the use of group testing. Oral reading and individual observation of pupils, however, remain the most effective form of analysis. Pupils who show particular difficulty in any of the tests should be observed individually.

Standard tests in reading and language comprehension are much more helpful in intermediate grades, since the maturity of the child's reading ability permits more accurate measurement. The use of standard reading tests is recommended to determine the child's reading age in silent reading. Certain tests may be helpful in measuring reading vocabulary, speed of reading, and some useful study skills.

However, many essential reading abilities are not measured by present standard tests. The informal analysis is still the best way to observe many of these abilities, and it is the only way to observe the suitability of instruction for a pupil or a group of pupils.

Important questions to answer in the informal analysis in the intermediate grades are the following:

1. Does the child have adequate listening comprehension to understand the materials used in the classroom?

2. Is the pupil using reading for many purposes?

3. Are the books used in the classroom at the right level for effective learning?

4. What faults and difficulties appear in his oral reading?

5. Are his word-mastery abilities adequate to assure growth?

6. Is he effective in silent reading and study?

    a) Are his vocabulary abilities adequate for his tasks?

    b) Is his recall adequate on questions, oral or written work, or class discussion?

    c) Is his speed of reading and speed of work satisfactory and adapted to the task?

    d) Is he competent in elaborative and critical thinking related to his reading?

Listening comprehension

Whenever a child has difficulty in reading, the first concern is whether the difficulty lies in the mechanics of reading or in lack of ability to understand the material if it is read to him. A standard test designed to measure listening comprehension is the *Durrell-Sullivan Reading Capacity Test*.[1] If the child is up to grade on this test but below grade in reading, it would appear that the difficulty is in the mechanics of reading. However, it is well to test the child on the materials used in the classroom to discover if oral-language background is adequate to handle those materials.

Materials from the readers and the social studies or science books should be used. Often it will be found that the child can comprehend stories in readers since his vocabulary will be adequate for general comprehension, but the ideas in the social studies books may hinge on vocabulary or ideas outside his experience. Read a selection of several paragraphs. Then ask oral questions to which the child writes

1 Donald D. Durrell and Helen B. Sullivan. Published by World Book Company.

single word or phrase answers. If it is suspected that the difficulty in writing provides too great a handicap, test the pupil individually and record his success with oral answers. Multiple-choice tests may be used if reading difficulty is avoided by oral reading of questions and answers.

The degree of handicap to comprehension caused by weakness in reading may be determined by comparing the child's answers to questions about materials read silently to his answers when he listens to the materials read.

Inattention rather than lack of comprehension may be responsible for inability to recall in either listening or reading. Care should be taken to give the purposes for listening and reading, with the task of the listener indicated in the introductory explanation.

Initiative and interest in reading

Interest and initiative may be rated in the same manner as "vigor of attack in reading" described on page 97. A more detailed inquiry about the pupil's use of voluntary reading is desirable in intermediate grades, since the child should have acquired a variety of individual uses of reading. An inquiry might be made by preparing a check list for the pupil to fill out, with opportunity for listing titles or topics of special interest.

Which of these do you read regularly? Check the ones you usually read, and indicate on the lines below some of the titles or topics which interest you.

1. Newspapers: Comics _____; sports _____; local news _____; national or world news _____; weather _____; crime _____; other _____.

Newspapers read regularly: _____

_____

2. Magazines read regularly: _____

_____

What parts do you read? _____

3. Story books: from library _____; from home or from friends _____; number read in past two months—less than 5_____; 5–10 _____; more than 10 _____.

Type liked especially: adventure _____; mystery _____; historical _____; animal _____; etc.

List some books read recently: _____

---

4. Books or articles on sports _____; crafts _____; travel _____; mechanics _____; animals _____; things to make or do _____; science _____; religion _____; hobbies _____.

What hobbies do you have which you read about? _____

Another general estimate of attitude toward reading may be made by having the child rate his preference for school subjects. This is done by making a list of the subjects taught in the school and asking the child to indicate his first, second, and third choice. Note if the subjects that require reading are rated high.

If a child does little reading of fiction, but a great deal of nonfiction reading, the fact should be noted. The rating scale may separate fiction and nonfiction reading.

Oral reading

It is somewhat more difficult to estimate the level of oral reading through informal tests when the child is reading above third-grade level. Individual selections in intermediate-grade books vary greatly in difficulty so that estimates of grade level made from reading such selections are inaccurate. The important thing to note, however, is the suitability of the textbooks for the child. The teacher should select lessons typical of the textbooks in the various subjects and listen to each pupil read them. If word difficulties, either in meaning or pronunciation, appear as frequently as one word in twenty running words, it is likely that easier books must be found or that some method of teaching must be used which will decrease the vocabulary burden.

The items to observe in oral reading are the same as those listed on page 100 for primary grades. Special attention should be paid to word attack: What does the pupil do when he meets hard words? Is he fairly accurate in figuring out the pronunciation of difficult words? Does he want to know the meaning of new words? Or is he primarily concerned about getting the disagreeable task of oral reading done as quickly as possible?

Silent reading and recall

Silent-reading level is best determined by the use of standard tests. Some tests include scores for vocabulary, comprehension, and speed. If they are available, these scores should be recorded on the analysis chart.

The suitability of a social studies or a science textbook for pupils may be studied by testing the vocabulary and comprehension problems encountered. A typical day's lesson may be skimmed for words or expressions which might be unknown to the pupils, with ten or more words selected from each page. The meaning of these words or expressions may be tested in any of several ways. The teacher may simply ask the children if they know the meaning of the words. The pupils make a column of numbers and are told, "This sentence says, 'The famine caused many families to emigrate.' Number 1 is *emigrate*. If you know the word, write a plus; if not, a minus." Then a child is asked what the word means, and pupils check the correctness of the definition.

If a closer check is wanted, the pupils may write the definitions or may match words with definition lists. Such tests of writing or matching definitions should be taken with the books open so that the child can see how the word is used in the sentence. If a day's lesson contains too many words for a child to remember from teaching—more than eight or ten words are too much—the material is too difficult.

A second check on the suitability of the material is measuring comprehension after silent reading. This is done by preparing ten to fifteen questions over the essential facts presented. The answers may be multiple-choice or short answers which consist of single words or phrases. If a child is unable to remember essential facts, the material is probably too difficult. Of course, the difficulty of the questions will vary. Care should be taken in preparation of questions not to use words beyond the child's reading vocabulary.

Recall is easiest when multiple-choice questions are given, harder when the pupil must write short answers, still harder when a series of answers must be given to a single question, and hardest when an oral or written summary is demanded without the aid of questions. Informal tests of these levels are relatively easy to make, and they may be used in connection with a series of social-studies lessons. If the information of the first lesson is checked by multiple-choice tests, the second by a series of questions requiring short factual answers, the third by a few general questions which require listing of several items, and the fourth giving a written summary, the results may be compared and the effective level of recall for each pupil estimated.

The pupil should adjust his speed of silent reading to different situations. Speed of reading in simple narrative material should be much faster than the reading of factual material in social studies or science. Reading to follow directions will be quite slow, while skimming for various purposes should be very rapid.

Testing speed of silent reading in narrative or study reading is easy. The pupils are told, "Begin at the top of page 66 and read as rapidly as you can until I tell you to stop. Then make an X at the end of the line you were reading when I call 'stop.' Then you can read on to the end of the story on page 68. Read as fast as you can, but be sure to read well enough to answer questions afterwards." At the end of two minutes, say "Stop. Put an X at the end of the line where you are now. Then read on to the end of the story."

The number of words read may be computed by counting the lines read, multiplying by the average number of words in the lines, and dividing by two to get the number of words per minute. If a more accurate measure is wanted, the teacher may count the number of words in each line and put the cumulative totals at the end of the line. The following selection indicates the method:

Henry goes to a large lake in summer.	8
Last summer a motor boat sank near	15
his house. The boat had ten men on	23
it. The man who was running the boat	31
brought it very close to the shore	38
when the water was low. He hit a big	47
rock under water. It made a hole in	55
the bottom of the boat. The water	62
came in very fast. All of the men	70
swam to shore.	73

Be sure to have a series of questions to be answered after the story; otherwise some children will have phenomenal speeds on later tests. If a child cannot answer questions satisfactorily after the story, his speed should be rechecked.

Speed of work in content subjects may be observed in the daily lessons. Some children are regularly slow in completing their assignments.

Imagery in the reading of fiction is difficult to observe accurately, but it should be checked when pupils show an aversion to reading fiction. The simplest way to do this is to select a paragraph from a story which has been read and ask the pupils to describe the scene they see in their minds. If the paragraph tells about a group of boys playing in a back yard, such questions as the following should be asked: "When you were reading, did you have a picture of the scene in your mind? Tell us about it." This general question may be followed by more specific ones such as, "How big was the yard? What was in it? Were there trees? What kind? Did you see the house? Tell about it. Were there other houses near by? Was there a fence around it? What kind?"

Any questions of detail may be asked; but questions should be avoided which cover facts given in the story. The task for the teacher is to see the amount of imagery added to the story by the reader.

The testing of imagery may take the form of a general discussion, with each child telling what he sees, the sounds heard, or other conditions which are observed by the child. The question may also be asked, "Are you describing some place you know, or is it some place you imagine?" Not a great deal is known about imagery, but it is certain that avid readers of fiction have excellent imagery. Further discussion of imagery may be found in Chapter 14 under "Teaching the Uses of Imaginative Reading."

Other factors of silent-reading ability may be observed: lip movements or whispering while reading silently; head movements in which the head moves with the eyes along the line; eye movements which indicate phrase perception in silent reading. See Chapter 9 for a discussion of these factors of silent-reading ability.

Eye movements may be observed by counting the number of jumps the eyes take in reading each line. If the child takes five or more eye movements in the average line, if the eye movements are irregular or slow, it is an indication that the reading is too difficult or that phrase perception is poor. Eye movements are best seen by sitting facing the child, with his book held high enough to make it easy to see his eyes. The self-consciousness which comes in such observations may interfere with normal eye movements, but any unusual conditions may be checked if the teacher will observe the child's reading at other times.

Word analysis and spelling

Ability in word analysis requires individual testing, although certain aspects of it may be observed through the use of group tests. Make a list of twenty to thirty words from the more difficult words in the next few lessons in the textbooks used in the grade. Ask each child to read these words aloud, noting the method of attack and recording successful pronunciations.

Notice particularly if the child analyzes accurately by syllables. Does he guess at the word from general form? Does he add or omit sounds? Does he divide syllables accurately? Does he attempt to sound one letter at a time?

If a more accurate measure of the child's ability in word recognition and analysis is desired, the test found on pages 393–394 in the appendix may be duplicated for use. However, the teacher will find that the test that is made up of words from future lessons will be a more satisfactory estimate of the child's difficulty in the classroom work.

The ability to hear sounds in words may be measured by asking the child to spell unfamiliar words which are spelled phonetically. This may be done by selecting such words from the spellers in higher grades, or from the dictionary.

The list at the top of the next page is from the *Durrell Analysis of Reading Difficulty*.[2]

2 Donald D. Durrell. Published by World Book Company.

1. intervent
2. carpolite
3. tonometer
4. introvert
5. blastment
6. ligulate
7. polarize
8. stimulus
9. titration
10. explicate
11. isotherm
12. astrolabe
13. epithet
14. dissonant
15. retrograde

In scoring phonetic spelling, a word is considered correct if all of the sounds are included. For example, *dissonant* would be marked as correct if it were spelled *disonant, dissonent,* or *dissunant.* A score of ten or more correct would indicate that the child's ear for sounds in words is adequate for his word-analysis needs.

Spelling is particularly hard for children who have word-analysis difficulty. A study of the child's spelling errors will reveal his instructional needs. If he adds or omits sounds, more careful instruction in listening for sounds is necessary. If he spells correctly by sounds but is troubled by wrong choice of vowels, digraphs, silent letters; if he selects the wrong homophone (*ait, ate, aight,* or *eight*) or makes other non-auditory errors, he needs more accurate visual perception with word meaning.

Visual perception may be tested by making flash cards containing twenty words which are beyond the children's spelling vocabulary and asking the children to write them after an exposure of three seconds. Some children will, of course, remember the spelling by rapid subvocal spelling of the word rather than by visual memory, but an informal visual-perception test of this kind is a good rough measure of the ability.

The ability to use the dictionary is sometimes troublesome for children. Speed of locating words may be measured by providing a child with a list of words (not in alphabetical order) and recording how many he can find in two minutes. He can indicate his location of the word by recording the page on which it is found. The ability to use diacritical marks may be measured by giving the child a list of unfamiliar words which are so marked and asking him to pronounce them.

Another ability in word recognition which is important to children is ability in recognition of unknown words. If children are asked to look for unfamiliar words and make a list of ones they do not know in three pages in a difficult science or social-studies book, the good readers will usually have the longest list. The poor readers cannot find the words they do not know. It is useful to check this ability with children.

Study skills

Many types of study skills may be tested or observed informally. Tests for various levels of recall have been suggested in the section on silent reading. Children may be tested on the ability to outline, to skim, to use an index or table of contents, to do various kinds of thinking in relation to reading, or to use several of the various library skills.

The ability to outline may be analyzed by the ability to choose the best title for a paragraph, to write acceptable titles for paragraphs, to fill in minor topics when the main topic is given, and to outline a paragraph or a short selection. Title fitting may be measured by supplying three or more titles for each of a series of paragraphs in a social-studies book and discovering which children can choose the best title. Wrong titles may be on the topic, but too general, fitted to only one or two details, or otherwise unsuitable. A series of items in an outline may be scrambled; the child's task is to reorganize them correctly. Or the pupils may be asked to make an outline of several paragraphs read.

Skimming may be tested by making a series of questions over a selection and finding out how many answers the pupils can locate in a given time. Such questions should call for the location of simple facts and should be phrased closely to the words of the selection. More difficult skimming might call for the location of paragraphs in a longer selection—paragraphs which answer certain questions, describe a process, give reasons for a decision, and so on.

Ability to do elaborative thinking about reading may be measured by lessons which call for ideas or activities related to the reading. For example, after studying about transportation in the colonial period, the child might be asked to make lists of topics for research or further study; lists of questions about the period—questions not answered by the text; lists of activities that might be carried on in the classroom; or lists of comparisons and contrasts between then and now. Ability in elaborative thinking may be informally observed by the teacher in the regular classroom discussions which call for interpretation, generalization, inference, or other types of reaction to the materials read.

Speed and accuracy may be observed in other aspects of school work that require detailed reading, such as success in written problems in arithmetic, ability to follow directions in laboratory work or in workbooks, and skill in following directions given orally.

Analysis chart for intermediate grades

The analysis chart on page 122 suggests a method of summarizing the findings of the tests and observations. A great many more tests have been suggested than are found on the chart. The teacher will need to determine what abilities are most important to the pupils in her room, and to include them in the program of testing and observation and in the summary chart of instructional needs. The same variations of recording instructional needs suggested in the primary-grade summary may be used here.

REPRESENTATIVE READING TESTS

California Reading Test. Tiegs, E. W., and Clark, W. W. Los Angeles: California Test Bureau, 1950. Grades: Primary, 1–3; Elementary, 4–6; Intermediate, 7–9. Four Forms. Time: 20–50 minutes. Reading vocabulary, various kinds of comprehension.

Durrell Analysis of Reading Difficulty: New Edition. Durrell, Donald D. Yonkers, New York: World Book Company, 1955. Grades 1–6. Time: Approximately 60 minutes per pupil. Materials for individual analysis of reading difficulties.

Durrell-Sullivan Reading Capacity and Achievement Tests. Durrell, Donald D., and Sullivan, Helen B. Yonkers, New York: World Book Company, 1945. Intermediate, grades 3–6; Primary, grades 2–3. Capacity Test measures understanding of spoken language: vocabulary and paragraph meaning. Reading Test has two forms: Test 1 measures vocabulary; Test 2 measures paragraph meaning; and there are optional tests of spelling and written recall.

CHECK LIST OF INSTRUCTIONAL NEEDS (Intermediate Grades)

School_____ Grade_____ Teacher_____ Date_____

					Oral Reading							Silent Reading and Study													Word Mastery Abilities					
												Speed					Recall and Use													
Age	M.A. or Listening Comprehension	Reading Age or Grade	Initiative-Interest	Level	Phrasing	Work Attack	Ignores Errors	Word Meaning	Expression	Enunciation	Insecure	Textbooks too Difficult	Word Errors	Stories	Content Subjects	Skimming	Attention	Specific Questions	General Questions	Unaided Oral Recall	Written Recall	Outlining	Elaborative Thinking	Discussion	Word Attack	Syllable Analysis	Ear for Sounds	Spelling	Identifying Unknown Words	Dictionary Abilities

Gates Advanced Primary Reading Tests. Gates, Arthur I. New York: Bureau of Publications, Teachers College, Columbia University, 1943. Grades 2–3: three forms. Time: 40 minutes. Word recognition and paragraph reading.

Gates Primary Reading Tests. Gates, Arthur I. New York: Bureau of Publications, Teachers College, Columbia University, 1943. Grades 1–2; three forms. Time: 50 minutes. Word recognition, sentence and paragraph meaning.

Gates Reading Survey. Gates, Arthur I. New York: Bureau of Publications, Teachers College, Columbia University, 1939. Grades 3–10. Two forms. Time: 60–90 minutes. Vocabulary, rate, and comprehension.

Iowa Every-Pupil Tests of Basic Skills. Spitzer, H. F., Horn, Ernest, McBroom, Maude, and Greene, H. A. Boston: Houghton Mifflin Company, 1945. Elementary, grades 3–5; Advanced, grades 5–9. Four forms. Time: 55–90 minutes. Test A: Vocabulary and paragraph comprehen-

sion. Test B: Reading maps, use of references, index, dictionary, and alphabetizing (Elementary), or reading graphs, charts and tables (Advanced).

Iowa Silent Reading Tests, New Edition. Greene, H. A., and Others. Yonkers, New York: World Book Company, Elementary, grades 4–8. Four forms. Time: 49 minutes. Rate of reading, comprehension, word meaning, locating information.

Metropolitan Achievement Tests: Reading. Allen, R. D., and Others. Yonkers, New York: World Book Company, 1949. Grades 1, 2, 3–4, 5–6, 7–8, in different batteries. Three forms. Time: 45–70 minutes. Vocabulary and paragraph comprehension.

Stanford Achievement Test: Reading. Kelley, T. L., and Others. Yonkers, New York: World Book Company, 1954. Grades: Primary, 2–3; Intermediate, 4–6; Advanced, 7–9. Three to five forms. Time: 30–40 minutes. Word and paragraph meaning.

SUGGESTIONS FOR FURTHER READING

Anderson, Irving H., and Dearborn, Walter F. *The Psychology of Teaching Reading.* New York: The Ronald Press Company, 1952. Chapter 1.

Betts, Emmett A. *Foundations of Reading Instruction.* New York: The American Book Company, 1946. Chapter 21.

Bond, Guy L., and Wagner, Eva B. *Teaching the Child to Read.* New York: The Macmillan Company, 1950. Chapter 17.

Dolch, Edward W. *Teaching Primary Reading.* Champaign, Illinois: Garrard Pres, 1950. Chapter 16.

Gates, Arthur I. *Improvement of Reading,* Third Edition. New York: The Macmillan Company, 1947. Chapters 8, 14, and 15.

Harris, Albert J. *How to Increase Reading Ability,* Third Edition. New York: Longmans, Green and Company, 1956. Chapters 7 and 8.

Kottmeyer, William. *Handbook for Remedial Reading*. St. Louis: Webster Publishing Company, 1947. Chapter 6.

McKee, Paul. *The Teaching of Reading in the Elementary School*. Boston: Houghton Mifflin Company, 1948. Pages 268–281, 337–341, and 398–413.

McKim, Margaret G. *Guiding Growth in Reading in the Modern Elementary School*. New York: The Macmillan Company, 1955. Chapter 13.

Russell, David H. *Children Learn to Read*. Ginn and Company, 1949. Chapter 15 and pages 346–351.

Russell, David H. "Evaluation of Pupil Growth in and through Reading," in *Reading in the Elementary School*, The Forty-Eighth Yearbook of the National Society for the Study of Education. Chicago: University of Chicago Press, 1949.

Yoakam, Gerald A. *Basic Reading Instruction*. New York: McGraw-Hill Book Company, 1955. Chapter 16.

CHAPTER 6 Grouping for Instruction

DIFFERENT KINDS OF GROUPING for instruction are required for an effective reading program. There are many values in individual and small-group instruction: The materials may be fitted closely to the child's reading level; intensive practice may be provided on needed skills; the degree of individual responsibility is high; and opportunity for oral practice is multiplied.

But there are also many values in class instruction: The common interests and activities increase the sense of belonging to a group; there is an economy of teacher effort when a single activity may be shared by all; and many areas of knowledge may be imparted to the whole class as effectively as to a small group. Skills learning generally requires small-group or individual instruction; the building of knowledges and appreciations may be done in large-group situations.

Whole-class activities

Large-group whole-class activities are appropriate when oral, visual, or various types of multiple-sensory presentations are used. Listening vocabularies of slower pupils are much larger than their reading vocabularies, so that oral presentation may utilize a much wider range of materials. Much of the context in oral reading is carried by nuances of expression so that the meaning is conveyed even when strange words are used. Visual materials convey meanings of their own and may be enjoyed equally by children of different levels of achievement. How much an individual member of an audience learns is not dependent upon the size of the audience.

The following types of activities allied to reading may be used effectively in whole-class activities:

Demonstrations	Story hour
Field trips	Recordings
Exhibits	Radio or TV programs
Displays	Group reports on units
Motion pictures	Class planning
Listening to poetry	Discussion of school problems
Plays and dramatizations	Explanations, directions
Choral reading	

Small groups with pupils of varied ability

Many types of educational objectives may be attained when the groups are made up of children with a wide range of reading and intellectual abilities. Such groups are especially good when thinking and planning are the main activities. Since correlations between elaborative thinking and intelligence are not high, many slower pupils may make effective contributions in planning. Generally, such groups are brought together because of common interests. They may be continuing groups or "clubs," or they may be temporary groups. They may all have a common interest in animals, airplanes, astronomy, weather, baseball, or fishing, or they may have chosen the same area of interest in a unit in social studies or science. They may be a committee assigned to a particular problem.

They may find reading materials which fit their ability levels and may transmit the results of their reading orally or through illustrated materials. Play reading may be done in groups of varied ability since children have time to learn the new words in their various parts.

Children needing oral-reading practice may be combined in a group with each using materials suited to his own reading level. If the reading is around the same topic, an especially desirable audience situation is attained.

The social values in the use of groups of varied abilities are such that the teacher should use much of this type of grouping. Group work is more effective if the number is kept to five pupils. Groups of seven or more, except in play reading or a similar "controlled" activity, are seldom effective.

Small-group work is particularly effective in unit teaching in social studies or science. The class may be divided into many small groups in order that pupils may work together or do independent research if they so desire. This type of instruction requires the availability of a wide range of reference materials and should extend over a period of two or three weeks. The teacher will need to suggest divisions of responsibility unless the pupils have had practice in the development of units. However, committees of pupils may plan how the individual tasks will be done and how the final reports will be made.

Small-group instruction with pupil teachers

Skills instruction in the primary grades is especially suitable for small groups taught by pupil teachers. Children in these grades are eager to learn and willingly accept pupil teachers who are superior readers. The groups will vary from three to five pupils; the smaller the groups, the more opportunity for individual response. At this level most of the superior readers have had considerable experience as teachers in "playing school." These teachers may replace the regular teacher in giving extra practice in many stages of reading readiness, such as letter matching and letter names. They may lead in various kinds of "games" in word recognition and word analysis and may help in oral-reading practice.

The teacher will need to observe the work of the pupil teachers and provide counsel and assistance at points of difficulty, but most pupil teachers will prove very helpful. Groups may be asked to choose a pupil teacher. Generally it is better if all of the eligible pupil teachers are given the opportunity to teach a group; so the "available" list of pupil teachers should be somewhat flexible. This small-group work should be "extra practice" and should not replace the regular contact between teacher and pupil in small-group instruction.

Pupil teachers of superior reading ability may be used in intermediate grades if the teacher is skilled in making such work acceptable. They may serve as consultants to help a group of slower pupils with difficult words encountered in silent reading. When assigned materials are much too difficult for a very slow group, the pupil teacher may present the lesson orally and explain unfamiliar words or passages. They may direct word-analysis practice or dictate spelling words to small groups. Or they may serve as "secretaries" or recorders in group study activities.

The pupil teacher is more effective in following routine activities and providing skills practice. The development of meanings and concepts is better done by the classroom teacher, although some pupil teachers will be highly effective in explaining particular meanings of words or sentences. Generally the pupil teacher will need prepared materials, such as lists of questions, lists of words, charts, flash cards, and other devices selected by the teacher. When a child or group of children is aware of the need for extra instruction, and when that instruction is helpful in attaining higher achievement, a pupil teacher is always acceptable. However, if the extra practice seems pointless or comes as a penalty, the pupil teacher will have trouble.

Groups of pupils may be led by members of the group who take turns in the position of teacher. This is particularly suitable for oral-reading practice after the word and phrase difficulties have been presented by the classroom teacher.

Any member of the reading group may serve as teacher when the following steps have been taken: (1) The teacher has identified the word and phrase difficulties in advance and has given practice on them. (2) The stage has been set for reading by the teacher's introduction to the story. (3) The pupil teacher has been provided with lists of questions which will be asked at various points and the answers recorded for her to see later. (4) The length of passages to be read has been indicated by the teacher. After the reading, the teacher may return to check the results, listen to comments, and answer questions on the story.

Paired practice or teams of three

There are a great many situations when interest is heightened, comprehension is increased, and general achievement improved through pupils working in pairs or in teams of three. Many kinds of learning in reading are unnecessarily lonely, even though the child may be sitting in a room full of children. There is seldom any type of learning which is not enhanced by children working in pairs. Children in primary grades may work in pairs on many kinds of word-recognition practice, on reading-readiness activities, in helping each other with words in silent reading, in checking each other in workbook activities. They may enjoy various types of contests when paired with a child of equal ability. Sometimes it is desirable to pair a rapid learner with a slow one, setting up a tutoring situation for various kinds of skills help.

In intermediate grades, children like especially to work in pairs or in teams of three. If they are given various types of assignments in advance, they enjoy finding the answers together. They may work together on arithmetic problems, agreeing on how problems should be set up and checking their answers against each other. They may dictate spelling words to each other and check their difficulties. Word pronunciation may be learned by one child having a list of words diacritically marked and the other pronouncing the words from an unmarked list. They may be given glossaries for a social-studies lesson and thus will work together in finding the words in the book and noticing how they are used.

Various types of use-of-the-dictionary practice may be done in pairs, and even library reading is more fun if somebody else is reading the same book. If a number of books on the same topic are being read by the class, two or three people may read the same material and decide on the most important points. Various kinds of contests between pairs or teams of three of equal ability give an occasional lift to some types of work.

While the child must have practice in independent work, there are few objectives of learning in the elementary school which are not better attained through group and team work. Children may be grouped or paired by the teacher so that one child does not continually lean on others to get his work done. Choice of partners or of members of teams may be limited at times to children on the same reading level. At other times the teams may be chosen from the entire class. In certain situations children may be paired for reading level, for enterprise, for interests, or even for certain personal qualities. The success of paired practice depends in part upon the congeniality of the pairs.

Individual reading

Extensive independent reading by a child is valuable training for improvement in reading. It alone is not adequate for children with learning difficulties, since such children need guidance in overcoming faulty habits and establishing vocabulary mastery and other skills. Rapid learners and superior readers undoubtedly gain more from extensive individual reading than from using the readers and textbooks suited to the average of the class. The usual test finding of low achievement in relation to mental ability of superior pupils will be overcome when the child is encouraged to read independently on materials which challenge him.

As soon as a child is fairly secure in independent silent reading, he should be encouraged to read stories by himself. So that the vocabulary will not bother him, special books may be selected for the child when he makes his first ventures in independent reading. He may need to have his interest lifted by the teacher, who asks him about what he has read thus far. She may recall amusing points of the story, reread certain parts, or set the stage for the next division of the story. Every child in primary grades should spend some time in the library corner, and many pupils may even look up special topics of interest to report to the class.

While workbooks and seat work are often presented as individual instruction, most of these activities are more effective with slow learners when children help each other through paired work. The important thing is the alertness in learning rather than the individual mark or comment a child may receive on each page. Care must be taken, however, that each child shares the work rather than copies from his neighbor.

In intermediate grades, individual reading becomes highly important, not so much in the daily textbook study as in learning to use reading independently. All of the school subjects and many club activities and individual hobbies present opportunities for independent reading. The classroom may be much enriched through having pupils look up additional information on future lessons and display the results of their learning.

Teachers who find unit instruction too complicated can at least direct individual children to special responsibilities in the content subjects. While only two or three children may be engaged in special topics in connection with a chapter in social studies or science, the teacher should see that each pupil has this kind of opportunity occasionally. When rapid learners complete their lessons, or when they are permitted to work in advance of the class in spelling and arithmetic, the time thus made free should be used for special assignments. In some schools each child has a specialty which requires various sorts of reading and related activities. It is usually found that pupils do their routine work more rapidly in order to get to the work of their specialties.

Various kinds of records may be kept of the child's leisure reading. Some teachers encourage each child to keep a notebook or card file on the books read, recording the title, author, main characters, plot, points of special interest, and the child's reaction to the story. Another method of recording uses a large chart with pockets under each child's name. In these pockets are placed slips which record the books read, with pertinent comment.

From time to time, the child's progress in independent reading should be examined to see if he needs encouragement to a greater variety in his reading. While book reports to the class may be dull and formal, some teachers find ways to help children improve the method and quality of reporting. Usually the reports are better if several children who have read the book plan a joint report, dramatize certain events in it, or tell of the situations of particular interest without "giving away" the whole story. Some group or individual reports may take the form of a series of illustrations, an appropriate book jacket with an invitation to readers, or an illustrated booklet for the library table. A number of book clubs can be formed so that the child can report to his group without taking the time of the entire class, some of whom may not be ready for the book.

Individualizing textbook assignments

When it seems necessary to use a textbook for an entire class, there are many ways in which it may be adjusted to the levels of ability of the group. The very slowest children may need to have the lesson read orally to them by the teacher or by a superior reader selected by the group. Difficult words will need to be explained and the group encouraged to ask questions when they do not understand. Children who are somewhat higher in ability, but who will find many words and concepts difficult, may need preliminary word-meaning practice. This practice is given orally by the teacher who then provides the pupils with a glossary of the words discussed. Other children may need only the glossary to help them with words.

Children in the top reading groups may read the lesson without help, other than the introductory statement by the teacher which sets the purposes for reading. Such pupils will probably learn more and will be greater assets to the class if they are provided with assignments or textbooks that deal with the topic on a more advanced or more richly illustrated level.

Vocabulary is not the only problem which besets the child who must use textbooks too difficult for him. His need is for study guides which help him understand, remember, see relationships and pertinence of the lesson. Various levels of study guides and methods of their use by study teams are presented in Chapter 13.

Homogeneous grouping for reading

Some schools have attempted to give special emphasis to instruction in reading skills by having the reading period at the same hour throughout the elementary school. Each teacher specializes in one level of reading achievement, and the pupils go to the room of the teacher who instructs on their level of achievement. To avoid too great differences in age groups, grouping is sometimes separated by primary and intermediate grades. The teacher uses books, charts, games, workbooks, and other materials suited to that reading level.

The advantages claimed for the method are that it gives a special emphasis to reading skills, it assures proper adjustment of material, and it makes the burden of providing for individual differences easier. Teachers who have slower learners may be given smaller groups, while those who teach more rapid learners have larger groups. The teaching of spelling is sometimes combined with the reading period. The child is not deprived of social contacts with children of his own age, since he spends the rest of the day with them.

When there are so many ways to group for effective instruction within the classroom, it is difficult to understand why homogeneous grouping throughout the school is thought necessary. If it is used, the need for small-group work still remains. Children of the same reading level may have very different instructional needs. All children need to feel the individual responsibility and have the rich opportunities for individual expression that come in small groups.

Furthermore, homogeneous grouping still must take into account the various learning rates of children. A single pace cannot suffice for all. It will retard some by being too slow and will confuse others by being too fast. However, if schools that use homogeneous grouping will work out ways of adjusting to individual needs, children's reading skills may be served well. Experiments in various types of school organization to improve the effectiveness of instruction should not be condemned without careful examination. Partial homogeneous grouping, bringing together children who are much below reading level in their classes, is often a desirable practice.

Suggestions on grouping for instruction

The teacher may find the following suggestions helpful:

1. The advantage of grouping lies in its possibilities of adjusting the lessons to fit individual learning needs. If these adjustments are not made, there is little point to teaching in small groups.

2. The teacher cannot delegate all of the reading instruction to pupil teachers. Each child should have a normal share of the teacher's time, with much of the small-group work being extra practice.

3. Since there are many forms of small-group instruction, the teacher should try them all and select the most successful. She can then make modifications to increase the effectiveness of the activity.

4. There should be considerable variety in grouping. Sometimes the class will join in whole-group activities in reading, and sometimes they will be with groups of their own reading level. Sometimes they may have a pupil teacher. Sometimes they will be with children of various reading levels. Sometimes they will work in pairs and sometimes they will work alone. There should be no attempt to work out a standard pattern and conform to it daily. Part of the advantage of small-group work is in the interest which comes with novelty.

SUGGESTIONS FOR FURTHER READING

Carter, Homer L. J., and McGinnis, Dorothy J. *Learning to Read.* New York: McGraw-Hill Book Company, 1953. Chapter 9.

Harris, Albert J. *How to Increase Reading Ability,* Third Edition. New York: Longmans, Green and Company, Inc., 1956. Chapter 6.

Kottmeyer, William. *Handbook for Remedial Reading.* St. Louis: Webster Publishing Company, 1947. Chapter 8.

McKee, Paul. *The Teaching of Reading in the Elementary School.* Boston: Houghton Mifflin Company, 1948. Pages 353–354.

McKim, Margaret G. *Guiding Growth in Reading in the Modern Elementary School.* New York: The Macmillan Company, 1955. Chapter 10.

Russell, David H. *Children Learn to Read.* Boston: Ginn and Company, 1949. Chapters 15, 16, and pages 327–346.

Tinker, Miles A. *Teaching Elementary Reading.* New York: Appleton-Century-Crofts, Inc., 1952. Chapter 11.

7 Motivation of Reading Instruction

NOTHING IS MORE IMPORTANT in an instructional program in reading than that every lesson—every exercise—be so motivated that interest and attention will be maintained at a high level. A child must have a desire to read. He must also have an interest in increasing his reading ability as a means of satisfying various practical and emotional needs. Unless he is able to keep his attention on reading, much of the teaching is wasted. Rate of growth, development and retention of skills, and amount of voluntary reading depend largely upon the level and type of motivation. This is particularly true in the case of children who have encountered failure in the course of their school careers because instruction was improperly adjusted to their learning needs. Inattention, misbehavior, and laziness result from assignments which seem purposeless to the child.

Education should provide the learner with voluntary habits of growth in effective living. Any type of motivation, whether in reading or any other activity, should be judged by its success in achieving this goal. Certain kinds of motivation may increase child effort at the expense of interest. In this class belong coercive types, such as threats of restriction or punishment or inattention or low effort.

Other types of motivation, such as rewards and contests, tend to arouse more interest in winning games than in accomplishing the real task at hand. Such motivation makes the child dependent upon the teacher or the class for initiating his work. A desire to read independently is not inculcated by such methods. Furthermore, all motivation in the teaching of reading should have as its fundamental purpose a systematic increase in the child's desire to read.

Bases of inattention

If a child is inattentive in class, teachers tend to blame the child's parents or various psychological factors beyond their control. A medical examination will sometimes reveal conditions which produce quick fatigue, resulting in loss of attention. Usually, however, inattention is due to faulty lesson planning. When children lose track of their work and slip into daydreaming, slovenly posture, aimless play, or misbehavior, they are merely indicating that the day's work is inadequately motivated.

Before seeking any other cause of inattention, the teacher should appraise her lesson plans. It should be remembered that usually attention parallels real interest. At certain times a child may evidence extreme fatigue or engage in discourteous behavior. Shortly after, he may display fine attention, cooperation, and regard for others simply because a new task is interesting and challenging.

It sometimes seems that parents have allowed their children to acquire undesirable attitudes toward school work. Yet the teacher need not wait for some miraculous change in the child's home life before undertaking plans to overcome inattention and aversion to work. Occasionally emotional conflicts and poor home conditions may account for inattention. However, well-motivated learning has a salutary effect on emotional disturbances. The expert teacher knows that removal of confusions in reading will result in progress and that interesting and purposeful activities will relieve emotional blocking and remedy bad habits. When home conditions are unsatisfactory and the child's emotional life is empty, a well-motivated reading program may become an oasis in an otherwise barren emotional desert.

When a child with little apparent interest in learning, or with behavior difficulties, is sent to a psychologist or psychiatrist for intensive study, the usual recommendation is that the child be given security, a sense of achievement, and a well-balanced program of activities. This describes the classroom activities of an intelligent teacher.

Objectives in motivation

It is in the planning and class management of reading instruction that the most significant values in reading are won or lost. These values will be found in three by-products of the program. A good program will increase and improve all of them; a poor program may weaken them or lose them altogether.

1. Zeal for improvement in reading skills
2. Initiative in voluntary use of reading
3. Desirable personal and social attitudes

While these three aspects of motivation will be presented separately, they bear a relationship to each other: negative or positive attitudes in one will carry over to the others. Zeal in learning skills is affected by the richness of the program in the uses of reading and by the spirit of the group. Both in turn are affected by the success of the motivation of the skills program.

Motivation of reading-skills instruction

Every child wants to learn to read. However, many children who have met with little success in reading appear to have given up hope of making progress. They show their discouragement in many different ways; by inattention and easy distractibility; by an attack which lacks vigor; by misbehavior; by lack of persistence; by unwillingness to try; by general hopelessness about reading. Such children will make little progress; even when they attempt to work at reading, only a small proportion of their powers is available to the task.

Success in skills learning depends primarily upon a feeling of progress. Both the teacher and the child want to see progress, and both are happier if specific progress can be seen daily, or at least weekly. Patience with lack of progress is a doubtful virtue in teaching. It is one of the superior arts of teaching to design methods by which the child can see his progress in small units of growth and have the lift given by continued success.

Suggestions for enabling the child to see his progress in skills learning are the following:

1. *The instructional material must be on the right level for the child.* When the materials are too difficult, the reading lesson becomes an exercise in frustration and confusion. The result is further discouragement. Specific methods for testing reading materials for suitability of instruction are found in Chapter 5. Throughout this book there are many suggestions for adjusting silent and oral reading, vocabulary instruction, study aids, and independent interests to the level of the child.

Although it is easy to remember the needs of the slow learner, it is equally important that the rapid learner be challenged by reading tasks. This challenge usually means special topics and reference reading instead of the usual assignments in the content subjects. Unnecessary practice on various skills, holding the child back to the daily lessons, and other work designed for the average learner, make school work for the rapid learner largely practice in sitting.

2. *The rate of learning must be suited to the pace of the child.* If new words or skills are presented too rapidly, or the time and amount of practice is inadequate for mastery, confusion results. There is a big difference between teaching and learning. A common comment is, "Yes, he was taught his letters, but he didn't learn them."

If teaching does not result in learning a skill, it is likely that the pace is too fast, the level of instruction too difficult, or the method of instruction wrong. The best measure of the proper rate of word presentation, for example, may be determined by inventory testing. If twenty words have been taught, but only five retained, the rate of introduction of new words should be stepped down. Often, by teaching half as much, the rate of learning will be doubled.

One should not assume that learning rate is a fixed, unchanging standard for each child. Better instruction, improvement of background abilities, removal of confusions, will improve the learning rate. Again, it must be remembered that the rapid learner will require a faster-than-average pace if he is to keep his zeal for learning.

3. *The reading task must be divided into several separate skills.* While the child may not see his progress in general-reading ability, it is helpful to attack a few things at a time. The nonreader can see his progress in learning the names of letters, in noticing sounds in words, in attaching sounds to letters. The primary-grade reader, when given specific help, may see his progress in word analysis, word recognition, the use of context clues, phrasing in oral reading, security and speed in silent reading.

A similar specific attack will help the child in intermediate grades see his progress in word analysis, word meaning, ability to identify unknown words, various dictionary abilities, speed of reading, ability to skim, oral or written recall, organization of materials, and various specific study abilities.

4. *Small units of instruction in particular skills may be set up to help the child acquire a feeling of reaching a particular goal.* This is easy in such things as word recognition, learning the names and sounds of letters, and the application of word analysis to new words. The materials may be set up in lists, charts, or small booklets which can be completed in a few days. A task which is divided into a series of steps, with each step providing a feeling of completion, is much easier to complete than a long single task or a series of unnoticed steps toward a remote goal. It is more difficult to see progress in general skills such as phrase reading, use of context clues, comprehension, recall, and study skills. A sense of completion may be attained by setting up in advance a specific number of exercises to be done.

5. *Personal records of achievement may be charted by the child in a reading-record book.* This book may contain a list of new words learned; charts of word-analysis elements known; the number of pages read or workbook exercises completed; a graph of increase of speed in silent reading; the number of errors in oral reading on stories set aside for testing and retesting; the per cent of ideas recalled in paired-practice exercises; the growth in speed of locating words

in a dictionary; the speed of skimming recorded in the number of correct answers found in two minutes; and the scores on comprehension tests. Differences in difficulty of the various tests and materials may lower the scores on certain lessons, but the general progress will be evident.

Many of the charts will need to be prepared by the teacher and bound in a personal-progress book. They may include forms for making bar graphs, for filling in a block of work, for checking off specific work done, for recording independent or extra work. They should look neat and important, and should be admired often by the teacher. Personal charts are preferred to class charts; class charts may motivate the rapid learners and discourage the slow.

6. *The child should understand the relations of the specific exercises and the general program to his particular reading needs.* He should be aware of his difficulties and faulty habits, and should know the purpose of the particular lessons in relation to his difficulties. When his interest is enlisted in the corrective program, he finds ways to get extra help. Interest in improvement of learning leads the child to reveal his difficulties rather than to conceal them. He learns that confusion and lack of understanding should be reported to the teacher and that no penalty results from revealing his difficulties. As a result, the classroom situation is more favorable to learning.

7. *Variety in lessons is important in maintaining interest in skills learning.* Even simple changes tend to relieve monotony, such as rearranging furniture, changing the size and members of groups, using games and gadgets, engaging in simple contests, using materials of unusual shape or color, using materials from newspapers, magazines, or catalogues. In each phase of reading instruction discussed in this book, many suggestions are provided for adding variety to the lessons.

Various mechanical aids and devices, such as the tape recorder, lantern slides, motion pictures, flash cards, charts, and educational games, may be utilized in providing effective variety. One should observe, however, if the device provides more *novelty* than learning. The interest in the gadget sometimes may be subordinated to the learning process, with the result that the child has learned more about the game or gadget than he has about reading.

Motivation and initiative in the voluntary use of reading

The highest type of motivation is reading for some purpose which appeals to the child as important. The best assignments are those that call into play certain internal drives and satisfactions, or "instincts," as they were called by William James. Some of these drives are the desire for prominence and social approval, desire for praise from an admired person, interest in planning and other inventive activity. Other drives include carrying out plans through various types of activity, expressing altruism and sympathy by helping less fortunate children, investigating to satisfy curiosity, and imitating admired people or products. Many types of assignments utilize these internal drives.

Special reports in school subjects

The content subjects such as science, safety education, history, geography, health, music, art, nature study, and so on, provide many opportunities for special reports by individuals or groups. Assignments of this kind may be an integral part of the course of study and should be made far enough in advance to allow adequate time for preparation. They are particularly suitable for superior readers. The reports should be made interesting by exhibits, pictures, maps, drawings, or other varied activities. The child or group of children making the report to the class should preserve an air of secrecy in their study and planning so that "previews" will not dull interest in the final report.

School events and class activities

Various events in which a class is to participate, such as visits to museums, factories, and farms, or the showing of informational motion pictures, lantern slides, or exhibits, provide opportunities for purposeful reading. The reading may be followed by reports. The reading and reports should come *before* the events if the highest motivation is to be derived from them. When the event arrives, the class will be sufficiently informed to ask pertinent questions, to notice specific elements in procedure or product, and to appreciate more fully what they see. The reading of the entire class may center around these future activities if a sufficient amount of reading material is available on the various reading levels.

Many class projects utilize the children's interest in planning and carrying out plans. A great deal of reading may be motivated by planning an assembly program, an exhibit to be placed in a store window, an evening's entertainment for parents, a class newspaper, or a magazine to illustrate the high points of the year's work. Other class projects may utilize sympathy and altruism as motivating elements in reading, as when illustrated books are planned, toys are made, or suitable stories are collected for children in hospitals or less fortunate communities.

It is often possible to utilize events of wide interest as well as seasonal activities. A state or world's fair, an antarctic expedition, a disaster such as a flood or a tornado, the visit of a head of another nation, a popular historical motion picture, or any event sufficiently dramatized in the news may serve to initiate reading. The activities of the Christmas season or the Thanksgiving season, a community festival or anniversary, or any of the special "weeks" such as Fire Prevention Week or Education Week, may stimulate an accompanying reading program.

Sometimes it is suggested that the teacher find the pupils' interests and connect the reading to them. There are several reasons why this advice is rather useless. Courses of study in most subjects are usually predetermined. Thus there is no opportunity for free choice of interest centers. Even if the teacher were free to choose centers of interest in place of courses of study, there would be wide differences among the children in what they wanted to study, and these differences might be based on whim rather than genuine interest. Furthermore, since expressed interests may be extremely narrow or even undesirable, basing instruction on expressed interests would often close the doors to wider education of value to the child. The task of education is to increase the variety and depth of useful interests.

Finding individual interests

Individual pupil interests, however, may serve to guide independent reading. The interest inventory below may serve as a basis for conversation with the child. It is read slowly to the child and interspersed with comments such as "Do you like any of these?" or "Have you tried any of these?" or other remarks or questions which seem suitable. If an interest is manifested, it is well to discover whether it is truly an interest or merely a whim. This may be done by finding out by questions whether the child has pursued any activities connected with the presumed interest. If many activities have been carried on over a long period of time, it is safe to assume that the interest will not disappear even if the reading is difficult.

INTEREST INVENTORY

1. Hunting, fishing, camping, sailing, canoeing, hiking, scouting
2. Horses, cows, sheep, chickens, dogs, cats, rabbits, birds, etc.
3. Flowers, gardens, trees, wildflowers, stars, weather, rocks, rivers
4. Automobiles, airplanes, radio, television, wireless, railroads, bridges, construction
5. Carpentry, electricity, chemistry, photography, printing, signaling
6. Drawing, painting, carving, modeling, basketry, metalwork, etc.
7. Music, orchestra, piano, violin, dancing, dramatics, debating, speaking
8. Reading: poetry, plays, stories, mythology, Bible, biography, adventure
9. Collecting: stamps, stones, shells, bugs, flowers, coins; other collections
10. Cooking, candy making, fancywork, sewing, weaving, interior decoration
11. Card games, puzzles, checkers, chess, indoor games
12. Football, baseball, basketball, hockey, boxing, wrestling, etc.
13. Swimming, skating, riding, tennis, golf, archery, rifle shooting, skiing, acrobatics, bowling

14. History, geography, science, arithmetic, languages
15. What clubs do you belong to? What do you intend to do for a living?

When interests are discovered, the child may be helped to find reading materials suitable for his specialty. Illustrated magazines, books, catalogues, pamphlets, articles, film strips, and even advertising materials may be used. If a child is to travel with his parents during the summer, he will enjoy the trip more if he reads about the region or the country he is to visit. Every chance should be utilized to teach the child to use reading to enhance his activities.

A much more complete treatment of motivation of the program in teaching the child the uses of reading will be found in Chapter 14. Individual initiative in the use of reading is the end sought. High motivation through class-related activities is excellent, but the final use of reading is through voluntary individual effort.

Motivation and child-development objectives

As stated in Chapter 1, it is generally acknowledged that personal and social values are more important than the possession of skills and facts. No phase of education is more burdened with generality than the field of character values. In fact, the evasive quality of the words associated with personal development makes it almost impossible to convey meanings in the area. A host of terms come to mind: honesty, self-reliance, self-discipline, responsibility, dependability, orderliness, enterprise, sensitivity, generosity, courtesy, friendliness, sympathy, serenity, integration. Too often, the concern is for the mental hygiene of the child—"He needs security and affection"—as though he were to be a permanent psychological invalid in the care of society rather than an enterprising and generous person—a person who finds the world full of promise, his place in it significant, and himself a brother to mankind.

Personal and social qualities are by-products of the teaching of reading as they are of all learning. The reading program can build or undermine most of the desirable personal qualities and habits.

The three general objectives listed under this heading in Chapter 1 need to be examined in the light of the motivation of the reading program.

1. Building standards of good workmanship

Certainly the habits of good workmanship cannot be achieved by the slow learner who is defeated by each day's lesson. His self-respect is lowered, his attack lacks vigor, he has little or no initiative, he gives up readily when difficulties arise, his attention wanders readily, his impressions are blurred and his learning is only partial, and his posture and speech reveal his hopelessness. Delinquency studies always show a high incidence of low school achievement among their cases. When one considers the maladjusted educational programs which some children must suffer, it is a matter of wonder that they survive as well as they do.

The well-adjusted, highly motivated program of reading instruction gives a lift to all desirable personal qualities. Children who are aware of their progress, who look forward to continued growth, and who find each day's work satisfying and significant, seldom have difficulty acquiring habits of good workmanship.

It is equally important to notice the situation of the rapid learner who competes with slower learners on the same tasks. He may easily acquire a feeling of smugness, his work habits may become slovenly, he may learn to do things at the last minute, he may learn to get by on glibness and fail to hold himself to good disciplines when the work is difficult, or he may isolate himself from others. The rapid learner should be given tasks that will challenge him and, at the same time, teach him to be helpful and generous in his relationships with others. Good management of the skills program in reading is highly important to building standards of good workmanship.

2. Building initiative in a variety of desirable interests

Building initiative in a number of interests is the primary goal of the program in the use of reading, not only in the reading class but in the various subjects in the elementary school. If the child leaves the information of each lesson behind him as merely a task to be completed each day, his resources for enjoying and achieving are greatly diminished. If his reading is merely another form of "controlled day-dreaming," like watching television "westerns" or listening to radio soap operas, it is likely to be of little service.

Reading generally should be related to child purposes and activity. It should be an adjunct to living, not a substitute for it. It will be noted in the program for the use of reading, in Chapter 14, that there are many types of reading that may be useful: imaginative, aesthetic, and dramatic reading; reading related to history and travel, bringing into usefulness the long ago and far away; reading to add meaning and pleasure to the world about you; and reading for personal needs and aspirations.

3. Establishing habits of social responsibility

Since the effective reading program requires a great deal of mutual help, group activities, and social relationships, it offers constant opportunities for developing social sensitivity and responsibility. The unfair competition of the single level of assignment for all is the greatest single enemy toward social development. It is unfair both to the slow learner and to the rapid learner. Lesson plans which allow the child to remain on the same plateau in various reading abilities increase the contrast between individuals.

Since there is no way to avoid the differences in ease of learning among children, the only thing to do is to recognize the differences openly and to enlist the help of all in mutual assistance. The slow learner did not choose to have difficulty, nor did the rapid learner acquire his skill by his own merits. Differences in rates of learning must be accepted by children as matters of interesting variation if equal effort is made to learn. Pride and shame or praise and blame have no place in reference to ease of learning. Children who have the good fortune to learn easily should accept the idea that with high achievement comes high responsibility. The many suggestions in this book for providing for individual differences are designed to assist the teacher and children to make the classroom a place of mutual helpfulness in the pursuit of skills and interests.

4. Establishing ideals of improvement

It is decidedly difficult to improve accomplishment merely through discussion of ideals of workmanship, persistence, and the like. Permanent gain from this approach is small unless other motivation techniques are employed. However, the child's aid must be enlisted in improving certain conditions, such as slovenly posture, excessive talkativeness, time wasting, and similar bad habits which contribute to failure in reading by making sustained attention difficult.

Personal habits which interfere with performance should be met directly. The child should understand that such habits arise naturally, often from previous reading failure. If there are a large number of habits needing correction, they should be eliminated one at a time, and the child should know the ones chosen for elimination. He should not expect to overcome each poor habit on one "firm resolve," but he must understand that only by his efforts can such corrections be permanent.

The essential part of a corrective program is definiteness. Advice such as "Work harder" or "Pay better attention" is too general to be of value. Posture in reading, correct holding of book, slowness to start work, failing to keep at certain kinds of tasks, distracting the attention of others, and similar habits are more specific and can be helped readily. When an undesirable habit has been chosen for elimination, lapses should not go unnoticed. A simple gesture, a touch on the arm, or some other unspoken symbol of the teacher should be the sign to correct the situation. Such campaigns to correct faulty habits should be private agreements between the pupil and the teacher. They should not be opportunities for public concern of other children, unless the situation is such that children can help each other without personal offense.

It must be acknowledged that sometimes the faulty habits arise out of poorly motivated and poorly planned reading instruction. In such case, any attempt to assist children in self-correction of faulty habits is bound to fail. It is remarkable how many poor personal habits of children disappear in a well-adjusted and highly interesting reading program.

5. Using contests, rewards, and punishment

Most children find contests stimulating if there is an equal chance to win, if the contests are over in a few minutes, and if the situation is one of good humor. Contests in which groups of equal ability work at desirable skills tasks during a reading period add zest to learning. Unequal or longer contests with rewards of privileges or special recognition have little place in reading instruction. Certainly, contests should be used sparingly in reading instruction, since they divert attention from higher purposes in reading.

Various forms of spoken and unspoken recognition of good work are constant helps to vigor in learning. While effusive and lavish praise is to be avoided, opportunities for quiet acknowledgment of good work come many times an hour in the classroom. Children should be encouraged to notice and comment on good work of other pupils. The sincerity and frequency of such pupil comments are indicative of a classroom with high group morale.

There is little place for punishment in reading instruction. At times the child gives the appearance of willful inattention. If a quiet comment does not remedy the situation, the child may be removed from the group and be required to work alone. Instruction without attention results in habits of inattention. Between willful inattention and coercive discipline, the latter should be chosen. However, the teacher should first examine her planning, since an interested learner seldom interrupts a learning situation without strong reason. Difficulties which seem to demand punishment can often be traced to failures in lesson planning and the use of variety in motivation.

SUGGESTIONS FOR FURTHER READING

Lee, J. Murray, and Lee, Dorris May. *The Child and His Curriculum.* New York: Appleton-Century-Crofts, Inc., 1950. Chapter 4. Pages 64–77.

McKim, Margaret G. *Guiding Growth in Reading in the Modern Elemen-* *tary School.* New York: The Macmillan Company, 1955. Pages 501–517.

Mehl, Marie, Mills, Hubert, and Douglass, Harl R. *Teaching in Elementary School.* New York: The Ronald Press, 1950. Chapter 4.

CHAPTER **8** **Oral Reading**

ORAL READING is a major consideration in the primary grades, and it is of special importance at any level for children with reading difficulties. This is because faulty habits, difficulties, and confusions become immediately apparent in oral reading in a way to reveal reasons for a child's lack of progress and difficulties in comprehension.

Oral reading has, in addition, many other important values for reading instruction. It motivates reading, as evidenced by the desire of primary-grade children to read aloud to the group. With a true audience situation, it induces exchange of ideas and a feeling of group unity. It is essential to instruction based on pupil reports and discussions of library materials, as in the content subjects. When carefully directed, it widens speaking vocabulary and tends to improve speech and conversation. Full enjoyment of poetry and drama is impossible without effective oral reading. It has important uses in both vocational and leisure-time activities. Parents with imagination and initiative find that oral reading serves a variety of useful purposes in their family life.

An obvious disadvantage of oral reading for classroom use is that only one pupil can perform at a time. This drawback can be offset somewhat by use of small groups in which each child may read more often. Another disadvantage of oral reading is its tendency to reduce silent reading to the slow oral-reading rate and to encourage lip movements and word pronunciation in silent reading. These will later require remedial attention.

Importance of audience situation

In every phase of oral reading the audience situation must be maintained. Ordinarily two conditions prevent attainment of the audience situation: (1) revealing the plot of the story during the preparatory work and (2) allowing children to look at their books while others read orally.

Children must always have a reason for listening during oral reading. If the plot has been revealed, the reason for listening has been lost. In this chapter are outlined various types of oral assignments to provide reasons for listening, such as preliminary study without disclosing the plot of the story or the development of a new listening situation through the study assignment.

The second factor that disturbs the audience situation—looking at the book as others read orally—has little justification at any level of reading instruction. Above the second grade the silent-reading rate is usually faster than the rate of oral reading. Therefore if children are required to "keep the place," they are being taught faulty silent-reading habits, such as slow reading, lip movement, and silent pronunciation, as well as inattention to content.

In grades one and two there is little reason for allowing children to look at the book while others read. Slow learners usually cannot follow the place in a book or give close attention to the individual words while the more advanced pupils read. The more advanced pupils are required to use faulty silent-reading habits if they follow the slower ones in their reading.

Word analysis during the oral-reading lesson often spoils the pleasure of the group in audience reading. A child should be helped immediately on mispronounced or unknown words. Comments of teacher and pupils during audience reading must be directed only toward the content of the story. Difficult words may be noted for future study if they are of sufficient importance to be included in the child's sight vocabulary. Any child will have adequate opportunity to apply his word-analysis ability in independent reading and study. At that time he is not emotionally confused by his display of difficulty and is likely to use his word-analysis ability to better advantage.

Interest cannot be expected in oral reading when the outcome of the story is known in advance, or when the activity serves only to "catch" children on mispronounced or unknown words, to answer trivial questions, or simply to fill the reading period. Each oral-reading lesson should be purposive as to both motivation and emphasis on reading skills.

Planning an oral-reading program

Carefully planned lessons based upon specific needs are essential to the success of oral-reading instruction. Attention must be given to skills specifically basic to oral reading and also to speech, such as volume and flexibility of voice, enunciation and pronunciation, expression, and breath control. In addition, the oral-reading lessons should be utilized for detection of certain faulty habits in silent reading, such as word-recognition difficulties, inadequate or incorrect phrasing, inattention to punctuation, and the omission or addition of words.

Small-group instruction

Oral reading should usually be done in small groups, as described in Chapter 6. This plan permits greater practice for each child. Before starting small-group instruction the teacher should be well acquainted with methods of administration, methods of selection and adjustment of materials to pupil needs, and the types of organization of classroom work. To obtain uniformity of interest in the entire class, lesson plans need careful development, types of instruction must be suited to the group, and there must be adequate provision for checking comprehension during and after reading.

Nature of lesson plans

The lesson plans for oral reading will, of course, depend upon the type and purpose of the assignment and the needs of the pupils. For example, when the entire class takes part in reading a story, the following typical steps are gone through:

1. The story is scanned by the teacher for words that may give difficulty in either meaning or recognition.

2. Exercises are given on the recognition of these words as outlined in Chapter 10.

3. Exercises may also be needed in reading these words in phrases and sentences.

4. Provision is made for motivating the lesson. Ordinarily this consists of a brief statement showing the relation of the lesson to general classroom activities, the nature of the plot, information to be discovered, or directions for listening with a specific purpose as the story is read.

5. It is usually well to indicate the amount of material each child is to read so that each pupil will have a fair amount of practice.

6. An exercise for checking meaning and comprehension is given. If the story has been well motivated and the audience situation maintained, often no need arises for comprehension checks after the oral reading.

7. If a group finishes the reading before the scheduled time, provision is made for other activities, such as review lessons in word meaning or word recognition, drills for various types of errors, rereading for expression, or games that aid reading.

Major types of assignments

Four general types of assignments are suitable for oral reading: (1) those requiring true audience reading; (2) those requiring intensive study of selections for various purposes; (3) those designed to improve phrase reading; and (4) those designed to improve voice and oral expression. These will be considered in the following sections of this chapter.

Methods for improving audience reading

It is important in audience reading that the child who is to read aloud study the selection before presenting it. Of course, the members of the audience should not have read the story. In the assignments suggested below, provision is made for the development of smooth oral reading, for the preservation of the novelty element, and for giving the audience a reason for listening.

Sight reading

In sight reading children read the new story without previous preparation except for word, phrase, and sentence drills. Since sight reading does not permit previous silent study of the selection, special emphasis must be placed upon phrase and sentence exercises based on the story. Thus pupils should encounter no new words and should be able to read reasonably smoothly without previous preparation.

The stories should not be known to the children prior to class reading. If this method is used in connection with basal readers, books should not be given to the children except during the reading period. As teachers know, books available at the beginning of a year are often read completely by some children during the first few weeks. If these books are used for oral-reading lessons, there is no compelling reason for certain children to give attention.

The divided-story method

A story for reading by a group of five or six children is cut into twelve to eighteen parts and pasted on cards for easy handling. The story may be cut from a discarded book or magazine. Two copies of the story will be needed, since part of it may be on the back of a section to be glued to a card. The cards should be numbered, corresponding to the order of the parts in the story.

Each child is given one or two cards to prepare for reading orally. When every member of the group has studied his cards and is sure he can read them without hesitation and with good expression, the cards are read orally in turn. In this plan each child is held accountable for only the words in his selection. If desired, the difficult words and phrases in the story may be studied by the group prior to reading.

Pupil preparation of short selections

Pupil preparation is particularly valuable in upper grades where the children have good word mastery. Suitable materials for this type of reading are newspaper clippings, short biographical selections, notes from encyclopedias, short selections from books of essays, and original compositions, poems, and extracts emphasizing special topics. Teachers themselves may make collections of short units related to such topics as holidays, famous people, transportation, and arts.

The reading lesson centers around a single topic, with easy and difficult selections suitably assigned. After the pupils have studied their selections, each reads orally to the class. If an article is too long to be read orally, the pupil may write a summary or select significant paragraphs for class presentation.

Reading of dramatized material

In oral reading of dramatized material each pupil prepares to read the lines of one character. The child will read the whole play while studying his part. However, no loss of interest results because the novelty of impersonating a character usually serves to sustain interest. This type of oral reading is especially desirable for corrective work in voice, speech, and expression. Many selections suitable for this type of reading are listed in Chapter 14.

Assignments for intensive study of selections

Research demonstrates that children usually obtain from an initial reading only a small fraction of the meaning of a story. Furthermore, unless help is given, rereading produces little additional meaning. Instruction to meet this problem depends mainly on the teacher's ingenuity in motivating a second reading of a story. Various devices have commonly been used to motivate detailed reading, such as simple questions, suggestions to "find the part of the story you like best," and the naïve pointing of morals by such questions as, "Do you think it was nice of the boy to cheat the old man?" or "Do you think the boy should have helped the dog out of the trap?"

This method, however, hardly provides sufficient motivation for one oral reading and certainly does not stimulate interest in a second reading of any story. Several types of assignments for motivating oral reading when the story has already been studied are found in Chapter 13, on study skills. The exercises below indicate a few of the types of lessons under this general classification.

Improving the organization and selection of ideas

Specific assignments may be prepared to aid children in recalling the details of a story for later use in oral and written summaries to be given independently. For such an assignment the first direction would be given: "On the board you will find a list of events that happen in the story you are about to hear. They are not in the right order. We shall read the story by sections. After each section is read, find the event that goes with it and write it on your paper."

On the board are written statements of significant happenings in the story, in some such style as the following:

    A. The boy saw two men running.
    B. The boys opened the door and looked out.
    C. They found a tree that had been cut down.
    D. They found a package of nails.
    E. The box fell into the water.
    F. The men started to open the box.

To save the time of writing the statements, the child may indicate his choice of statement by copying the capital letter which precedes it.

A somewhat more difficult assignment of this type would consist of asking the children to write a headline or title for each section of the story as it is read. If the story is divided into ten sections for oral reading, each child should have ten numbers on his paper and write his title for each section as read. He should also write a title for the story as a whole. This assignment will be made more dramatic if the children are told that they are writing newspaper headlines or perhaps captions for a motion-picture story.

Noticing the structural elements of a story

After a story has been read silently, it may then be read orally for one or more of the following purposes: to notice good action words, descriptive words or passages, apt combinations of words, topic sentences, transition statements, and other structural elements. As each paragraph is read, the pupils report orally the elements that seem particularly good. The teacher also adds comments. This type of assignment is useful in the intermediate grades, particularly as an aid to written composition.

Enriching imagery

It is quite possible that the pleasure one derives from a story depends upon the imagery accompanying the reading. Children vary considerably in the richness and type of imagery experienced during reading. Reading and also listening are, of course, creative activities. The imagery experienced by a child while listening or reading depends partly upon previous contacts with the words, phrases, and ideas of the story and partly upon new associations to which his attention is called. Even the simplest statements may suggest many pictures.

On hearing a statement such as "The man ran down the steps," a child may add numerous details, such as the man's age and appearance, the speed of his running, the direction taken at the bottom of the steps, the appearance of the building from which he came, the general surroundings, the width and type of street, the general weather conditions, and the presence or absence of automobiles and people.

Few investigations have been made of ways of improving imagery in reading and listening; yet it is likely that the power could be increased by instruction. To promote richness of imagery, it is suggested that the following type of lesson be employed as a listening assignment in oral reading. Begin by saying, "I know you have read the story yourselves, but I wonder whether you have seen all the pictures in the story. After Henry reads the next paragraph, let us stop to see whether we can find any more pictures than we saw the first time."

After the paragraph has been read, questions may be asked in order to stimulate the children to add other descriptive elements. Such questions might concern the appearance and dress of the characters, the distance and direction of travel, the kind of weather, the sounds to be heard, the emotions of the characters, and other details pertinent to the paragraph.

Suggesting activities related to the story

Oral reading that calls for close attention and is effectively motivated usually results from assignments that involve or anticipate some class or individual activities, such as drawing or dramatizing.

Three illustrations of assignments that will involve certain activities are given here:

1. As you listen to this story, think of five or six pictures which sum up its most important parts. When you have finished reading, discuss with other pupils the pictures you found and decide on the best ones to draw. Then draw pictures which contain the main points of the story.

2. As you listen to this story being read, think of similar things which have happened to you or to people you know. Write down your thoughts so that you can have them for our discussion after the story is read.

3. As you listen to this story, think of the things we would need if we were to make a play out of it. What would we put on the stage? How would we dress the characters? What would we have them say?

Assignments such as these serve to develop the habit of expecting reading to contain ideas for further activity. They also stimulate thought and conversation and may serve as motivation for oral and written composition.

Phrase reading in oral assignments

In a complete program of oral-reading instruction there are times when attention should be directed to problems of expression rather than to the meaning of the story. Before any selections are used for practice in the mechanics of expression, they should have been read for meaning, using one of the lesson types already discussed. Poetry and drama are particularly useful for such practice, although other types of reading material may be chosen.

In reading to improve phrasing the pupil doing the reading of course derives the most benefit. For this reason small-group work is particularly desirable in order that each child may have frequent reading opportunities. Since the audience gains little benefit from the practice, this type of oral assignment should be used sparingly, perhaps only when the children are outstandingly deficient in the mechanics of reading and expression.

Rereading for measurement

In remedial work with individual pupils or with small groups, oral reading of material previously used will provide a measure of progress. Upon the child's first oral reading of the selection the teacher records the pupil's errors and files this record for later comparison. The record should include time required for reading, difficulties with individual words, addition and omission of words, and similar difficulties. Comparisons made with the second reading will show the degree of improvement which the child has made. In individual tutoring such oral rereading is important, and occasional tests of this kind should be made in the primary grades to provide an objective record of each child's progress. Such records are best made on a copy of the story.

Phrase reading in relation to speed

For improvement of mechanics of oral reading, attention should be paid to voice, expression, and interpretation rather than to speed. If the child knows he is being timed while reading, he will often manifest insecurity and tenseness, both of which shift attention from expression and meaning.

Among the factors which tend to reduce oral-reading speed are difficulties in word recognition and in perception of words and phrases, repetitions of words and phrases, addition and omission of words, losing the place, and difficulties in breath control and voice.

These basic abilities are the ones that call for the teacher's special attention.

Symptoms and causes of slow phrase reading

Occasionally a child tends to drawl vowel sounds of words in oral reading or paces his reading to the slow motor habits acquired when reading was laborious for him. If the phrase drills outlined on the following pages and the exercises in expression and interpretation (pages 169–170) are not sufficient to break up these habits, use of timed selections may be helpful.

Another cause of a slow reading rate is the habit of pointing along the lines with the finger during oral reading. This practice tends to emphasize small units and to pace the reading too slowly. While finger pointing is sometimes recommended for primary-grade children in order to establish a left-to-right reading habit, the resulting slow pacing and the shortened reading units offset any advantages of the method. The use of a marker under the lines is to be preferred. Several types of markers are suggested later in this chapter. See pages 164–165.

Head movements also tend to reduce oral-reading rate. If the child forms a habit of swinging his head from side to side at a uniform rate, he unconsciously reads at this rate. This habit is usually overcome merely by calling the child's attention to it, or, in severe cases, by having the child read with his chin resting on his hand or some other support.

The need for improvement in phrase reading is indicated by word-by-word reading, many eye movements per line, an expressionless voice, and a slow rate. Often the basic difficulty lies in slow or faulty word recognition. When exercises are given to speed up recognition, phrase reading improves naturally without further help. The use of phrase exercises, as described below, will often improve speed in oral reading and both speed and comprehension in silent reading, reduce oral-reading inaccuracies, eliminate habits of addition and omission of words in oral reading, and improve attention to punctuation and expression in oral reading.

Techniques for improving phrase reading

The exercises below have been found useful in improving phrase reading, assuming that certain fundamental reading conditions have been met. Materials must be of appropriate difficulty, without too many new words or ideas to interfere with smooth reading. Words included in phrase drills should have been previously taught through the word-recognition exercises included in Chapter 10, and their meanings should be already known.

Phrase work is essential to reading progress. The exercises should be followed by their immediate use in the succeeding reading lesson, either oral or silent. Many sample exercises on word recognition presented in Chapter 10 are immediately adaptable to phrase exercises.

The relationship between correct phrasing and meaning should be emphasized in all phrase exercises.

Phrase flash cards

Phrases from stories to be read may be placed on large flash cards for drill work after the individual words have been taught in recognition exercises. Phrase flash cards are presented by the usual short-exposure method. The technique recommended is to place a phrase card in a holder, hold a large blank card in front of it, then raise and lower the large covering card quickly so as to give the brief exposure desired.

This technique is more satisfactory than holding the phrase card in the hand and exposing it by turning it over. In the recommended method the print of the phrases is stationary, while in the other it moves. However, the second method can be satisfactorily used.

Sometimes it is found that the learning of phrases by flash cards does not transfer to the normal reading situation. The child can read flash cards but is not able to recognize the same phrases on the book page. This can be corrected somewhat by having the child underline or encircle on prepared typed lists the phrases presented by flash cards. Also, the phrases as they appear in the story may be singled out by the use of a mask over the page, with holes cut out to reveal the phrases. This mask device is illustrated in Chapter 10.

Phrases on the blackboard

Phrases from stories to be read may be written (printed) on the board for practice. Unless provision is made for covering and uncovering the phrases quickly, this drill will not be as effective as that with flash cards. But the child does obtain practice in seeing and reading whole phrases. If several children read in turn from the same list, the teacher should skip about in the list to guard against mere memorization by order.

Phrases on lantern slides

Lantern slides containing phrases may be prepared by the method described for word-perception slides in Chapter 10. See the description of lantern-slide methods on page 212. These phrases can be flashed readily by covering and uncovering the lens of the projector with a card.

Phrase exercises with the tachistoscope

The phrase tachistoscope insures the quick perception of phrases required for smooth oral and silent reading. The phrase tachistoscope (see page 201) resembles the device used in word-recognition exercises (page 200), except that the aperture for exposing words is wide enough for phrases. Phrases may be typed on tachistoscope cards in random order or the phrases of an entire story may be presented in sequence.

Use of spaced material

The material to be read is arranged with the phrases separated by extra spaces in a manner such as the following:

By this time	the big bear	had disappeared
into the woods.	Dick ran	across the field
as quickly as he could	and soon came	
to the edge	of the woods.	

After the story has been presented in this way, the child turns to the book and reads it with the phrases unmarked. The practice thus carries over directly to the material in the book. Gradation of the emphasis on the phrasing may be accomplished by first separating the phrases by five spaces and later by only three. The child should be trained to observe the entire phrase carefully before he reads it aloud. This exercise will provide practice in increasing eye-voice span.

In separating a story into phrases, either by typing or by pencil markings, the teacher will find it difficult to determine the beginning and the end of phrases. Certain phrases will appear long, while other divisions will leave individual words dangling by themselves. The best practice for marking the phrases is to mark by voice units and to have no phrases with fewer than two words or more than six. The teacher should not be too much disturbed if the phrases are not of uniform length.

Phrase exercises that direct eye movement

A manila envelope 9″ by 12″ in size is prepared as follows: The bottom and the top are cut off evenly so that both ends are open. Two inches from the top of the envelope front a slot ¼″ wide is cut the entire width of the envelope. The drawing on page 163 shows the appearance of the envelope when prepared. On a sheet of paper 8½″ by 11″ are typed or printed phrases. Five or six spaces are allowed between phrases across the page, and two lines down the page, as indicated on the next page.

If the story is a long one, several sheets may be glued together. The phrases thus prepared are inserted in the envelope and are drawn slowly past the slot. Each phrase appears separately and moves across the opening so that eye-movement practice as well as drill in phrase reading is provided.

Reading phrases marked in a book

The phrases in a book may be marked by light vertical pencil lines in order to guide the children in phrase reading. After the pupils have read the book with the marked phrases, they should transfer to

By this time

       the big bear

              had disappeared

into the woods.

           Dick ran

              across the field

as quickly as he could

             and soon came

to the edge

          of the woods.

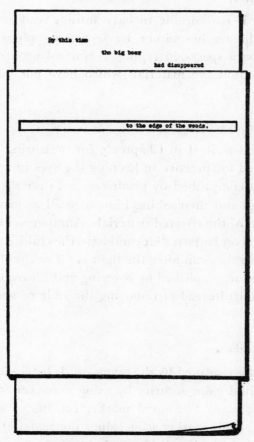

Device for Directing Eye Movement

a book with unmarked phrases so that they will have practice in reading the phrases without the crutch of the penciled divisions.

Recognition of phrases as read by the teacher

As the teacher reads, the children make light pencil checks in the book at pauses between phrases. At first the phrases will need emphasis, while later only slight pauses need be made between them. This is a good exercise to develop consciousness of the need for reading in phrases.

Reading in unison

Occasionally it is desirable to have unison reading of materials prepared by the teacher either by separating phrases by pencil marks or by extra spaces in typing. Advanced groups of children may read in unison the materials which have not been separated into phrases.

Eye-voice-span exercises

The method described in Chapter 5 for measuring the eye-voice span can be used for practice in keeping the eyes in advance of the voice. This is accomplished by placing a card over the material the child is reading, and then asking him to recall as many additional words as he can of the covered materials. Another method is to present the material on lantern slides and have the children recall all the additional words they can after the light is off or the slide removed. This can also be accomplished by covering and uncovering the front lens of the lantern instead of removing the slide or shutting off the light.

Use of line markers

Often a child is confused by the many words before his eyes at one time. Such a child gains security by using a marker to exclude the lines not being read. The usual marker consists of a card placed under the line. This marker, concealing the material below, gives greater emphasis to the line being read. Another type of marker consists of a card with a slot which reveals one line of print at a time. (See first diagram below.) The length and the width of the slot will vary with the size of the type and the width of the lines on the page.

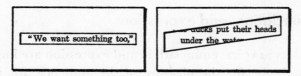

The third type of marker has the slot cut diagonally across so that the end of a line appears at the right side of the marker, while the beginning word in the next line appears at the left side of the marker. This type of marker reveals the phrase being read and also aids the child to overcome a difficulty in returning the eyes to the beginning of the next line. (See second diagram above.)

In individual remedial work it is often desired to point out a single phrase to the child. The marker in the illustration below may be used for this purpose. It is built in the manner of a slide rule and may be made of strong manila paper. A strip is cut $1\frac{1}{2}''$ in width and the long edges folded over $\frac{1}{4}''$. A slot for phrase reading is cut in the strip. A second strip of manila an inch wide is then inserted under the folded edges and adjusted to phrases of varying lengths.

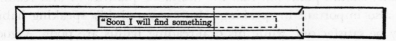

Other methods of phrase reading

Books with especially large and clear print sometimes help in phrase reading since they give an impression of ease in reading. However, if the print is too large, phrases may be broken too much. Therefore if large print is used, it should appear on wide pages.

Often dramatization and the reading of poetry improve phrase reading. Sometimes the only phrase work needed by certain children consists of the suggestion to catch large units of words at each look. In all phrase work it is helpful to explain how the eyes move in phrase reading as compared with word reading. The child then has little difficulty in understanding the purpose of the work.

Other methods which help phrase reading are outlined in the section on voice and expression immediately below.

Voice, enunciation, and expression

Good habits in voice, enunciation, and expression are important in all oral reading — for the pleasure of the audience, for improving general speech habits, and for proficiency in learning words and in deriving meaning from material read. If a child's pronunciation of a word is uncertain or if his enunciation lacks clearness, he will experience difficulty in retaining the word and understanding it in later reading. Faulty enunciation also affects perception of differences and similarities in words, thus delaying word mastery. Faulty enunciation is a common source of spelling difficulties.

Meanings of many sentences and the beauty of poetry are not appreciated until the child reads with proper rhythm and emphasis. Feelings of pleasure and pride in the clarity of one's speech in oral reading often carry over to conversation and to speaking before audiences.

In giving practice for improving expression in oral reading, the teacher should point out that the desirable qualities of oral reading are also important in speaking. However, a child's speaking habits may be satisfactory, while his oral-reading habits are poor. A good reading voice (and especially a good speaking voice) is often one of of the most important acquisitions that a child makes in school.

Methods of improving voice pitch

A high-pitched voice in oral reading is most frequently a result of tenseness and insecurity due to difficult material or to the emotions arising from the situation. Word difficulties can be removed by using simpler materials and by giving exercises in word recognition and phrase perception. The tenseness then disappears, and the voice approaches the right speaking tone.

High-pitched voices sometimes result from poor motivation and a low reading interest. Again, they may develop from too intense pressure of classroom work or from unconscious imitation of the teacher's voice. Usually the pitch of a person's voice is habitual rather than natural.

A child's reading tone may be changed without injury to his vocal apparatus. A teacher need not hesitate to help a child modify his voice to obtain the easiest and pleasantest tone for oral reading. Almost every person has several pitches of voice for different occasions. Usually the voice is higher during fright, anger, and other strong emotions. It is also raised during attempts to be especially convincing. Some persons' voices vary with situations, such as talking to superiors, talking over the telephone, speaking before a friendly audience, dictating to a stenographer, or talking to children.

Some plans that have proved to be helpful remedies for high-pitched voices are given below.

Removal of word-recognition difficulties

Word-recognition difficulties may be removed by selecting materials that are not too difficult and by use of word-recognition exercises prior to the reading. It can be observed that pitch of voice almost always rises to parallel the difficulty of the reading material. High-pitched voices cannot easily be changed when insecurity and confusion accompany the child's reading.

Showing the need for a lower pitch

To show the child his need for lowering the pitch of his voice, take him to the piano and compare for him the pitch of his reading voice with that of his conversational voice. This is done by noting his tone on the long vowels and having him prolong them until the pitch is found. The teacher should demonstrate the difference in tones by reading in a monotonous tone at a higher pitch and then at a lower pitch, keeping the regular tone for contrast by striking the piano keys. To show the difference between a child's reading and speaking voices the teacher may imitate him. However, in imitating him, she must exercise great care since this practice may embarrass the child.

Use of piano to find a natural pitch

To help the child find his natural pitch, again use the piano. Have the child sing various notes to determine his range of pitch. Determine the lowest and the highest tones he can comfortably produce. The proper pitch for his voice is three or four notes above the lowest one he can speak or sing easily. It should certainly be below the middle of his voice range. It should be remembered that in reading, the expression comes partly from varying the pitch, this variation usually being upward from the normal tone. To give practice in reading at the lower tone, the teacher strikes the piano note corresponding to the child's proper reading voice, and the child practices reading on that tone.

Use of exaggerated examples

Many coaches of amateur plays use the exaggerated example to show the actors the desired effect. The teacher reads with her voice pitched as low as possible and asks the child to follow her example. The reading may be done with a very high pitch or a very low one, thus giving the child practice in reading with flexibility of voice. Of course the pupil's effort will not be as exaggerated as the teacher's, the result thus being approximately the desired one.

Exercises for improving expression

Dramatization or part-reading of stories containing much conversation, with special attention to expression, will help to overcome voice difficulties. In such reading the effort is to interpret the material in ways natural to the situation. In his attempts to present sentences and expressions in a normal manner, a child's fear of an unnatural voice is often overcome.

Monotonous tone and inadequate expression in reading are often accompanied by difficulties in voice pitch. Attention to pitch will also aid in correcting the other faults. For the corrective exercises suggested below the reading materials should be familiar to the pupils. In corrective voice work for oral reading, familiar stories will enable the child to use some previously acquired meanings as an aid to expression.

Reading of poetry and plays

Use of poetry and plays helps to overcome monotonous tones. Attention is given to interpretation, and errors in reading the lines are immediately checked by other pupils. The fun of reading a play comes from careful interpretation of the lines. For some children reading poetry is particularly difficult. Either they engage in monotonous scanning of lines or they ignore meter and thus break up the rhythm. Selections for voice work should enable children to read easily without exaggeration of metrical units.

Sentences with words marked for emphasis

As preliminary practice to show the importance of emphasizing the proper words and varying the voice accordingly, it is well to demonstrate how meanings of short sentences depend upon emphasis. As an example, take a simple sentence such as the following: *"He* dropped a box of crayons." "He *dropped* a box of crayons." "He dropped a *box* of crayons." "He dropped a box of *crayons.*" Children find a great deal of pleasure in this sort of exercise. They learn to understand the importance of emphasis on particular words through voice modulation in determining the exact meaning of a sentence.

Next, the child should read paragraphs with words to be emphasized previously underlined by the teacher. He should read the material silently before trying it orally. Later the child himself should underline the words to be emphasized, and finally by a preliminary reading should learn to select the words for emphasis without underlining them.

Steps in overcoming fear of an audience

If high-pitched or monotonous voices result from fear of the audience, several remedies are available. The child becomes less aware of the audience when one of the following plans is used:

1. An imaginary radio broadcast at which the person reads behind a screen

2. A puppet or marionette show in which the audience watches the action of the puppets while the pupil reads the lines accompanying the action

3. Reading material to accompany shadow plays

4. Reading from a lantern slide with the room darkened

5. Reading into a microphone placed in a separate room

6. Reading into a sound-recording device and then listening to the record of one's own voice

Techniques for correcting faulty enunciation

Faulty enunciation may be due to careless speech habits or to structural defects. If the child has an articulatory speech defect, special corrective work is needed. However, if the enunciation difficulties are due merely to careless habits, it is possible to correct them for purposes of oral reading, even though the new skills may not transfer to speech. The suggestions for remedial work given below and on page 171 assume that the faulty enunciation is merely a result of careless speech habits.

Calling attention to the sound elements of words

The ear-training exercises recommended in Chapter 11 will help the child if his poor enunciation is due to lack of attention to word sounds. In such exercises it is particularly important that the child sense the value of each syllable in a word and include all the syllables in his reading. Words should be presented in syllables, both visually and orally, with special attention to correct vowel sounds.

Reading in whispers

If a child is required to read in whispers, he finds it necessary to make unusual use of lips and tongue, since the voice then cannot cover enunciation defects. Whispered reading should not be for too long a period, for this kind of reading necessitates great effort and results in strain and fatigue, particularly if the child must be heard several feet away.

Enunciating difficult words

Practice in enunciation can be made specific by using words that the child commonly enunciates inadequately. If the teacher will see that the enunciation drill is designed to correct his specific errors, a child will usually pay close attention and will practice on his own initiative.

Calling attention to proper use of the speech organs

The child may watch his lips in a mirror as he speaks in order to notice whether or not he uses his lips adequately. In cases of serious difficulty it is important to show the child the exact positions of lips, teeth, and tongue in making certain sounds. Some teachers motivate the work on enunciation by calling attention to the diction of certain motion-picture actors or actresses who have particularly good enunciation.

Having the child listen to his own enunciation

Listening to one's own reading is possible only if a sound-recording device is available. When a child can listen to his own reading voice, his specific faults and the desirability of overcoming them are brought to his attention in a dramatic way. It is usually necessary to point out difficulties with particular words, inadequate emphasis on final sounds of words, slurring syllables within words, ignoring little words, and other errors in enunciation that have previously been observed.

SUGGESTIONS FOR FURTHER READING

Bond, Guy L., and Wagner, Eva B. *Teaching the Child to Read*, Revised Edition. New York: The Macmillan Company, 1950. Pages 267–274.

Broom, M. E., and Others. *Effective Reading Instruction in the Elementary School*. New York: McGraw-Hill Book Company, 1942. Chapters 5, 6, 8, and pages 265–301.

Horn, Ernest, and Curtis, James. "Improvement of Oral Reading," in *Reading in the Elementary School,* The Forty-Eighth Yearbook of the National Society for the Study of Education. Chicago: University of Chicago Press, 1949. Chapter 12.

McKee, Paul. *The Teaching of Reading in the Elementary School.* Boston: Houghton Mifflin Company, 1948. Chapter 18.

Paul, Vera A. "Improvement of Oral Reading," in *The Teaching of Reading; A Second Report,* The Thirty-Sixth Yearbook of the National Society for the Study of Education. Bloomington, Illinois: Public School Publishing Company, 1937.

CHAPTER 9 Silent Reading

AN IMPORTANT AIM of elementary-school instruction is mastery of silent reading. Fluent and accurate silent reading is essential for success in school, college, and many vocations. It also opens the doors to a world of information and pleasure. The person with unsatisfactory silent-reading skills will find that all of his later education will be difficult, and he will tend to ignore the rich social heritage preserved in books.

The individual who plans his leisure reading intelligently has infinite possibilities for personal growth. Independent, planned, silent reading produces many desirable results—development of one's vocational abilities, increased enjoyment from new fields of knowledge, enhanced pleasure from travel, enriched understanding of the everyday world, expansion of interests, establishment and strengthening of friendships, enlarged rewards from conversation, stimulation of general effort, and greater mastery of emotions and actions. These results, of course, do not come solely from mastery of silent-reading skills, but they are unlikely to develop fully without control of these skills. Reading for effective living results from a program combining security in skills with experiences leading to initiative in the uses of reading.

This chapter deals primarily with simple silent-reading abilities, such as attention and comprehension, improved speed, and vocabulary growth.

A classification of the uses of reading and methods of teaching these uses are found in Chapter 14. At the end of the chapter are suggestions for planning a year's program in the uses of reading. Study skills in the content subjects are presented in Chapter 13.

Differences between silent and oral reading

While silent and oral reading have many skills in common, success in one does not insure equal success in the other. Comparison of results on oral-reading and silent-reading tests often reveals entirely different habits in the two types. A child who is painstaking and accurate in oral-reading vocabulary may ignore difficult words in silent reading. Children who find oral reading interesting and understandable often show inattention and insecurity when asked to read silently.

After the third grade, oral reading is usually slower than silent reading, pupils being no longer impeded by the vocal organs and being able to translate printed words directly into ideas without pronunciation of individual words. Habits of saying words during oral reading carry over to silent reading as lip movements and whispering. These habits need elimination to insure pupils' fluency in silent reading.

The table shown below shows a comparison of oral-reading rates and silent-reading rates for grades 1 through 6. It is based upon data from studies that were made in the Boston University Educational Clinic.

Rate in Words Per Minute

Grade	1	2	3	4	5	6
Oral Reading	45	80	110	135	150	170
Silent Reading	45	78	125	156	180	210

Silent-reading instruction in beginning reading

Silent-reading instruction begins in first grade at the same time as oral reading. The two cannot be separated in the reading process. As soon as the child recognizes a word, he has "read" it silently, even though his oral reading comes a split second later. All vocabulary instruction which puts word meaning foremost, emphasizes the silent aspect of reading and makes the oral pronunciation of the word a secondary process. By improper methods that emphasize the name of the word or the sound components of the word, it is possible, of course, to develop word calling with little attention to meaning. In good teaching, there is little conflict between the skills required by oral and by silent reading.

There has been some academic controversy about the value of non-oral versus oral methods of beginning reading. The differences between the two methods are merely of degree, since all non-oral methods must contain large elements of oral reading. Any written language based upon a phonetic system requires a close relationship between spoken and written words. The system is one of written speech. To ignore the relationship would be to give up the values of phonetic written language and resort to ideographs unrelated to the sounds in the spoken word. Since English words look so much alike, the system is grossly inadequate as an ideograph system. To teach it as such produces "reading disability" in most children after a few sight words are presented. So-called "silent-reading" and "non-oral" methods have large amounts of oral reading in classroom practice.

Silent-reading transfer skills in beginning reading

One of the commonest problems among first-grade pupils is insecurity in silent reading. Children like oral reading. Hearing the sound of their own voices gives them a sense of importance and of accomplishment. They have a greater security in oral reading since their errors are observed and they are helped at once. If they stop reading in the middle of a sentence, if their inaccuracy in phrasing leads to confusion, or if their word errors indicate lack of comprehension, they are quickly set straight. Usually they are rewarded by a "Good!" or "Fine!" immediately after finishing the oral reading of a sentence. Silent reading, in comparison, is a much duller process, filled with pitfalls which may discourage the child.

Over-emphasis on word analysis, or materials so difficult that oral reading becomes "word wrestling," may eliminate meaning from reading entirely, and make attention to meaning—the primary process of silent reading—almost impossible for the child. When he attempts to read silently, he continues his oral word-wrestling. Too much drill on the *name* of the word in word-recognition practice may empty words of their meanings. Most beginning readers tend to lean so much on oral reading that it is necessary to give special emphasis to silent-reading practice which provides security in the first stages.

There are many ways that teachers can provide secure silent-reading practice in beginning reading. Some of these ways are described below.

1. Responding to the meaning of a word as well as its name

In establishing a sight vocabulary, the child must know the name of the word, but it is equally important to maintain the meanings or qualities of the object being named. The teacher is emphasizing the *name* of the word when she holds up a flash card and asks, "What is this word? Yes, *shoe*. Now find *shoe* on this chart. See if you can find *shoe* on the blackboard. See if you can find another place where it says *shoe*. Now draw a circle around every *shoe* you can find on your paper." But she is asking the child to respond silently to the meaning of the word when she holds up a flash card with the word *shoe* and says, "Would you like one of these for lunch?" The delighted giggles and positive shout of "No!" indicate successful silent reading. Many methods of teaching silent reading of words are illustrated in Chapter 10.

2. Responding to directions read silently

Directions read silently require that the child know a number of command words such as the following:

Point	Show	Put	Find	Bring	Move
Look	Tell	Take	Draw	Come	Clap

By combining the above words with other words in his sight vocabulary, the child can respond to the silent reading of such directions as these:

> Point to the door.
> Look at the flag.
> Show me your pencil.
> Tell me how many girls there are in the room.
> Come to the front of the room.
> Put your hands on the table and close your eyes.
> Clap your hands if you are a boy.
> Draw two circles on your paper.
> Take your book and find a picture of a dog.
> Bring your book to me.
> Move your head up and down.

Directions such as these may be printed on flash cards and presented rapidly. Or they may be printed in a list on the blackboard with the teacher pointing to the various directions in random order. If it is evident that some children are merely copying the actions of the others, the teacher can ask such children to read the direction orally.

3. Responding to questions read silently

Oral responses to questions read silently require that the child know a number of words that commonly introduce questions, such as *Where, How many, Who, Can, Does,* and the like. By combining these words with other words in the child's sight vocabulary, all children or individual children may be asked to respond to such questions as these:

> How many feet does a horse have?
> Who is going to have a birthday this week?
> Does a cat like to drink milk?

These questions are used in the same manner as the silent reading of directions. If individual children only are to respond, the teacher may call the child's name, or indicate the child by pointing to his name on the blackboard. Questions are an excellent way of giving a child meaningful practice on the difficult "wh" words—*who, what, where, when, why, which*. Questions may center on a single topic such as an interview: "What is your name? How old are you? How many brothers and sisters do you have? Where do you live? Where were you born? What did you do last Saturday?" Plans for a party may be presented, such as, "When shall we have the party? How many people shall we ask? Whom shall we ask? What will we have to eat? Where will we go?"

A similar set of questions may be made over a story which has been read or told to the children.

4. Responding to questions accompanying silent reading

The teacher prepares a list of oral questions which accompany the sentences in the story, and gives these questions in advance of each sentence. For example, the following questions might be used with the story "Bobby's Wish." [1]

The story begins like this:

> Mother and Grandmother were getting lunch ready. Betty was helping Mother and Grandmother. They were getting the milk and cake and sandwiches out of the box. Father was sitting under a tree. Baby was sitting under the tree with him. . . .

The questions to be asked by the teacher before the child reads each sentence are as follows: "What were Mother and Grandmother doing? Who was helping them? What were they getting out of the box? What was Father doing? Where was Baby and what was he doing?" and so on.

The child first reads the book silently. Then he either shuts the book or covers the sentence he has just read and gives the answer to the question.

[1] Donald D. Durrell, Helen B. Sullivan, and Kay Bishop, *The Big Surprise* (Yonkers, New York: World Book Company, 1950).

5. Working in pairs to answer questions prepared by the teacher

If children work together on silent-reading tasks, they usually tend to keep more alert than when working alone. Children read the questions to each other; then they read silently until one finds the answer. The other checks to make sure he is right. It is better at this level if the teacher uses multiple-choice questions so that the child will not have to write an answer. Or she can give a list of questions with answers in random order in an opposite column; the child will draw a line from the question to the answer. Or she may have the questions on a sheet of paper with the answers on slips of paper or oak tag; the child will place the answer beside the question.

6. Placing events of a story in order

Placing the events of a story in order also works better in pairs. A list of happenings in the story is placed on strips of construction paper. The children first read the sentences on the strips. Then they read the story, rearranging the strips as they come to each of the events.

The same thing may be done with a series of pictures drawn by more-advanced learners to illustrate the story. It is important that the pictures clearly illustrate the event, or at least are given titles which may be put in order.

7. Working in pairs in doing workbook exercises

Many workbooks are designed to give practice in silent reading, with the child following directions to demonstrate his comprehension. It is well if two children work together, checking with each other the understanding of what is to be done. Workbooks in which a child reads for five seconds and then colors for two minutes are to be avoided. It is better to reverse the process, with more reading and very short responses. Even the yes-no type of question is to be preferred to the "much coloring" type of reading workbook. The same thing may be said for checking comprehension by having the child draw a picture series to indicate comprehension. The child who is slow in learning reading would profit more by multiplying the reading practice.

8. Maintaining attention through help of introductory statements

Several suggestions for different types of situation-setting before silent reading are found on pages 184–187. These suggestions include several types of introductory statements such as discussion and questions. Only the more persistent and attentive readers in the class will be able to read an entire selection following a preliminary statement.

All of the foregoing suggestions are dependent upon the child's having an adequate sight vocabulary for handling the reading. If the silent-reading material contains unknown words, attention will be diverted from the meaning task. All silent reading in the beginning stages should consist of words that the child can read orally. Even then it is well to give preliminary word and phrase practice immediately before the silent-reading lesson. At this early stage, a child will not be expected to be skilled in "working out" unknown words for himself. Even if he could, the process interrupts his thoughts. If the reading has a very slight hold on the child's attention, he should be encouraged to ask the teacher for help immediately on words that he finds difficult.

More advanced learners may serve as "word consultants" for a group of slow learners who are working at silent-reading tasks. As the child's skill in word analysis and silent-reading attention advances, he may be asked to work out words for himself. In fact, it is desirable to insert in a selection words that are readily solved by phonics.

Lip movements in preprimer and primer levels need not worry the teacher too much if the child gets the meaning. However, such reading is not true silent reading. Sometimes the lip movements can be suppressed by having the child hold something between his lips, but this merely gets rid of the outer sign of continued oral reading. The various word-meaning-recognition exercises (see Chapter 10) and silent-reading response cards are better ways to establish true silent reading.

Just how quickly a child can eliminate all inner speech in silent reading is unknown. Perhaps this inner speech persists in a subconscious level for several years. The comparison of oral- and silent-reading rates would indicate that it persists into second-grade reading. Rapid responses by the child to the meaning of words and sentences is the best way of eliminating lip movements at the early stages of reading.

Silent-reading instruction beyond beginning reading

When the child can maintain his attention in silent reading throughout a typical primer story, he may be helped to maintain and improve his comprehension by many types of less detailed assistance. The best motivation for improving comprehension is the simple desire to read and enjoy the story. However, even the best-motivated reader needs to be observed from time to time to see that he is not learning habits of ignoring unknown words and being content with having many vague spots in his reading. When the motivation is lowered by a less interesting story, or when it is made difficult by the generalizations of social-studies books which must "mention and move on" so that they can cover a broad area, more assistance is necessary.

While Chapter 13 will deal with many aids to study in content subjects, most of the suggestions in this chapter will deal with silent-reading aids that are useful in both literature and content subjects. In both, the adjustment of materials to a suitable reading level is required. Any material too difficult for oral reading is much too difficult for silent reading. Such materials should be relatively free from word and concept difficulties. Where word difficulties will necessarily be encountered, preliminary help is given on difficult words. A glossary is provided to help the child remember meanings as the words are encountered in reading.

Chronic inattention

When the motivation is lowered, habits of inattention creep into the reading. Every adult reader occasionally awakes to the fact that he is reading without comprehending; he can return to the exact spot in reading where his mind "left off." Children have the same difficulty. Sometimes, however, their minds leave off at the beginning of the first sentence, and they are unaware of the fact until study time has ended. Chronic inattention in silent reading can become so serious that a child is almost completely unable to keep his mind on reading. A child's inability to keep his mind on reading is often reflected in frustration in schoolwork that requires reading. It also forces low scores on educational and intelligence tests. The child's sight and meaning vocabulary may be excellent and his oral reading may be clear and expressive. However, he will be unable to recall what he reads simply because meanings of words are not entering his mind.

Levels of recall

Remembering what is read is a relative matter. It varies not only in amount and quality but also in level of availability to the reader. While there may be many shadings of difficulty in each level, the abilities named on this page and the pages that follow—to identify the correct answer, to answer general and specific questions, to summarize or give unaided recall—are some of the major stages in recall.

1. Ability to identify the correct answer

The ability to identify the correct answer is a very low level of recall, requiring only the ability to select or verify answers presented by others. It is the *true-false* or *multiple-choice* level where the memory is greatly aided by the presentation of the answer. It is also observed in a situation in which the child is unable to answer a question. However, when the answer is given by another, he exclaims,

"Oh, I remember that now!" Although multiple-recall tests may be made difficult by increasing the amount of interpretation required, the identification process does not assure the availability of the information at other levels.

2. Ability to answer specific factual questions

Here again, in the ability to answer factual questions, the memory is aided by the questioner. The questions refresh the memory and carry the pupil through the structure of the selection. However, the answer is not given and must come from the memory of the pupil. The questions may be made more difficult by requiring inference or interpretation.

3. Ability to answer general questions

A child who can answer specific questions may not be able to handle questions that call for multiple answers, such as listing or enumerating causes, products, plans, illustrations, or other development of general ideas. Five or six general questions may reveal the structure of the selection, thus aiding the memory. With this much prompting by the teacher, a child may show a fairly high level of recall.

4. Ability to summarize or to give complete unaided oral or written recall

In the ability to summarize or to give unaided recall the child is required to tell the story from memory without the structural aid of questions, either specific or general. This is rather difficult for many children who are able to show almost complete recall on multiple-choice or short-answer questions. Correlations between multiple-choice recall and either oral or written unaided recall are seldom above .40. This fact indicates a low relationship between the abilities.

The preparation and use of graded study guides presented in Chapter 13 will prove helpful in bringing the pupil from low levels of recall to higher ones.

These various levels of recall indicate that there are also various levels of comprehension. Comprehension and recall are so intimately interwoven that it is difficult, and perhaps unnecessary, to separate them. Many times a child is unable to recall certain facts because the questions that he is asked do not have in them the same words and phrases that were used in the selection. This inability indicates only a verbal memory. Thus a "right answer" does not necessarily mean that the child understands what he has read. Differences in comprehension (or understanding, or interpretation) depend upon the amount of experience the child has with the ideas or experiences being described. Experiences also determine richness of imagery in silent reading. All of the suggestions below are intended to improve both comprehension and recall.

Introductory statements to aid comprehension

Silent-reading interest and comprehension may be greatly aided by laying the groundwork for reading through any of several ways. Children are better able to maintain attention when they have some idea of what they are to look for. Questions and discussions prior to reading have a far greater importance than the practice of some teachers would indicate. The list of suggested methods (below and on pages 185–187) of introducing a story or a lesson is given so that a teacher may have a variety of approaches and may suit them to the selection being studied.

1. Vocabulary study as aid to comprehension

Since preliminary vocabulary study is often necessary, it may be used to assist the reader in following the selection. For example, if the story contains such words as *thwarted, obstinate, persevere, manuscript,* the teacher may illustrate the words through experiences known to the child and then say, "Somebody in this story was thwarted in an unexpected way. You find out who the person is and how he was thwarted." Or, the teacher might say, "There was a very obstinate person in this story. You are going to find out why this person was so obstinate." In this way the words which might give the child some difficulty are changed to words which add interest to the selection.

2. Mystery questions to guide reader

A series of questions may indicate the structure of the selection without giving the story away. For example, the teacher may say, "This story is about some boys who wanted something very much. See if you can find out right in the beginning what they wanted and why they wanted it. The story goes on to tell how they tried to get what they wanted. They tried three different ways, and you will see what these ways were. Then there is a surprise at the end. Perhaps the boys got what they wanted, and perhaps they got something else. Perhaps they liked it and perhaps they didn't. The story will tell you at the end."

3. Preliminary picture study

Children always like to look at pictures, those in the book or those presented outside the book. By looking at the pictures and asking questions about them, the child's interest for the story may be whetted.

In factual material, pictures may be presented from sources other than the book. A discussion of these pictures by the children may serve to introduce the story and create an interest in the events of the story.

4. Discussion of experiences related to content or problem of story

If the story relates a common experience, such as humorous things that happen to a child, embarrassing events, mysterious noises, things that disappear, or other similar problems, the teacher may ask the children to tell such experiences. Then she may turn to the story which relates still another similar experience. If the story deals with travel, camping, holidays, parties, accidents, dangers, such things are discussed before the story.

5. Presenting story as acts in a play

Since children have had experience with plays divided into acts, or have observed divisions of television performances into acts, it is helpful to divide the story into acts and to present titles for them. A brief discussion of what might take place in each act is helpful. Essentially, this is giving an outline of the story. Headings in the selection in the book may provide the outline, and these may be discussed in order to show the structure. Since a child usually likes to know how long a story is before he begins to read it, a preliminary study of dividing the story into acts will enable him to see his progress as he reads.

In some types of fiction it is possible for the teacher and the pupils to discuss the scenes without revealing what takes place in each scene. Those children who read primarily for plot and action and skip descriptive passages will be particularly helped by the setting of scenes.

6. Oral reading of part of story

The teacher may help the pupils to get a clear start on the story by reading the first few paragraphs to them. Then the children may go on in silent reading, or there may be a short period of guessing about what happens.

With very small groups of children who read at about the same rate, the teacher may give them a boost during the reading of the story by assigning further oral reading of the less important phases of the story.

7. Reading of selected sentences in story

A good method of introducing a story is for the teacher to pick out several of the more interesting sentences in the story and read them to the entire group of children. The teacher should take care to select the kind of sentences that could add an air of mystery or perhaps a suggestion of fun to the story but do not give the plot or the action away.

8. Oral presentation of similar stories

Short informational or amusing stories may be read or told by the teacher. These should be similar in some essential way to the story which the children are to read silently. They may be about the same location, the same problem, the same emotional situation, the same period of time, or they may be written by the same author. Then the children are told that their story is another story of the same type, place, or time.

9. Motion pictures, film slides, or television programs

Visual aids such as motion pictures, film slides, and television programs may serve as an introduction to reading if a good film library is available. The pictures should be presented before the story is begun, if the greatest interest is to be obtained. Every librarian has observed the increase in demand for certain books which follows motion-picture or television presentation.

10. Map and time studies

The teacher will find that map and time studies are very helpful in locating in the child's mind the time and place of the events that are to be read or studied. These studies should precede social-studies material.

Aids to comprehension during silent reading

All of the graded study guides to be used with pairs, teams of three, or larger groups presented in Chapter 13, give suggestions for assisting children in comprehension during silent reading. While they are more suitable for informational material in content subjects where comprehension is often difficult, they may be used in narrative reading when necessary. It is usually undesirable to interrupt the reading of fiction by a series of factual questions. However, if a child needs to have help from the teacher in maintenance of attention, such help should be given.

Several suggestions which may be used in the reading of imaginative stories are given below.

1. Assistance with imagery during the selection

Small groups of children who read silently at about the same rate may be asked to stop at various points in the story. The teacher then joins them and asks questions about the pictures they have in their minds. This is particularly helpful when the book has no pictures. Suggestions for checking the vividness and extent of imagery are found on page 117, in Chapter 5.

2. Suggesting illustrations for the story

At selected points in the story the group is reading, a child may be asked to list the pictures which would be needed in order to tell the story up to that point. If the children are working in pairs, they should be allowed to discuss the pictures and make their lists together.

3. Answering questions about the story

A child, or a small group of children, is given questions to answer while the child or the group reads. If the children are very poor readers, they should look at the questions before each unit of reading and find the answers as they go. If they are better readers, they may answer the questions after the selection. Such questions should add interest or interpretation to the story.

Some of the types of questions which may be used in the reading of fiction are the following:

1. *Questions that call for the child's reactions to the story.* "Would you like to be in Bobby's place?" "Would you like Carl for a friend?" "Would you like to have the dinner that Mary and Billy had?" The child should be prepared to answer the question orally in later discussion.

2. *Questions that call for reasons for action.* "Why did they go to the camp of the Indians?" "Why were they afraid?" "Why did they take Henry with them?"

3. *Questions that require generalization.* "Which of these titles would be best for this paragraph?" "Which of the questions on the board does this paragraph answer?"

4. *Questions interspersed in the reading.* If the child is reading from typed material, questions may be inserted after each paragraph or at suitable intervals in the story. If he is reading from a book, he may be expected to answer questions after each paragraph. Or, perhaps, numbers of questions may be indicated at the end of lines in the book, with the child looking at the questions on a study sheet. Children who are inattentive in silent reading are kept alert by such a series of questions. If the child moves a cover over the page as he reads, the need for looking back to find the answer will be emphasized by the need for lifting the cover. This type of exercise is often used in tutoring a single child.

Questions after silent reading

Questions which come after silent reading are too late to help the child in comprehension. His reading is already done, and his comprehension task is completed. If the questions deal with factual material, they serve to measure comprehension. The results may indicate that the child needs help in future lessons. Only the knowledge that such questions are coming will serve to keep the child alert during the reading. This form of coercion may help some children, but it is too general and too remote to be of much use if the child has serious difficulty.

Discussion after reading, however, may be helpful in showing to the child interpretations, applications, inferences, and relationships which he might have missed during the reading. Questions of this type are presented in Chapter 13. More appropriate for the reading of fiction are questions that deal with the child's reactions to the story —to the characters and situations in it. These questions can relate to similar experiences that have happened to the child or to people he knows; to similar situations in other stories; and to the evaluation of the story situations or the actions of the story people.

Improving speed of silent reading

No attempt should be made to improve speed of silent reading until the habits of accurate, attentive reading are established. It is doubtful if any attempts should be made to emphasize speed of reading in primary grades. Pressures for improving speed of reading must be used with caution in all levels of reading. The number of words or pages per minute is not as important as the yield per minute in memories, images, ideas. Stress on speed of silent reading must not be made when it results in ignoring difficult words and passages, lowering the attention in reading, diminishing comprehension, ignoring the imagery, or eliminating thought or reflections about the material.

If the slow speed of reading is due to such faulty habits as lip movements and whispering or general mental apathy, several steps may be taken to improve the speed of reading. Flash cards that require oral or action responses, described on page 203, will be helpful. More mature readers will need the skimming tasks outlined in Chapter 13.

While the best basis for improving speed of reading is the desire to learn the end of an interesting story, children may be helped to improve their speed in a number of ways. The speed tests described in Chapter 5, if given once or twice a week and the results recorded on a graph, will be adequate to motivate the children to greater speed of reading.

Questions should always be asked after speed tests, and perhaps a penalty score of 20 or 30 words should be subtracted from the computed speed for each question missed. Questions should be relatively easy and should cover only the main points of the selection read. Such speed tests should be over simple narrative, and the material must not contain many difficult words or concepts. If the speed tests are limited to two or three minutes, at most, and if the material is suitable, no great nervous strain is found. However, if any of the children are bothered by these speed tests, the tests should then be used very sparingly.

The various gadgets for increasing silent-reading speed—reading pacers which move a cover over the page at predetermined rates, mechanical shutters which expose phrases or lines, or films which do the same thing—are not particularly suitable for elementary-school use at present. The problems of the immature reader are primarily those of vocabulary, comprehension, imagery, recall, and thinking about reading. The various reading-pacing devices offer no help in these skills and may actually build poor habits when the materials are unsuitable. They may be helpful in individual or small-group tutoring when adequately safeguarded by a teacher who watches the comprehension factors carefully. Most of these reading-pacing devices are much more helpful for mature readers who can adjust their read-ing speed to their comprehension without help from the teacher.

Eye-movement exercises seem to have little place in elementary-school instruction. It is doubtful if they have value at any level of reading. Eye movements are controlled by thought processes, and they vary greatly with the difficulty of reading or the mental task re-quired by the assignment. The photographing of eye movements is not helpful in the analysis of reading at the elementary-school level. The strained situation of casual observation of eye movements by di-rect observation is multiplied greatly when eye movements are being photographed. The results of photographing eye movements are of doubtful validity.

When casual observation shows that the child is irregular in eye movements, has too many per line, or uses many regressive move-ments, the cause is usually found in word difficulties or insecurity in reading. If there are no word difficulties, then some help in quick word or phrase perception may be given. The cardboard tachisto-scope described on page 200, or the one included in the *Durrell Anal-ysis of Reading Difficulty*,[1] may be used for flashing words or phrases

---

[1] Donald D. Durrell, *Durrell Analysis of Reading Difficulty*, New Edition (Yonkers, New York: World Book Company, 1955) .

that are already known to the child. A shutter on a lantern-slide projector may be used for the same purpose. Such exercises are particularly helpful if they provide for responses to the meaning of the word, or if they are presented in oral context. They may be used for slow learners for vocabulary review.

SUGGESTIONS FOR FURTHER READING

Adams, Fay, Gray, Lillian, and Reese, Dora. *Teaching Children to Read.* New York: The Ronald Press, 1949. Pages 238–268.

Broom, M. E., and Others. *Effective Reading Instruction in the Elementary School.* McGraw-Hill Book Co., 1942. Chapters 9 and 10.

Hildreth, Gertrude. *Learning the Three R's.* Minneapolis: Educational Publishers, Inc., 1947. Pages 325–330.

Smith, Nila B. *One Hundred Ways of Teaching Silent Reading.* Yonkers, New York: World Book Company, 1925.

CHAPTER **10** Word Recognition in Primary Grades

THE MAIN TASK in reading instruction in the primary grades is that of building a secure and wide sight vocabulary, so that the child can handle the creative task of building images and ideas from the words the author uses. As soon as the child has difficulty with words, his thought processes are interrupted. He cannot enjoy reading; he is so lost in wrestling with words that the ideas that he might get from the reading are neglected, comprehension is vague, and recall is inaccurate and fragmentary.

The three word skills to be taught in primary grades are word recognition, word meaning, and word analysis. Each of the three skills has an important place in the program; the omission of any one would retard or even prevent growth in reading vocabulary. Word-recognition practice by simple look-and-say methods is self-defeating unless it is accompanied by methods that keep the meanings high, and by the background skills of auditory and visual perception of word elements.

Without attention to meaning, reading becomes word-calling; without a background of phonics, reading becomes a guessing game. With phonics alone, however, reading becomes nonsense syllable analysis.

Some general suggestions for teaching
word recognition

Most teacher's manuals in primary-grade reading systems provide the teacher with many materials and suggestions for teaching word recognition. If children fail to make adequate progress in word recognition when these materials are used, the following suggestions may indicate ways of removing the difficulty:

1. *The number of words to be taught in each lesson should be suitable to the child's learning rate.* If the learning-rate test described in Chapter 3, pages 50–51, shows that the child can learn only three words a day, the presentation of five or six words each day will cause confusion. If the child remembers only five of the last twenty words taught in the daily lessons, it is obvious that the rate of presentation of new words is too fast. Adjusting to learning rate always requires small group instruction in which the children are of approximately equal learning rate.

2. *The child's auditory and visual perception of word elements must be adequate.* The importance of such skills as reading-readiness background was discussed in Chapter 3, and suggestions for teaching them presented in Chapter 4. Children who make rapid progress in word recognition are familiar with forms and names of letters. They also notice separate sounds in spoken words. Pupils who do not possess these skills should be given the reading-readiness background during the first few weeks of school. Attempts to teach a sight vocabulary without these skills will result in confusion. Suggestions for teaching word-analysis skills beyond the reading-readiness period are found in Chapter 11.

3. *Word meanings must be kept high.* Most words in the primary readers will be in the child's oral vocabulary. But in the process of learning to read, the meanings must be attached to the visual form of the word. Care must be taken to emphasize meaning. Many of the exercises in this chapter direct the child's attention to the meanings and images evoked by the word. The section on silent-reading trans-

fer skills in beginning reading in Chapter 9 also offers many ways of maintaining attention to meaning.

Some general problems in word recognition

Children may attempt to recognize words by the general appearance of a word rather than by exact letters. Often a part of a word stands out and serves as a cue for recall of the whole. Cues used by children to recognize words often lead to errors. The word *dog* is commonly misread as *girl*, probably because the *g* is the cue for the latter word. A first-grade boy with reading difficulty volunteered to write "Come with me to the tree," and wrote "o-w-e-t-h-ee." He then said, "*O* is a bad one because you never can tell whether it means *come* or *go* or *boys.*"

One is never sure which part of a new word the child observes. The list below shows errors made by children when certain words were presented to them. It is significant that every error of recognition contains letters or phonograms of the stimulus word.

WORD PRESENTED	CHILDREN'S ERRORS
and	an, sat, fan, animal
away	was, way, when, awake
back	bark, lack, book, take, Dick, Jack, look
comes	came, can, come, house, some
kitten	cat, little, kitchen, kittens
many	and, away, may, make, my
night	right, bright, light
on	an, go, in, Oh, one, no, not
out	but, cat, cut, not, put, you
cook	book, look, take, talk
walk	away, like, milk, wall, take
wash	fish, was, washed, wish, with, which
work	would, word, down, with, wake
went	want, what, wheat, when, with

Such tabulations of children's recognition errors reveal some relationship between the word presented and the word as read by the child. Generally the error results from failure to notice the word's

exact appearance and a tendency on the part of the child to ignore
minor characteristics of the word. Sometimes the initial letters furnish
cues; at other times the final letters seem most prominent to the child.
General word length or peculiar letter characteristics, such as double
t's in the middle of the word, will at times attract the child's attention. A few errors result from mistaken meanings, such as confusing
the word *cat* with *kitten* or substituting *mouse* for *rat* or *bunny* for
rabbit.

Sometimes the child pays no attention to the word, but notices
some other condition which serves as a cue. For example, a child who
had successfully read the word *children* on a flash card was unable
to read it in a book. He insisted he had never seen the word before.
He was presented with the flash card of the word and was asked how
he recognized the word as *children*. He replied, "By the smudge over
in the corner."

The child who is unfamiliar with the form and names of certain
letters will often ignore them in new words. If the child does not
know the names of all letters, teaching them will assist him in observation of words.

The chief psychological justification for avoiding the teaching of
letters before reading is based on the belief that it results in over-
analytical word study and slow, laborious word-by-word reading. The
same argument is used against word sounding in the regular teaching
program. The tendency to over-analysis can be offset by the various
quick-recognition methods described in this chapter. Phrase drills
especially will reduce over-analysis, as will many exercises for expression in oral reading.

Preparing exercises for word recognition

In this chapter will be discussed many types of exercises for pro-
moting accuracy, security, and growth in word recognition. These exercises have been tried out in regular classrooms, in remedial classrooms, and in individual tutoring. The teacher should select those
most suited to her level of instruction and classroom needs, as in-

dicated by the inventory testing. The sample exercises are intended to serve as patterns rather than to be duplicated for use.

In preparing exercises for drill in word recognition the teacher will find it helpful to bear in mind the following general suggestions:

1. So far as possible, the exercises should be self-explanatory; the child should be able to use them without much direction from the teacher. This requires that the directions for the exercises be simple. If an exercise consists of several steps, these should be presented in easy short sentences.

2. The material should preferably be planned for repeated use. Time is required for preparing exercise material, and it certainly should not be discarded after a single use unless it has proved to be ineffective. An exercise that may have required an hour or more to develop may be completed by the child in a few minutes. It is sometimes feasible to prepare the exercises in such form that the child's responses are put on a separate piece of paper and the actual exercise is used with several different children.

3. Several types of exercises should be prepared for each group of words to be taught in order to avoid monotony in the work, especially when extra practice is needed for slow learners. The child with wandering attention may require several short exercises during the reading period, while a child with greater attentiveness may need only a single exercise.

4. Exercise material should be filed so that it is easily located and convenient for use. Various types of exercises for each word group may be filed together, so that all material on those words is available together. Words related to a particular story or activity may be grouped together and recognition exercises filed in one envelope. Special lists of troublesome words, such as those beginning with *th* or *wh*, may be put in a special envelope.

5. Exercises assigned to particular children should be chosen to fit specific needs. The exercises recommended later in this chapter are designed for several purposes: for increasing attention to differences between words, for emphasizing word endings, for increasing perception of words, and for overcoming the difficulties common to

children at various stages of reading achievement. The child's needs should guide the selection and construction of exercises. Each reading system reveals a certain type of error; the experienced teacher discovers the supplementary materials needed for her particular system.

6. Eyestrain should be avoided. Common causes of strain are crowding of words in lines or columns, poorly printed exercises, too many exercises on the page, and masses of word lists. Experience with various types of exercises will reveal those tending to confuse a child and to reduce his interest.

7. The child should be able to follow his progress in word recognition. Each new word learned to the point of recognition should be added to his personal list. Competition between children can be avoided by having these lists kept by the children themselves or by the teacher. The child who sees his own growth and accepts the exercises as designed for his needs has a basis for confidence and security.

Types of word-recognition exercises

It is difficult and perhaps undesirable to classify the word-recognition exercises presented below, since many of them care for numerous difficulties. But word-recognition exercises can be grouped according to certain main categories, and that has been done for convenience in reference.

Inventory tests

Inventory tests should emphasize words that were mastered with but little instruction. After twenty or thirty new words have been taught, each child should be tested on his ability to recognize and pronounce all the words at sight. The words may be presented in a list, or in sentences or paragraphs; the latter procedure is preferable. Duplicate copies of the test material can be used for record blanks. Check all words that cause hesitation or difficulty. Capable children who have passed the test may test the slower ones.

Following is a list of words to be tested, with a paragraph containing them:

cook	country	hang	clothes
stone	afternoon	return	wear
climb	bother	fire	weather
mountain	finish	swim	wouldn't
hike	forget		

Wouldn't you like to go for a hike in the country tomorrow afternoon, if it is good weather? Don't forget to wear your old clothes, so we won't have to bother to hang them up when we go in for a swim. We will build a fire on a large stone and cook our dinner on it. When we finish dinner we can climb the mountain and return before dark.

In preparing inventory paragraphs, previously-taught words may also be used. If the words cannot be used in a single story, add the extra ones in other sentences. Note the time required for reading, thus checking each child's improvement as compared with that of the group.

Context cues for word recognition

Every child should be able to use the context in word mastery. In many situations the context alone should indicate the word meaning. The following drills, for the daily lesson, should stimulate greater use of the context in mastering words.

Assume, for example, that the words *follow, measure,* and *happened* are to be taught. Prepare sentences in which key words may be easily guessed from the context. All words should be known to the child except the words to be learned. The following are sample sentences:

1. The boys could not leave the dog behind. Wherever they went the dog would *follow* them.

2. "I wonder how tall you are. I wish we had a ruler so we could *measure* you."

3. "See all the people running around the corner. What do you think has *happened?*"

The word knowledge gained though such exercises will transfer more completely to regular reading if the sentences used are taken from stories that are to be read. An oral outline of the story will help the pupil correct certain obvious errors. If he knows the story concerns a *horse,* he is not likely to think it deals with a *house.* The oral outline should not reveal the point of the story.

Quick-recognition methods

If a word is to be read smoothly in phrases, it must be recognized accurately in one tenth of a second or less. If longer time is required, word-by-word reading results. For testing recognition and for practicing quick perception, a quick-flash device, such as a word or phrase tachistoscope, is desirable. A teacher may make a word tachistoscope from oak tag by following the diagram below.[1] On page 201 is a diagram for making a phrase tachistoscope with a wider opening.

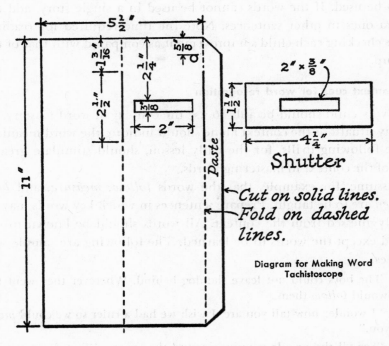

Cut on solid lines.
Fold on dashed lines.

Diagram for Making Word Tachistoscope

Words previously taught by various recognition exercises should be typed or printed clearly on cards for the tachistoscope. The shutter should be closed and this direction given: "Watch closely to see

1 A tachistoscope with ruled cards for the use of the teacher in preparing her own exercises may be purchased from World Book Company.

whether you can tell what the word is. Ready." Then flash the word quickly. Although the motion of the teacher's hand may be fairly slow, the narrow slot in the shutter passes the opening rather rapidly. Proper speed can be developed by moving the shutter up and down ten times in five seconds, the motion for each opening thus requiring approximately one-half second.

If the child cannot see the word the first time, he may have a second trial. If he is unable to recognize it on the second trial, open the shutter and let him read it. Then the next word is flashed for recognition in the quick-exposure interval.

The tachistoscope may be used by a pupil teacher in small-group work, especially if the pupil teacher has mastered all the words to the point of quick recognition. If the pupil teacher has not attained complete mastery, he should use the word list concealed from the child taking the test. The pupil teacher thus knows the word that is coming. If the response is cor-

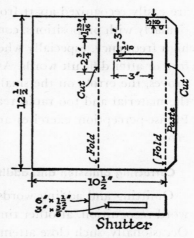

Diagram for Making Phrase Tachistoscope

rect, he can present the next word without checking by opening the shutter.

If a tachistoscope is not available, a slightly slower method for exposing words may be used. Words are typed or printed in columns separated by vertical intervals of about one-half inch. A card is placed over the list, and the top word is exposed rapidly and covered again as quickly as possible. After the first word is recognized, the card is slipped down to the next word and the procedure repeated. This device is not so satisfactory as the tachistoscope, but it is superior in individual work to the flash-card presentation commonly used.

Practice in phrase reading

Many children require help in reading in phrases. Word-recognition exercises often must be followed by practice in phrase perception.

Since the need for such exercises is especially important in oral reading, they have been discussed in Chapter 8. However, phrase exercises logically follow the quick-perception practice described in this chapter.

Correction of errors on easy words

Certain children make mistakes on small, common words which are easily recognized apart from the context. Such errors occur particularly with prepositions, conjunctions, articles, and other words of high frequency, especially when such words appear immediately before or after difficult words. As recognition of the difficult words im-proves, the errors on the small words disappear. Lack of interest in the material and too rapid reading may account for the difficulties. Phrase-perception exercises are of value in correcting this type of error.

Correcting omission and addition of words

Omitting and adding words in reading is sometimes due to poor word recognition, at other times to inattention and lack of interest. Occasionally, such close attention is paid to meaning that words are read into the selection which seem to the pupil to belong there. Phrase-perfection exercises will help in correcting these errors also.

Visual-motor methods

Kinesthetic methods are often recommended for children with severe reading difficulties. Usually they involve elaborate exercises and devices, such as tracing, writing in the air with the eyes closed, writing on the board with the eyes closed as the teacher guides the hand, tracing sandpaper letters and words, and similar dramatic procedures. Such methods may be useful for children with extreme reading difficulties, but ordinarily they are too time-consuming for the results produced.

The visual-motor methods are sometimes effective for children who fail in word discrimination and in reverse letters and letter sequence, or who tend to add or omit syllables and sounds. To use these methods, the child must know how to write or print all the letters. Printing or manuscript writing is preferred, since it is similar to the letters used in print. However, any of the regular handwriting systems may also be used.

The visual-motor method may be used with individual pupils or adapted for use with groups. It may be used by pupil teachers in small-group work if it has been previously demonstrated by the teacher in the regular class.

The visual-motor method consists of the following steps:

1. Place the word on a large flash card. Show the word to the children and give this direction: "This word is *from*. Say it aloud. Look at it very carefully. When I turn it down, you are to write it as fast as you can. Look carefully and be sure to get it just right. Ready." Then turn the card down quickly and have the children write the word from memory.

2. After the children have written the word, show the card again and say: "Look! Is your word just like that?"

3. Have the child cover the word he has written; then say: "Now here is the word again. What is it? Yes, that's right. When I turn it down, write it again as fast as you can. Ready." Turn the word down. Check as before to see that the word is correct. Then present the next word.

In this method the first words shown should be short words containing elements that commonly appear in other words. Word elements which can already be written easily will help the child in learning new words containing those elements. Thus the word *information* will be relatively simple if the elements *inform* and *tion* can be written.

There are variations of the visual-motor method. Here are some of them:

1. Words may be shown on lantern slides rather than on flash cards.

2. For advanced or extremely rapid learners words may be presented in the tachistoscope with an instantaneous flash.

3. Children may write words three or four times without seeing the flash card, covering their previous writings to insure use of memory rather than automatic copying.

4. After two or three words have been thus taught, they may be dictated in a short sentence which also includes words previously taught.

5. Children with marked difficulty in remembering the visual appearance of words may receive preparatory drill in copying the word directly from print. In this way they acquire an impression of the general shape of the word.

6. Use of a typewriter often helps the child who writes slowly. When the typewriter is used, the child should be given instruction on the keyboard so that he becomes familiar with the location of the letters.

Teachers who have not used visual-motor methods should not hesitate to try them. They have been successfully used for a long time in some schools. The written-language approach to reading, involving the writing of words before reading them, has been practiced for more than forty years in the Henry Barnard School in Providence, Rhode Island. Writing of words prior to reading is part of the Calvert system, a correspondence course for children.

It is a common observation that young children desire to write long before they desire to read. They prefer the real activity of writing and copying to the prosaic finding of names for strange scrawls called printed words written by someone else. To the young child a written word is merely a series of ink marks on paper. Visual-motor methods do not work miracles, but they do increase attention to word forms and serve to vary regular methods of word presentation.

Samples of other word-recognition drills and devices

The following exercises may be used either for group work or for individual tutoring. They are difficult to classify, for they are intended to serve several purposes. Some emphasize meaning, others deal with perception skills, while still others involve various psychological factors.

1. Word-matching exercise based on a picture dictionary

The procedure in exercises of this type is as follows: The child has a large card on which appear pictures with words underneath them. He is given tiny cards with the same words on them. He studies the pictures along the top of the large card and matches his small word card with the picture it represents. He then puts the card beneath the correct picture. This exercise helps the child to notice all the letters, since he pronounces each word as he puts it in place. Whenever it is necessary, colors, in place of pictures, may be used to teach color names.

2. The word-picture game

The procedure for the word-picture game is as follows: Arrange pictures representing certain words, either in rows or at random on a 9″ by 12″ card. Under each picture draw a box $\frac{1}{2}$″ by $1\frac{1}{2}$″. Prepare cards of the same dimensions as the boxes and on them print the words represented by the pictures. Put these word cards in an envelope together with two or three extra ones for which there are no pictures. Clip the envelope to the picture card. On the reverse side of each picture card may be written the names of the children who have performed the exercise correctly. The teacher can thus check progress quickly and easily.

3. Picture and word cards

On cards measuring 4″ by 6″, six pictures representing objects such as a gray cat, a turkey, a boy fishing, a rabbit, a garden, or a school, are pasted. Several words related to each picture are printed on cards 1·' by 3″, such as (one word on a card):

milk	gobble	brook	carrots	flowers	children
kitten	feathers	line	bunny	watering	rooms
gray	Thanksgiving	pole	eating	lead	books
saucer	dinner	worms	pink	hose	paper
purr	bird	catch	white	plants	pencil

A few extra word cards are provided with words such as *talk, kitchen, camel,* and the like. Shuffle the cards. Have the children separate them quickly, placing each card with the picture it matches.

4. Using a mask

Cut from a discarded book the page that is to be used as a sample. Cut a piece of paper to fit the page. Hinge the paper with mending tissue or gummed labels to the side of the page so that it will turn back readily without bending the page. Hold both the page and the attached paper against a window and draw little boxes on the paper

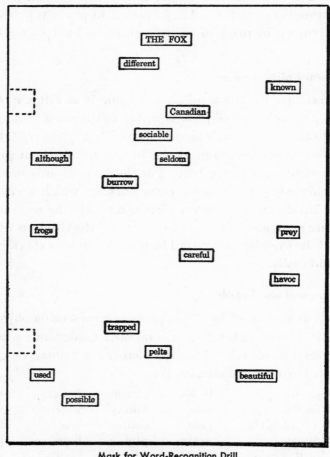

Mask for Word-Recognition Drill

around difficult words for preteaching. Cut out the boxes so as to expose the words. Leave the remainder of the text covered as shown in the diagram on page 206.

The new words thus selected are taught and the meaning enriched by use of the regular methods suggested. Then present to the pupil the sheet with only the newly taught words showing. Have them pronounced. Turn the mask back, exposing the full page. Have the child read the page.

5. Word-enrichment drill

Pictures are chosen to illustrate different meanings of certain words. The pictures are mounted on 9″ by 12″ cards, and beneath each is written a descriptive sentence containing the word illustrated. The teacher holds each picture before the class and discusses its meaning. The child thus learns to recognize the word and apply its meaning at the same time. The following illustrates the procedure:

> Picture of a train of cars (streamlined).
> "Here is a streamlined *train*."
> Picture of a boy training his dog.
> "See John *train* his dog."
> Picture of a bride in wedding dress.
> "The lady has a *train* on her dress."

6. Picture identification

Paste a 6″ by 9″ picture on a 9″ by 12″ sheet of colored paper. On white paper type three columns of words, *all* of which the children know. Several words in each column should be related to the picture; the others are nonstimulus words. Number the words. Paste the list of words under the picture. Each pupil divides a sheet of paper into three columns. He is shown the picture with the word lists and told to write in each column the numbers of the words he sees in the picture.

This exercise is designed to test ability to follow directions, as well as to recognize words which refer to the picture. Simple directions may be typed on the sheet, enabling the children to perform the exercise independently.

7. Word discrimination

Words that are similar in appearance are typed in a row across a sheet of paper. The rows are labeled with letters, while the words are numbered, as for example:

A. 1. parent   2. perfect   3. permanent   4. pertinent
B. 1. design   2. desire   3. despise   4. despair

The teacher has a list of the words; the children have slips of paper. The children write the number of the word in each line as the teacher pronounces it. For example, the teacher says, "Line A, *permanent*." The child writes *3*. The teacher says, "Line B, *design*." The child writes *1*.

8. Wordo, an adaptation of Bingo

Cut cards 7½″ by 6″. Consider the 7½″ sides the top and bottom of a card, and draw a line across the top 1″ from edge. Rule the card into five columns, each 1½″ wide, extending from the line at the top of the card to the bottom. Then divide the card into five rows, each 1″ high, starting at the bottom of the card. Type selected words in the spaces formed by the vertical and the horizontal lines as on a Bingo card. Two cards are illustrated on page 209.

Rule several cards and on them type the same words, varying the order so that no two cards will have any identical columns or rows of words. The same words are typed on a number of small cards, and as the teacher reads the word on a small card, the children cover that word on their large cards. They may use paper circles, if wooden counters are lacking.

The child wins who first covers five words horizontally, vertically, or diagonally. Any number of sets of words may be practiced for quick recognition. One child may play with the teacher, although the game is better when several are playing.

9. The tachistoscope

Words to be tested for recognition are printed on cards. The rapidly moving shutter allows only a quick glance at each word. Usually a word is not claimed for the child's sight vocabulary until recog-

W	O	R	D	O
were	they	there	want	them
that	which	the	why	then
with	what	Free center	went	this
those	will	while	whose	when
where	white	tell	wind	wall

W	O	R	D	O
them	want	they	there	were
why	that	which	then	the
this	with	Free center	what	went
when	those	will	while	whose
wall	where	wind	white	tell

nized at a glance. All the words previously taught in analysis drills should be presented in this rapid-flash device to insure transfer of skills. Pupil teachers may be taught to use the apparatus for group instruction.

10. Story method for review

A new story is presented on the difficulty level of material in the basal reader. Most of the vocabulary will already have been studied. A few new words related to those taught may be included, to test analysis skills. Review words are put into the tachistoscope and flashed for quick recognition; words from the new story are flashed in phrases; finally the child is given the card with the new paragraph. He should then be able to read the new paragraph quite rapidly and smoothly.

Several stories on the same level, but with different content, may be written to provide additional practice. These stories should be pasted on strong cardboard. They may be made more interesting by use of illustrations and colored cardboard. The teacher should prepare a few of these stories at a time and file them. On a slip pasted lightly on the back of each story she may keep the names of children who have read it. A check on the child's reading is thus provided. When one group has completed them, the paper may be removed and the cards filed away for the next group. Cards for various vocabulary levels may be differentiated by color. The different colors enable the teacher to sort the cards easily and to discover on what level the child is reading.

11. Tachistoscopic drill with small words

Prepare word cards containing little words, such as *if, it, on, no, to, is, in.* Some children recognize long words quickly, but have difficulty with short words. Often these short words occur together in phrases and result in choppy, irregular reading. Practice on such phrases as *it is on the, if it is in, for it is the, up on the top,* results in smoother reading. These phrases are presented in the tachistoscope in the same manner as are words.

12. Multiple-choice method

Prepare large flash cards, each containing a word to be taught. Prepare and duplicate lines of words similar to those to be taught, such as the following:

```
clear.....clean.....close.....lose.....lean.....chose
blank.....black.....dark.....clock.....block.....drink
recognition.....radiation.....registration.....reputation
undaunted.....undecided.....undesired.....unbridled
```

Show the large flash card for one word, such as *chose*. The teacher says, "This word is *chose*." The group pronounces the word. The teacher repeats the word, then turns down the card. Each child finds the word on the first line on his paper and draws a ring around it. The other words are presented in the same manner. Have children exchange papers and check incorrect answers as the flash cards are shown again.

A number of variations of this method can be used. Two key words are placed in a row. Variant forms of the same word are placed in a line. It should be emphasized that the flash card is turned down before the child is allowed to hunt for the word. The teacher should see that the words to be circled fall in different places in the rows.

13. Flash-card drill

Make large flash cards for words to be taught. Show the flash card, pronounce the word, and enrich it through any of the suggested methods. Have the children look at the word carefully as they pronounce it. Place the word before the class, on the chalk tray or other convenient place. Make certain each child can read all new words. Type paragraphs containing the words just taught. Hand a copy to each child to read.

When flash cards are used in word-recognition exercises, it is essential that words taught be transferred to print immediately. A child may recognize a word on a flash card and still not know it in print. Reading short paragraphs insures transfer of words from the flash cards to close work.

14. Sentence-analysis method

A sentence, each word of which occupies a separate flash card, is placed on the chalk tray. All the children read the sentence. Each child points to a card, pronouncing the word at the same time. The teacher places the words in random order. Each child then picks up a card and reads the word. New sentences may be framed with the same words.

Words and sentences may be printed or written on the blackboard instead of on cards, and the pointer used to indicate individual words to be read.

15. Lantern-slide methods

Prepare lantern slides with words printed on etched glass or on cellophane masks between glass slides. Show each word on the screen or wall, pronounce it, enrich it through any of the suggested methods, and have the children pronounce it. Among the new words intersperse old ones needing review.

Present new words several times during the lesson. Do not teach more new words at one time than the child can master. Provide for immediate use of the words by a slide or sheets with sentences or paragraphs.

16. Word-meaning exercise

Paste a picture on a card. Beneath it type a short descriptive story. In an envelope place a 3" by 4" card with seven or eight typed questions based on the story. Phrase these questions so that the child must know the word meanings to answer the questions correctly, such as:

> Which word tells what the mother is doing?
> Which word tells what was happening to Sam?

On a second card make a list of words which are synonyms of those in the story. Have the child copy the words that answer the questions. The words on which the children fail should be discussed and enriched.

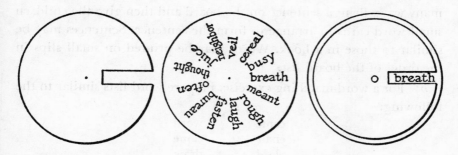

17. Word wheel for teaching nonphonetic words

The word wheel aids retention of nonphonetic words which must be memorized. After the child has learned the words and can say them as the wheel revolves, he is allowed to spin the circle and pronounce the words as a review drill.

A word wheel is easily made of two disks cut from oak tag, as shown by the first two circles in the drawing above. A slot is cut in one disk (the circle at the left) and selected words are lettered on the other disk (the circle in the middle). The two disks are fastened together at the center so that they will revolve. One word at a time is then exposed through the slot, as shown in the circle at the right.

18. Word-discrimination exercises

Most of the recognition exercises described in this chapter help in understanding the forms of words and the differences between them. There are, however, some children who require specific drill on word and letter forms. Word-and-letter-matching exercises ordinarily demand no reading, but mere matching of words, letters, or word parts. They have no reading value, being designed merely to teach differences in the visual form of words. Such exercises aid in the discrimination of letters and simple words prior to actual reading.

Samples of word-and-letter discrimination exercises are given below and on page 214.

a) Provide two sets of the same words on slips of paper or oak tag and have pupils match them. To avoid waste of time in handling the material, give only a few pairs at once. Ordinarily six or seven pairs will be sufficient for matching exercises. This drill may be varied in many ways. Print a sentence on the board and then give the children small word cards to arrange to form the sentence. Sentences may be similar to those in a book. Words may be printed on small slips in the order of the board list.

b) For a word-matching exercise, prepare word lists similar to the following:

came	word
chair	came
word	draw
make	chair
draw	make

The child draws a line from the word in the first column to the same word in the second column. Or the words in the first column may be designated with capital letters, while those in the second column may be numbered. The child then writes the exercise on a piece of paper, putting down the letters of the words in the first column and places opposite these letters the matching numbers of the words in the second column. This arrangement makes possible repeated use of the material. This exercise can be used either on the board or on the lantern slide, with the child indicating his responses on paper.

The difficulty of exercises of this type may be increased by using words similar in form, as below:

A. pint	1. paint
B. paint	2. pant
C. point	3. pint
D. pant	4. part
E. part	5. point

Such exercises may use letters of similar form, such as *b, d, p,* and *u, h, m, n, r,* which the child ordinarily confuses. In other lists one column may contain consonant blends or phonograms, while the second column consists of words containing these phonograms or blends. This exercise will help to call the child's attention to particular parts of words.

A number of exercises combining visual discrimination with ear training will be found in Chapter 11 on word analysis in the primary grades.

Individual devices

Many types of flash devices may be made for capturing the interests of children with aversions to reading due to previous failures. Below and on the pages that follow are descriptions of several devices that teachers may find helpful in capturing the interest of the child who is having difficulty in learning to read and who shows little interest in learning.

1. Individual word books or picture dictionaries

Word books or picture dictionaries are used in many classrooms. There are two types of books which are effective in the improvement of sight vocabulary. In the first type of book, the child lists all the words he does not know. For these words he finds pictures to match. In the other type of book the child collects pictures of words he knows. The work can be motivated by use of a typewriter or printing press to prepare the words for the books. As the words are learned by quick-flash devices, they are transferred to the second book. As learning continues, the sheets are removed from the first book, and the number of words still to be learned decreases. All words in the second book should be reviewed at intervals to assure retention of the sight vocabulary.

2. Football game

Cut a football shape, $6\frac{1}{2}''$ by $9\frac{1}{2}''$, from brown paper. Draw the lacing and stitching with black crayon. Cut a slit in the long side 5" from the top. Paste a 4" by 6" card on the back, fastening down only the ends, leaving the center, the top, and the bottom free. (See the diagram on page 216.)

Make word cards similar to those for the tachistoscope. On these type the football terms and paragraphs from a story. As the child moves the card past the opening in the football, he finally reads a whole paragraph in sequence. This type of drill often works when more formal ones fail. In place of the football any article in which the child shows interest may be used. Engines, airplanes, or steamers may be cut from magazines for this purpose. The device is often worth the short time needed to prepare it. Many children enjoy preparing their own. Similar devices may represent Santa Claus, George

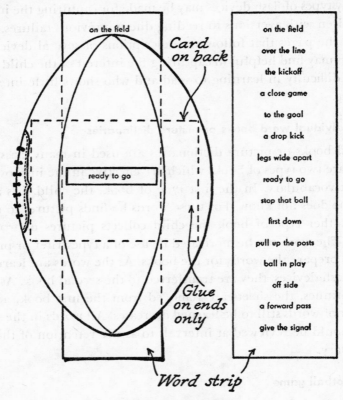

on the field

Card
on back

ready to go

Glue
on ends
only

on the field
over the line
the kickoff
a close game
to the goal
a drop kick
legs wide apart
ready to go
stop that ball
first down
pull up the posts
ball in play
off side
a forward pass
give the signal

Word strip

Diagram for Football Device

Washington, Lincoln, a log cabin, a flag, a heart, and the like, depending on the content of the story.

3. Mailbox game

The mailbox game provides motivation for children who are easily bored. Obtain a small jewelry box. Paste a piece of colored paper over the top and make a slit in this. Print "DEAD LETTER OFFICE" on the box.

Draw a mailbox, 6″ by 9″, on green paper. Make a slit for the letters. On the back paste a small paper candy bag cut to fit. The bag has expanding sides which will push out and hold many words. Make a post for the box out of strips of cardboard. Paste a support on the back of the box to hold it up.

Put in an envelope the words to be mastered. The three pieces should be kept in a large envelope.

The child puts the letters or words being taught on the desk. The tutor allows him to drop into the mailbox all the words he knows. These are later sent to some other child for study. The words he does not know go into the Dead Letter Office and are returned to him. Small children are especially fond of this game.

When the game is over, the child takes the letters from the Dead Letter Office, and the teacher reviews them with him. Words from the Dead Letter Office are put in a separate envelope in the large envelope. The next word lesson begins with these. Then they are mixed with the other words, go back in the mailbox, and later appear again.

Exercises for word meaning and enrichment

Words are more easily learned when possessed of "color" or surrounded by many associations. A word may be "dull" if it has only one meaning, such as a dictionary definition or a synonym given by the teacher or by the class. Such a word will be learned with difficulty and forgotten quickly. Even when the word is in the child's oral vocabulary, meanings may be driven from words by extreme concentration on word analysis, by constant repetition of the word in word-recognition practice, or by confusion and embarrassment during the reading period.

Teacher's manuals suggest many methods of keeping attention to the meaning of words. Some additional methods of enriching words include (1) conversation about exercises related to words, (2) words in oral context, (3) use of activities and centers of interest, (4) experience charts, and (5) visual aids to vocabulary. These exercises are described on the following pages.

1. Conversation about exercises or images related to words

The conversation or question method of enriching words may be used if the words for the day's lesson are within the child's experiences. The class should be encouraged to talk about their experiences in which use is made of the word. Effort should be made to bring in the colorful rather than the trite or commonplace. Examples of questions to start this type of exercise are given below.

The words *wheel, shine,* and *through* are presented on cards or on the board. Attention is called to them when they are discussed.

wheel: Do you know of anything that has wheels?
         How many kinds of wheels have you seen?
         What other kinds of wheels are there?

shine: Name all of the things that shine.
         What other words do you think of when you hear the word "shine"?
         How do you make things shine?

through: Can you think of anything that goes through things?
         (Suggest if necessary—car through a tunnel, stone through a window, dog through a hoop.)

2. Words in oral context

Words for enrichment may be presented by weaving them into a story or several short stories. When telling the story to children, pause at the key word, point to the printed form, have it pronounced, and then continue with sentence or story. The following examples illustrate the method, although it is well to add several other sentences to continue the story:

blew and *into:*

The boy was wearing a big straw hat. All at once the wind _____ [Point to *blew* and have children pronounce it.] the big straw hat across the road and _____ [Show *into*.] the pond.

All of the children went _____ [Show *into*.] the dining room. The candles on the cake were all burning. Louise drew a big breath and _____ [Show *blew*.] every one of the candles out.

The same method may be used with tachistoscopic presentation of words. The words may be flashed in a cardboard tachistoscope or on the screen if a film-slide or lantern-slide projector is used. As children become more familiar with words, the flash may be faster, and the amount of context clue diminished. If the word *dog* is being flashed, a context clue would be "The boy heard a scratch at the door; then he heard a bark. When he opened the door he saw a _____." (Flash the word *dog*.) A lower context clue for the same word would be "The boy heard a sound in the bushes. When the sound came closer he saw a _____." An even lower context clue would be this: "What do you think Jeff's father gave him for a birthday present? He gave him a _____."

3. Use of activities and centers of interest

Enriching word meanings through activities is especially useful with young or dull children. It may be recommended as a motivating device as well as for the word-enrichment value. Children who experience difficulty in learning and retaining words when the words are presented in other ways, will grasp meaning readily through activities.

Classroom projects will center around child interests and include such activities as building and furnishing a house or a museum, building a play farm or a model town, conducting a carnival or a circus, planting a garden, planning a vacation trip. The activities will involve use of words in a way to enrich meaning.

Special projects may be planned especially for the purpose of developing particular meanings of words. Here are some ideas for projects:

a) Use of a bulletin board
b) Sand table and construction work
c) Making books from picture and clipping collections
d) Trips to places of interest related to reading
e) Marionette and puppet shows
f) Dramatizations, pageants, operettas

4. Experience charts

Stories dictated by the children and printed on charts or on the board by the teacher are an effective method of keeping the meaning of words high. While experience charts are sometimes recommended as *the* method of teaching beginning reading, they appear to be more effective as a supplement to regular instruction in basal readers. When the child has a fairly good sight vocabulary, his chances of actually reading the sentences rather than merely remembering the ideas are greater. Experience charts are too whimsical in vocabulary choice and practice to enable the child to learn words. The teacher will need to modify somewhat the oral suggestions made by the children so that she can keep the reading vocabulary within sensible bounds.

Experience charts may follow various classroom activities suggested in *3* (page 219). The activities take the form of lists of things to be included in planning; children's suggestions for things to do; a summary of things learned yesterday or this morning; a number of sentences to describe procedures for making things; some questions to be asked of a classroom visitor or on a field trip.

5. Visual aids to vocabulary

Word meanings may be further enriched by well-planned use of the following visual aids:

a) Lantern slides showing various objects or activities related to words or sentences that are printed on flash cards or are printed on the board.

b) Collections of pictures related to printed words.

c) Models or objects, with an accompanying word list referring to parts or processes.

d) Catalogues of various kinds, picture dictionaries, and illustrated encyclopedias.

Word practice with responses to word meaning

After the initial presentation of words through word-recognition methods, pupils profit greatly by giving various responses to the meaning of the word. Such practice is highly effective in learning sight vocabulary. Children enjoy responding to meaning more than to a mere repetition of the name of the word; imagery is kept high and words are better remembered; definition is enriched by responding to various aspects, qualities, and uses of the thing being named. These word-meaning practices are especially useful for review of previously taught sight vocabulary and also for extra word practice for slow learners.[2]

1. Use of color cards in word practice

Each child is provided with several cards of different colors. For example, each child may have cards with these colors: red, brown, white, yellow. The following words are shown to the child and he holds up the color associated with the object named on the cards: *apple, cherry, chocolate, gold, squirrel, milk, snow, strawberries, corn, butter, clouds,* and so on.

Color cards should first be used for learning the names of colors. The teacher shows the name of the color, and the child holds up the appropriate card.

2. Use of number cards in word practice

Each child is given a set of cards containing the numbers one to four. They may be used with any meaning exercise where the response is a number. Here is an example: "How many legs has a _____?" Then show the following words: *bear, calf, cat, chicken, cow, crow, dog, duck, fox, frog, goat, goose, hen, horse, kitten, lamb, monkey, mouse, pig, pony, rabbit, rooster, squirrel, turtle.*

3. Use of Yes-No cards in word practice

Each child is given two cards on which are printed the words *Yes* and *No*. These may be used in a great many ways. "Can it run?" _____. Then show such words as *animal, cake, cat, chair, dog, doll, door, duck, father, fish, flower, hat, horse, hill, mitten, mouse, pig, pony, pencil, engine, farmer, fence, drum.* "Can you eat this?" _____. Then show *apple, wagon, eggs, corn, door, father, card,*

[2] Many of these exercises are adapted from materials prepared by Florence Betcher of Santa Fe Springs, California, and Clara Tupper of London, Ontario, Canada.

cake, shoe, coat, fruit, orange, pie, grass, cart, airplane, oatmeal, father, box, chocolate.

4. Placing words in different classifications

Placing words in different classifications has a number of possibilities, depending upon the imagination of the teacher. Words may be practiced through being placed in a great many classifications. Usually it is better to have at least three classifications into which the words may be sorted. Suggestions for sorting primary-grade words are as follows:

a) Do you eat it, wear it, or ride on it? Each child is given cards that say *eat, wear, ride.* The child holds up the suitable card for the following words shown: *coat, hat, orange, cake, automobile, horse, meat, candy, car, bicycle, carrots,* and so on.

b) Would you buy it in a grocery store, a hardware store, or a clothing store? Children are given cards with these words, or cards with pictures of the different stores, or cards with pictures of groceries, tools, or clothes. Then the teacher shows words that belong in any of the three classifications, and the child holds up the correct picture.

c) Where would you find it? This question offers countless combinations: at a circus, on a farm, in a lake, in the kitchen, on a train, in a toy store, in a baby's room, in a book, in a garden, in the woods, in the city, on a bed, in a medicine cabinet, in a cupboard, in a bureau, and so on. The child has the appropriate response cards, and he shows the correct one for each word shown by the teacher.

d) Other possibilities in word-classification exercises. For word-classification exercises words may be classified in a great many ways: who uses it or who does it; time of day, week, or year when it occurs; whether it is heavier or lighter than certain objects; the material from which it is made; something of which it is a part; what can be done with it; who owns it; what it describes; the speed with which it is done or moves; age, durability, value, sounds, odor, personal qualities, and any of the multitude of classifications suggested by a thesaurus.

5. Use of various types of oral responses to words

When the instruction is in small groups of not more than five or six children, meaning may be indicated to words shown by the oral responses of the children. Since the oral responses will be varied, the teacher should acknowledge each child's response if it is appropriate. Some of the various types of oral responses to words shown are the following:

a) *"What can it do?"* Typical words shown are *pony, fish, kite, truck, train, frog, star, fox, elephant.*

"What can you do with it?" Typical words shown are *hammer, knife, orange, toy, water, milk, jelly, dog, cow, basket, stairs, table, bed, rug, coat, mittens.*

b) *"What would you need to _____?"* Typical words shown are *play, ride, see, eat, sail, splash, color, burn, tell, time, smell, blow, drink, sleep, run, write.*

c) *Opposites.* "Tell a word that means the opposite of _____." Typical words are *up, night, little, white, yes, good-by, happy, old, cold, work, back, new, stop, boy, long, lost, under, shut, off, stay, fat, dark, city, summer, woman, before, high, asleep, laugh, pretty, empty, bright.*

d) *Synonyms.* "Tell a word that means the same as _____." Typical words are *fast, cross, gay, penny, little, brook, call, big, many, bring, children.*

e) *Associations.* "Think of a few more words that could go with the word you see. If you see the word *across,* you could say *across the room.*" Prepositions are particularly suitable for this exercise: *above, across, after, around, at, before, behind, beside, by, down, in, inside, on, through, to, under.* Adjectives might be taught by the following: "Read the word on the card. Then think of another word to go with it. If you saw the word *warm,* you could say *day* or *fire.*" Words suggested are *best, big, black, blue, brown, cold, dark, fat, good, gray, green, happy, high. little, long, old, pretty, red, sleepy. warm, wet, white.*

Other possibilities for oral responses are the following: ("Who can do it?") paint the house, fix the car, bring us milk, cook our meals, mend our toys, catch many fish, and so on; ("Where could you do this?") eat your dinner, find a book, go swimming, have a picnic, see a cowboy, play house, see an airplane, and so on; ("What could you see?") in the water, at the circus, when it rains, on the street, out of doors, through the window, down the street, in the store, on the table, in a nest, and so on.

SUGGESTIONS FOR FURTHER READING

Beery, Althea. "Development of Reading Vocabulary and Word Recognition," in *Reading in the Elementary School*, the Forty-Eighth Yearbook of the National Society for the Study of Education. Chicago: University of Chicago Press, 1949.

Betts, Emmett A. *Foundations of Reading Instruction*. New York: American Book Company, 1946. Pages 577–614.

Bond, Guy L., and Wagner, Eva. *Teaching the Child to Read*. New York: The Macmillan Company, 1950. Pages 224–234.

Gates, Arthur I. *Improvement of Reading*, Third Edition. New York: The Macmillan Company, 1947. Chapter 7.

Gray, William S. *On Their Own in Reading*. Chicago: Scott, Foresman and Company, 1948. Chapters 4, 5, and 6.

Harris, Albert J. *How to Increase Reading Ability*, Third Edition. New York: Longmans, Green and Company, 1956. Chapters 12 and 14.

McKee, Paul. *The Teaching of Reading in the Elementary School*. Boston: Houghton Mifflin Company, 1948. Chapter 2 and pages 317–334.

McKim, Margaret G. *Guiding Growth in Reading in the Modern Elementary School*. New York: The Macmillan Company, 1955. Chapter 9.

Russell, David H. *Children Learn to Read*. Boston: Ginn and Company, 1949. Chapter 10.

Yoakam, Gerald A. *Basal Reading Instruction*. McGraw-Hill Book Company, 1955. Chapter 9.

CHAPTER 11 **Word Analysis in Primary Grades**

"To PHONIC, or not to phonic," is a question of much concern to teachers of reading. The best answer, drawn from overwhelming research evidence, is "to phonic." But there are right and wrong ways of teaching phonics, and it must be said that our present knowledge of the most effective ways to teach word analysis is defective in many areas. Certainly phonics can be overtaught to the detriment of rapid and meaningful reading, but the lack of phonic instruction makes reading a confused guessing game.

The development of phonetic writing is considered one of the greatest advances of mankind. Instead of using thousands of symbols for objects and ideas, the Phoenicians simplified writing through representing speech sounds by twenty-two symbols. The relationship between speech sound and written symbol makes it possible to express all words in a very few characters. It also permits easy translation of spoken language into written language and makes possible equally easy oral reading of written language. If this relationship between sound and symbol is not established, the result may be utter confusion for the child whose sight vocabulary has grown beyond sixty or seventy words. The similarity of words based upon a relatively few symbols is such that the child's attempt to learn to read by remembering the name of each of the sixty or seventy words on a look-and-say basis would result in failure.

Steps in word-analysis learning

The mastery of reading a phonetic language depends upon a number of stages of development of visual and auditory perception of words.

1. *Hearing sounds in words.* The child must hear separate sounds in spoken words. If he does not notice the separate sounds in words, he cannot make any connection between sounds and written symbols.

2. *Seeing differences in printed symbols.* The child must see differences in printed symbols. If the letters look alike to him, the sound-symbol relationship cannot be established.

3. *Learning letter sounds.* When the sounds and symbols are clearly perceived in words, the sounds of letters and letter combinations may be taught. Some children see this relationship without direct teaching of phonics. When they have read several words beginning with *m,* their lips automatically take the shape for the *m* sound when they encounter a new word beginning with that letter. However, most children need to be taught the sounds of letters and letter combinations.

4. *Analyzing words by applying phonics.* The child must be given practice in applying phonics to analysis of unfamiliar words. This does not come automatically from learning the sounds of letters and letter combinations. This applies also to syllable analysis in the intermediate grades and word construction of larger elements in the higher grades.

Further stages in phonic development are necessary because of the unsystematic nature of phonics in written English. It is regrettable that after giving the child an introduction to phonic aids to reading, he immediately encounters countless exceptions and variations which may readily cause confusion. In the earliest words of the first grade some letters are silent; vowel sounds are particularly undependable, as are many consonants; the final silent *e* doesn't make the vowel long in *have, give, come, done,* and *love;* the same sound is spelled several different ways. In fact, the teacher of reading will find that there is a great flood of confusing difficulties in the application of phonics.

5. *Using context clues.* The child learns that phonics are clues and indicators, not infallible guides. He must use context clues to the pronunciation of familiar words. When words are outside his speaking vocabulary, when the context clue is inadequate, or when the phonics of the word is irregular, he must receive help in word pronunciation.

6. *Developing phonic ability and a "homophone" sense.* The child acquires a constantly growing sight vocabulary. At the same time he notices many of the complexities of the phonics of English. Having learned *right,* he is not surprised at *night, fight,* and *delight.* He then learns *kite* and *height,* thus developing a "homophone" sense—a recognition of the same sound in its variations in spelling.

7. *Developing a higher level of phonic ability.* As vocabulary increases, the recognition of word structure matures. Such words as *cabinet, engineer, homesick, perfume,* and *decorate* are read orally without hesitation. Words outside the speaking vocabulary of the child will often need dictionary support when the vowel sounds and the accented syllables are not immediately indicated by familiar patterns.

8. *Translating words into ideas.* At a higher stage of maturity in silent reading, the child will be able to translate words directly into ideas, with the sound structure of the words not even being noticed.

These stages of phonic development may be summarized in the learning process as (1) ear training, (2) learning letter forms and names, (3) learning letter sounds, (4) practice in analyzing words, (5) using context clues, (6) refining phonic abilities and acquiring a homophone sense, (7) developing a higher level of phonic ability, and (8) translating words directly into ideas.

A complete mastery of each stage is not required before the introduction of later stages. For example, while the beginning sight vocabulary is being taught in first grade, children will be given ear training, visual discrimination of words and letters, and the beginnings of phonics. Word-analysis teaching is needed at every stage of reading instruction, and we may not assume that the various steps of the teaching can be assigned to particular reading levels and ignored thereafter.

Supplementing the basal-reader program in word analysis

Most basal-reading systems present an orderly approach to word analysis, providing a variety of practice in ear training, visual discrimination training, and phonics. However, the basal-reader program cannot provide adequate practice for assuring mastery since many children require much more practice than does the average reader for whom the system is built. Furthermore, some of the basal-reading systems and some of the supervisors and teachers using them are undecided upon how much to emphasize word analysis. Some ways to supplement the basal-reading systems are described below and on page 229.

1. *Providing training in auditory and visual discrimination.* Training in auditory and visual discrimination, as outlined in Chapters 3 and 4, should be provided *before* the child tries to establish a sight vocabulary. A child who does not have the perceptual background simply becomes confused in trying to acquire a "sight vocabulary of seventy-five words," which is the usual prescription.

2. *Starting the phonics program early.* As soon as the child can identify separate sounds in words and knows the forms and names of letters, the phonics can begin. In fact, it can begin for a single letter or group of letters even before all of the sounds and names of other letters has been learned. The possession of an adequate perceptual background, not a "mental age of seven," makes phonics effective.

3. *Providing enough teaching in the phonics program.* In the phonics program the child should be provided with enough teaching to master such elements as an ear for sounds in words and the sounds of letters and blends, a knowledge of the names of letters, and the ability to apply phonics to the solving of new words.

4. *Freeing the child from unnecessary practice on phonics.* The rapid learner does not need to plod through all of the "reading-readiness" and phonics program at the same rate as the average or slow learner.

Use of supplementary phonics systems

The appearance of many supplementary phonics systems and the tendency of educational practice to swing from one extreme to another make it desirable to offer some precautions in regard to the teaching of phonics.

1. *Ear training with phonics.* Phonics is ineffective unless adequate ear training is given. If a child has not noticed the separate sounds in spoken words, it is useless to teach him the sounds of letters or blends.

2. *Learning letter forms first.* The child should know the forms of letters before phonics is taught. If he cannot tell *m* from *n*, or if *b, d, p,* and *q* are the same letter as far as he is concerned, the attachment of a sound to them is futile. It is recommended that the child learn the names of letters, as outlined in Chapter 4, before he learns the sounds of letters.

3. *Look-and-say with meaning.* Word-analysis practice must be counterbalanced by accompanying practice on look-and-say with meaning. Word analysis is not reading; it can drive the meaning from words.

4. *Practice on word analysis.* Word-analysis practice in solving new words should be given apart from the regular reading period, perhaps in connection with spelling. Opinion differs on how much effort should be spent in "sounding out" new words. Because of

variations and exceptions, and because many blends and phonograms appear in very few words, exercises in learning words by sounding have marked limitations. Time devoted to sounding out new words appears to be profitable when these conditions are present:

a) The words selected are "regular" in sound.

b) The words are within the child's speaking vocabulary.

c) The words are to appear immediately in the reading lesson. This is highly desirable, but not absolutely necessary, since the object is to establish a transfer skill.

d) The word is not used during the silent or oral reading in context. Words which give difficulty should be told to the child immediately in reading situations.

5. *Limitations of word analysis.* Word analysis has serious limitations. Errors in spelling and in reading arise as often from following rules as from failure to follow them. The value of word-analysis instruction is probably in improving the ease of learning a sight vocabulary rather than in giving the ability to solve new words. Sharpened auditory and visual perception is probably the main gain from phonics instruction.

6. *Limitations of phonics systems.* Elaborate phonics systems, particularly those employing a great stress on rules, those teaching a variety of phonograms upon which unfamiliar words are built, those presenting word parts in different colors or sizes of letters, and those generally making a great stress on word analysis are to be used with great caution, if at all.

The best basis for determining whether or not a child needs supplementary phonics instruction is to observe his word difficulties in oral reading. If his attack on words is reasonably accurate, using the phonics elements presented in his basal system, he needs no supplementary work in phonics. Certainly it is a mistake to push every child through any lesson series in phonics. Most of the commonly used basal systems provide a program adequate for the average and more than adequate for the superior reader. The teacher should select or build the necessary supplementary practice for slower learners.

In areas of controversy in regard to details of phonics instruction, until clear evidence is presented for the merits of a particular practice, the teacher will do well to follow her judgment of what works best for her. Certainly there are few things, even in this chapter, which are always true on all occasions for every teacher and every child.

It probably makes a little difference in the ear-training program whether the child is to listen for the name or for the sound of the letter in the word; whether an exact order is followed in the teaching of the sounds; or whether initial sounds are presented separately or are taught in connection with final sounds. In the phonics program it is probably inconsequential whether consonants or vowels are taught first—although consonants seem more dependable as to sound and therefore seem better to present first—or whether the consonant and vowel sounds are taught in connection with words or are taught as separate tasks.

Areas of ignorance always produce highly emotional crusaders for picayune details which they consider matters of great moment. The defense of a practice through justification by psychological principles is not proof of merit. Psychological principles are extremely flexible and may be marshaled on either side of any question. As panaceas are pressed upon the teacher, she should ask for impartial evidence of the merit of any system.

Word-analysis elements to be taught in primary grades

The specific word-analysis elements to be taught in each grade vary from one system to another. This is the result of the differences in beginning vocabularies and in the emphasis given the word-analysis program. Ordinarily, the basis for choice of word elements to be taught depends upon the frequency of occurrence of word elements in the vocabulary of the grade level. Since the child will need to handle all of the sounds in the primary-grade vocabulary, and since all appear at each grade level, the differences in the word elements chosen by the various basal systems are not of great importance.

In both ear training and phonics, there is probably a large amount of transfer. This means that after a child has learned several sounds, he will learn others more readily. He may even acquire them from his own observation in word-recognition practice. However, as long as word-perception difficulties appear in reading, direct instruction in phonics will be needed.

Grade 1

Auditory training. The child is taught to identify most consonant sounds and blends in the initial and final positions.

Letter names. Names of both capital and lower-case letters are taught as soon as possible; two weeks for the rapid learners, perhaps as much as two months for the slower ones.

Suffixes. These suffixes are usually taught: *s, es, ed, ing, y.*

Letter sounds. The sounds of all consonants and blends are taught.

Consonant sounds and blends. Consonant sounds and blends vary from one basal system to another. The ones most common to the initial position in words are *th, st, wh, sh, br, ch, dr, tr, cl, fr, gr, pl, sm, tw, fl, sw, sp.* The ones most common to the final position are *sh, ch, al, on, ck, ty, nk, lk, by, nt, rk, se, ty.*

Phonograms. These phonograms usually have high frequency in grade one: *in, and, ike, is, ake, oke, ook, own, ed, oy, ay, as, ed, ig, ouse, at, an, un, am, it, ome, ack, ank, ut, un, ell, all, ill, ame, og, ee, up, id, ool, en, oll, ot, op, ap, ing, ow.*

Grade 2

Auditory training. The child is taught to listen for sounds of word elements in all word positions. Instead of single sounds, he notices larger elements in words. Short and long vowels are also taught.

Prefixes and suffixes. The prefixes often included here are *con, ex, in, en, el, up, de.* The suffixes are *ly, ty, er, est, ion.*

Phonograms. The phonograms are *ue, eet, ive, oom, op, oot, unk, ight, eep, ich, ore, ent, oss, uy, ilk, ead, ease, om, ass, eat, ith, orse, out, arn, ird, ern, our, eak, ink, alk, arm, ove, ora, ick, ile, old, aid, int, ood, eet.*

Grade 3

Auditory training. Ear training continues on unfamiliar sounds as they appear needed in reading or spelling. Special emphasis is given on vowels in varied positions in words.

Prefixes and suffixes. The prefixes assigned here are *re, di, bi, be, per, any, un, for, el.* The suffixes are *ily, ier, iest, ant, ous, ious, ent.*

Phonograms. The phonograms are *onk, een, ought, igh, tion, atch, itch, ob, ix, eel, eek, ush, tch, eech, orn, eal, oast, ound, ut, ough, age, oil, ure.*

Wide individual differences in need for phonics instruction will appear in any grade. Slow learners in third grade will need many of the materials assigned to the first grade. Rapid learners in first grade often need word-analysis help which ordinarily comes in third grade or later. More capable third graders will need some of the syllable analysis assigned to the intermediate grades. The instructional need will depend upon the difficulties which appear in the child's oral reading.

Suggestions for ear training

Many of the suggestions given for ear training in beginning reading found in Chapter 4 may be adapted for use in later ear-training instruction. Some useful exercises in ear training are described below and on the pages that follow.[1]

1. Identifying sounds in words

Sets of cards are made containing the sounds to be practiced, for example, *ch, st, br,* and *pl.* Each child has a set of these cards. The

[1] Many of the illustrative lessons in word analysis in this chapter were prepared by Dr. Helen A. Murphy, Professor of Education, Boston University.

teacher reads a list of words and asks the child to hold up the card that contains the first two letters of the word pronounced. A suitable list for these word elements would be *chair, star, church, broken, please, stone, plant, bright, child, play, sting, brush, change, stop, break, place, study, choose, bridge, stamp, bring.*

It is not necessary that the words be in the child's reading vocabulary. In fact, it is better if they are not, since the child will then try to remember the visual forms of the word rather than listen to the sounds. The words should, however, be in the child's speaking vocabulary.

Although children enjoy the use of identifying sounds by showing cards, the child may indicate his identification of the sound in another way. He may write the first two letters of each word pronounced by the teacher.

2. Teaching short and long vowel sounds

A sample of a complete lesson for teaching the short and long sounds of *o* indicates the technique to be followed in teaching the child to notice sounds of vowels in words:

Some letters of the alphabet are called vowels. These letters are *a, e, i, o, u,* and sometimes *y.* [Write the letters on the board as you say them.] *Y* is a funny letter; sometimes it is called a vowel, and sometimes it is a consonant. Let's read the names of the vowels together. [Children read from the board.]

Vowels have many sounds. Sometimes they have a long sound, sometimes a short one. They have many other sounds too. We will listen for the short sound of *o.* Listen. It is the first sound in these words: *on, occupy, odd.* Say the words after me. [Repeat the list.] What is the first sound in these words? Yes, short *o.*

Listen to these words. They have a short *o* in the middle. Listen and say the words after me: *hot, mop, knock.* [Write the words on the board. Have the children underline the *o*'s.]

Let's play a listening game. I'll say some words. When you hear one with a short *o* in the middle, hold up your card with the *o* on it. Ready. These are all names of people: *Bobby, Betty, Don, Mary, John, Frances, Polly, Sally, Jim, Tom.*

I'll ask some questions. The answers all have short *o* in them. Let's see if you know the answers. Remember the short *o,* like the *o* in *hot.*

(a) What can a rabbit do? (hop). (b) What is the opposite of *cold?* (hot). (c) What sound does a turkey make? (gobble). (d) Who is Betty's brother? (Bobby).

Here are some words that have a short *o* sound. [Write on the board, *clock, lot, box.* Pronounce the words as you write them.] Can you name other words that end with the same sound? Be sure to name real words. [Write the words as the children say them. Have different children go to the board and underline the short *o*'s.]

Now listen for long *o*'s. Long *o* says its name, like the *o* in *rode.* Listen and say these words after me. They all have long *o*'s in them: *clothes, Joe, slope, spoke.* These words have long *o* too; say them after me: *hello, home, hotel, lonely, most, mower, notice, November.* What was the sound in all of the words? Yes, long *o.* Can you tell me the missing words in these sentences? All of the answers have long *o*'s. (a) Bobby dug a _____ (hole). (b) Mother's ring is made of _____ (gold). (c) Slices of bread are part of a _____ (loaf). (d) In the wintertime we have _____ (snow).

Let's play a game with long and short *o*'s. The *o* with the straight line over it is the long one; the one with the curved line is the short *o.* When the *o* in the word is the long one, hold up the long *o.* When the *o* in the word is short, hold up the short *o.* You will get a point for each correct answer. Ready: *body, Don, Halloween, knob, cocker, don't, hobgoblin, collar, joke, microphone, dot, jonquil, obtain, moment, honest, loan, goldenrod.* [Notice that the last word has both sounds.]

3. Teaching beginning and ending sounds

The following lesson illustrates methods of teaching *sh* and an initial and final sound in words:

Listen: *shelf, shellac, shepherds.* Did you hear *sh* at the beginning of each of these words? *Sh* sounds as if you were telling someone to be quiet. Here are other words that begin with *sh.* Say them after me: *sharpened, sheepskin, shadow, shamrock, shoemaker, shoveling, shrimp.* What sound did you hear at the beginning of each word? What letters make this sound?

Can you guess what I'm thinking of? The words begin with *sh.* I'm thinking of a word that means *not long* (short); something you wear on your feet (shoes); the opposite of *open* (shut); something to wear (shoes, shirt, shorts).

Listen again. See if you can hear *sh* in these words: *fish, trash, finish.* What part of the words had the *sh* sound? Yes, the end. Here are some other words that end in *sh*. Say them after me: *selfish, polish, leash, rush, swish.*

Let's play a game. We'll have two teams. You make one point for your team if you give a right answer. I'll say some words and you must say if you hear *sh* at the beginning, in the middle, or at the end. Listen carefully as I say the words: *finishing, sheep, shadows, fish, battleship, shop, Berkshires, shingle, shallow, British, sharks, brownish, wash, crashing, dishwasher.*

See how many words you can think of that have *sh* in them. Say the word, and tell me where the *sh* is—at the beginning, at the end, or in the middle.

4. Teaching different sounds for the same letters

It is well to call attention to the different sounds of certain letters, such as *s, c, g, j, qu.* A sample lesson for teaching the differences in hard and soft sounds of *g* follows.

G has different sounds. Sometimes it is hard like the first sound in *gate;* sometimes it is soft like the first sound in *George.* I'll say some words that begin with hard *g.* You say them after me: *gone, gallop, game, gather.* Now we'll say some words that have hard *g*'s in them, but not at the beginning: *August, ragged, organ, bullfrog, burglar.*

Now we will say words that have soft *g* at the beginning. You say them after me: *germ, geranium, gingerbread, gem, gypsy.* Here are some words that have soft *g*'s in them but not at the beginning: *badge, agent, angel, cage, dangerous, hinges, hedges.*

Let's play a game with words that have *g*'s. I'll say some words that have *g*'s. If the *g* is hard, write *h;* if it is soft, write *s* (or h-g, s-g) . Ready. *Porridge, gorilla, goldfish, giraffe, ghost, germs, engine, change, orange.* [Check after each word to establish the sounds.]

5. Identifying sound elements

Identifying sound elements requires the preparation of a pupil's record blank, listing some sounds that are in the word and some that are not. The child circles all sounds he hears in each word. For example, if the teacher is to pronounce the words *birthday, summer, between, dollar,* and *present,* the pupil's blank might be like this:

a) b m ch th ce ay (Child circles sounds in *birthday.*)

b) t s n m ey er (Child circles sounds in *summer.*)

c) k b sh tw one een   (Child circles sounds in *between*.)
d) b d t l an ar   (Child circles sounds in *dollar*.)
e) pl o e r s st nt   (Child circles sounds in *present*.)

6. Identifying words that contain certain sounds

The teacher gives each child in the group a list of ten words or she prints the list on the board. A sample list of the words is as follows:

about	best	called	faster	decided
find	party	having	winter	bread

Children may find and read or write from the list a word that has a certain sound. The sound, not the name of the letter, is given in these directions:

        a) Has a *v* sound in the middle.
        b) Begins and ends with *d*.
        c) Says *st* in the middle.
        d) Starts with a *br* sound.
        e) Starts with *c*.
        f) Ends with a *st* sound.

7. Practice with different vowel sounds

The teacher gives a child a list of guide words for each sound to be matched. Such a guide sheet might be as follows:

a as in *came*	*a* as in *hat*	*e* as in *he*	*e* as in *met*
_____	_____	_____	_____
_____	_____	_____	_____
_____	_____	_____	_____

bag	take	page	ten	cap	day
help	tree	had	pen	seed	three

The child notices the short or long vowel sound and writes it under the proper guide word. This may be varied by using the board for either the guide words or the list, and saying the words instead of writing them.

Sounding practice which emphasizes meaning

It is desirable to keep word meaning high while noticing sounds in words. Simple exercises which suggest ways of doing this are as follows: word practice related to basal-reader stories, completing sentences using words in the listening lesson, practice with opposites that contain appropriate sounds and rhyming words that fit content, adding endings to fit sentence context, completing words in context, and matching initial sounds with pictures.

1. Word practice related to basal-reader stories

The teacher directs as follows:

I want to see how well you remember the stories we have read. The answers to all of these questions will begin with the letter *b*.
   a) Who woke Bobby up? (Bing)
   b) Whom did Bobby and Bing wake up? (Betty)
   c) What kind of a birthday cake did Bobby want? (big)
   d) When did Jim get Dusty? (birthday)
   e) What were the sandwiches for the picnic in? (box)
   f) What did Bobby want to be? (bird)
   g) Who cut Bobby's hair? (barber)
   h) What was the barber's name? (Mr. Brown)

2. Completing sentences using words in the listening lesson

In teaching the sound *fr*, the teacher should print it on the board and tell its sound. Then she will direct the children in the following way:

These words begin with *fr;* say them after me: *freeze, fraction, frost, Friday, freckles.* Now you are to finish these sentences with words which begin with *fr*.
   a) The day after Thursday is _____. (Friday)
   b) In winter, water sometimes _____. (freezes)

c) Birthday cakes have _____. (frosting)
d) Apples, pears, and bananas are all _____. (fruit)
e) Davy Crockett lived on the _____. (frontier)

3. Opposites that contain appropriate sounds

The teacher says a word, and a child gives a word that means the opposite. This word must have a particular sound. For example, practice on the long *i* sounds could be given with the following words: *low* (high), *naughty* (nice), *narrow* (wide), *day* (night). The teacher can add others to the list.

4. Rhyming words that fit content

Rhyming words are arranged in pairs. Two incomplete sentences are given. The child reads the words and the sentences, completing each sentence with the correct word:

lunch—punch   Soon it will be time for _____.
                He made a hole with a _____.
matter—fatter   Do you think it will _____
                If you are a little _____?

5. Adding endings to fit sentence context

Words that children know should be used. Write sentences that can be completed by adding an appropriate ending to words in the list. A group of words which might give practice on *ly* are the following:

friend—slow—careful—sure—love

a) My dog is _____. (friendly)
b) The children walked _____. (slowly *or* carefully)
c) You must hold the baby _____. (carefully)
d) Mother said _____ you may go. (surely)
e) The day was _____. (lovely)

6. Completing words in context

Give a list of blends to be used in completing words. The child reads each sentence and then writes the correct blend to complete the word.

The following sentences illustrate practice on *fl* and *pl*. The teacher can add other sentences.

- *a*) The farmer __anted his garden.
- *b*) The baby was in the __ay pen.
- *c*) Birds can __y.
- *d*) Snow falls in little __akes.
- *e*) Bobby had a __ash light.

7. Matching initial sounds with pictures

Paste several pictures on a sheet of paper. Attach to the sheet an envelope containing small cards on which are written consonants or consonant blends. The child is told to find the first letter of the name of each picture and place it on the picture. After he has finished, he tells the name of the picture.

Visual discrimination of words

Reading calls for very precise visual discrimination of words. When an adult must read accurately such words as *particle, practical, piratical, participle, percentile, practicable, partition, parturition,* and *preterition* at very high speeds, it is evident that reading calls for highly accurate visual discrimination. Children encounter the same problems when reading such words as the following: *meat—neat; fire —tire; dead—bead; night—right—might—sight; some—come— came—same; print—point—paint—pint—part; butter—better— button; except—expect; was—saw; on—no.* All of the *th* and *wh* words look very much alike to the child.

Such visual discriminations are aided greatly by fitting the sound to the visual form of the word. The adult tests strange words by checking his visual form through pronunciation. The process is almost automatic, and until a reader arrives at a level—if he ever does —of reading ideas only, the accuracy of visual perception is always checked by this automatic sound-fitting process. Thus auditory perception sharpens visual perception, as do ear training, phonics practice, writing and spelling. Most of the word-pronunciation errors made by children, such as the addition and omission of letters, reversals, and letter substitution, reveal deficiencies in ear training and phonics as much as they do errors in visual perception. All of the types of word study, including attaching meanings to words in recognition practice, reinforce each other in the development of accurate word perception.

Practice in visual perception

Word perception is improved through specific practice in visual perception alone. The intent of such practice is to sharpen visual perception and to increase alertness. It should require memory of word forms rather than simple matching, and should be done quickly rather than analytically and labored. The exercises would be helpful even if neither meaning nor sounding were present, but wherever possible both should be used in connection with visual presentation.

Most of the exercises are variations upon identifying words exposed quickly. They vary in method of presentation of words, in method of the child's indicating his recognition, and in grouping of words so that certain parts of words are emphasized.

A typical visual-perception practice is the following: The teacher prints ten to twenty words on flash cards. The child has a work sheet containing rows of words from which the flashed word is to be selected. The teacher says, "This word is *wish*. Find it in the first row and draw a circle around it." The child finds the word in the following row of words:

fish   wash   wish   dish   wish   wishes

(The word may appear several times, with the child circling it whenever it appears.)

Variations in method of word perception
1. The words may be printed on flash cards.
2. They may be printed in a column or they may be written separately on the board. The teacher should erase the words or cover them quickly after she shows them.
3. They may be shown in a tachistoscope, either mechanical or lantern.

Variations in method of child's identification of words

1. Circling the word whenever it appears in the list.

2. Matching it with a single word in a column on a record blank.

3. Covering it on a "Wordo" card.

4. Identifying it in context in a sentence or paragraph.

5. Writing it from memory.

6. Spelling it orally—if the group is small and the child's turn comes often.

Variations in word groupings to force attention on particular word elements

1. Easy exercises to call attention to general structure:
   Word flashed: *coat*
   Record blank: father   three   coat   number   animal

2. Forcing attention to initial letter:
   Word flashed: *done*
   Record blank: bone   gone   lone   done   stone   tone

3. Forcing attention to word endings:
   Word flashed: *buttons*
   Record blank: buttons   buttoning   buttoned   button

4. Discriminating elements within the word:
   Word flashed: *card*
   Record blank: could   cold   cord   card   carted

The speed of flashing the word and the time allowed the child to select the right word will differ with the level of learning. Usually, a two- or three-second exposure of the word will be adequate. The child will ordinarily take a quick look at the word, then turn his attention to finding it. When the child is more familiar with words, the word may be flashed in a fraction of a second. Memory is emphasized by flashing the word, then asking the child to wait for a count of five or six before responding to it.

Even the earliest stage of visual discrimination requires the child to be familiar with letter forms. There appears to be little point to exercises which emphasize the general shape, length, or peculiar visual characteristics of words. If the sight vocabulary were to be limited to ten to twenty words, it might be helpful to call attention to "long words and short words," to "letters above and below the line," or to "block in" words to show their general shape. The child will be quickly disappointed to find that such clues do not work. The clues are typical of his own inadequate approaches to remembering words.

Word matching

Word-matching exercises which involve neither quick recognition nor memory may be useful at very early stages of learning, or in the initial presentation of word discrimination. They are too easy for most pupils after a few weeks in the first grade.

Such exercises allow the child to take his time in comparing the letters in the words. They are variations on either of these two forms:

1. make:	take	sake	make	lake	make	bake
2.	make	bake				
	sake	make	(The child draws a line between words
	bake	lake	that are alike.)
	lake	take	

These exercises are simple visual matching. They do not give the child the advantage of hearing the name of the word. They may be made to force attention to fairly close discriminations and to emphasize different parts of the word.

Another common practice is that of identifying small words within larger ones. In order to avoid phonic variations which mislead the child, such as finding *in* in *behind, no* in *knock, at* or *rat* in *rather*, it is well for the teacher to indicate the small word to be found by showing the small words in one column, followed by the larger words:

us	must
it	kitten
ear	hear
man	fisherman
in	print

Inventory of phonics

Although the child will learn to associate sounds with letters and letter combinations through the ear-training exercises which combine both the sound of the word and recognition of the visual form of the word, it is well for the teacher to discover if the child knows the sounds of letters, blends, and phonograms appropriate to his grade.

This is best done by individual testing. The teacher should place the sounds taught on a card and ask the child to give the sounds for them.

m s t f g w r *etc.*
st ch sh sp cl tw wh *etc.*
ake ight all ell ouse *etc.*

It is not enough to assume that because a child knows a few sounds, he knows all of the others taught. While there is probably a considerable amount of transfer from individual sounds to blends and phonograms, and much incidental learning through word recognition after a secure sight vocabulary has been established, it is well for the teacher to check a large per cent of all of the sounds that have been taught.

Group testing in the identification of sounds may be done by preparing record sheets similar to those used for identification of letter forms or names in Chapter 3, pages 55–56. However, the ability to identify sounds given by the teacher is not as valid as having the child give the sounds himself.

Direct teaching of sound elements apart from words is generally discouraged in professional books and teacher's manuals, primarily because of doubt of its transfer to actual use in word analysis. However, there are probably many situations in which children will be helped by such direct teaching. The minimum safeguard in such teaching is for the teacher to make sure that the child hears the sounds in spoken words—that he has an adequate ear-training background.

Ability to use phonics

There should be direct instruction in the use of phonics to solve new words. It is not enough to be able to give the sounds for various letter combinations. The child must be able to recognize new words made up of these elements. The words to be analyzed should be those within the child's speaking vocabulary so that he will be rewarded by recognizing a familiar meaning when his analysis is successful.

Ability to use phonics rests upon ear training. No attempt should be made to teach either the sounds of letters or the use of phonics until the child can identify separate sounds in spoken words. The commonest difficulty found among children who have been given phonics before ear training is lack of ability to use phonics. Even though the child may be very facile in giving sounds for letters, blends, and phonograms, he will be unable to combine the sounds into words unless he already has an adequate ear-training background.

Although many of the ear-training exercises suggested earlier in this chapter give practice in the use of phonics, especially those which combine auditory analysis with context clues, direct practice in solving words through application of phonics requires more advanced ability.

There are a number of ways in which this practice on phonics may be given. Some of these ways are described on this page and pages 246–247.

Solving words through the application of phonics

1. *Reading new words derived by changing the first letter of known words.* The child knows *back*. If he knows the sounds of *p, s, t, cr, st,* and *tr,* he should be able to read *pack, sack, tack, crack, stack,* and *track* through the application of phonics. If he knows *hill,* he should be able to read *fill, pill, will, spill,* and *still.* Words such as *grill, frill, thrill, gill,* and *dill* should not be used unless the child happens to

know their meaning. The sounding of such words, even though correctly pronounced, leads the child to nonsense drill and diminishes his search for meaning.

2. *Reading new words formed by adding known phonograms to initial letters.* The child knows the phonograms (or words) *eat, at, ad, and, op,* and *ot.* He should then be able to read such words as *heat, hat, had, hand, hop,* and *hot.* Other letters may be used to form new words with these phonograms, but the teacher should be sure that the words formed by using initial letters and phonograms are in the child's oral vocabulary.

3. *Reading new words formed by combining known words.* If the basic words are known, the child should be able to read these words: *forget, bedroom, outdoors, belong, hallway, become, classroom, highway, hilltop, moonlight, around, awake, daylight, homesick, outside, bathroom, bedtime, blackboard, everyone, everything, football, horseback, necktie, overcoat, playground, sometime, tonight, understand.*

4. *Reading derived forms of known words.* When the common suffixes are known, the child should have practice in reading words formed by adding the suffixes to known words.

Safeguarding meaning in use of phonics

In the desire to give extra practice, the teacher may be easily led into using words outside the child's oral vocabulary. Even though the words may have meaning later on, the temptation should be resisted to use words such as *puck, mist, flung, drake, quake, stile, mold, sought, plight, stroll, glide, flick,* and so on. The child should learn that the use of phonics is rewarded by immediately meaningful words. Even when the meanings of the words are familiar, the application of phonics may be nonsense drill, with the child doing a "double take" of first pronouncing an "empty" word, then immediately saying it again with a different expression as its meaning comes to mind.

Words derived by analysis should, if possible, be used immediately in oral context. For example, in the words formed from *ack,* the teacher may say, "Here is something you do before you go on a trip." The child then reads *pack*. The teacher may then say, "What things do you pack when you go on a trip?" "Here is something you put things in." The child then reads *sack*. "What might you find in a sack?"

After a lesson in the use of phonics, the words read may be put in sentences or in a paragraph. On reading the newly studied words in a paragraph, the child practices more rapid analysis and he also has the pleasure of finding that he has several new words which he can read.

Word-building practice

The child enjoys making new words through combining known word elements. A great many devices, games, and gadgets for seat-work are based on word building. The commonest fault of such practices is the formation of words beyond the child's oral vocabulary. Whenever possible, the words formed by these devices should be limited to those known to the child. They should be in his oral vocabulary if not in his reading vocabulary. When the game or device used is one which permits many combinations, the child should be taught to make only words he can use in speech.

Some of the exercises and games which follow emphasize meaning, while others do not. Preference should be given those that emphasize meaning, but others may be found useful in calling attention to the visual structure of words.

1. Building words that match pictures

Paste several small pictures on a sheet of oak tag. Use pictures of common objects immediately recognized by the child. Words to be attached to those pictures are printed on cards. The cards are cut apart between initial consonant combinations and phonograms, between compound words or any division phonetically correct. The pieces are put into an envelope attached to the picture. The child takes the word pieces and combines them to make the names of the objects. When the child has finished, he reads the words to the teacher.

2. Matching word parts to make known words

By using lightly ruled lines, divide a sheet of oak tag into ten sections 1″ by 3″. Print one word in each section, using ten words containing consonant blends and phonograms which have been taught previously. The following words are typical: *string, crack, sleep, bring, stand, slice, sheep, stick, choke.* Cut the words apart, taking care to cut all exactly vertically so that matching cannot be done by fitting the angle of the cut. Then place all of the pieces in an envelope.

The child is given these directions:

The little cards in this envelope fit together to make words you know. There will be ten words when you are through. See how fast you can put the words together. Remember, the words must be ones you know. When you have finished, you may read the words to me.

3. Making compound words

Groups of words may be presented on the board or on a card to be used by pupils. The children then combine the words in the first column with those in the second column to make words that they know.

A		B		C	
after	green	air	fish	any	some
bare	way	base	room	club	field
church	noon	class	town	lone	more
door	yard	down	ball	corn	where
ever	foot	gold	plane	any	house

The teacher may use the exercise above as an oral exercise or she may have the children write it as seatwork.

4. Adding correct suffixes

Prepare a paragraph in which the endings of some words are left blank. Ask the child to fill in the correct word endings. At the top of the next page is a paragraph of this kind.

John and his brother Ned went fish_____. They walk_____ to a small brook near their grandmother's house. They had fish_____ only a few minutes when they saw a toy boat float_____ by. John reach_____ for it with a pole and pull_____ it to shore. Soon they saw a small boy com_____ along the brook. He was hunt_____ for his boat and had been cry_____ because he could not find it. John gave him the boat and told him that he had pull_____ it to shore when he saw it sail_____ by.

A similar practice can be given with common suffixes. The teacher puts a list of known words on the board and gives the following directions:

Here is a list of words. You can make several words from each of them. Let's see how it is done.

She then uses a sample word with the individual or group—for example, writing the word *bake* on the board, and under it, with the help of the entire class, writing the words *bakes, baker, baking, baked.*

The sample is erased to prevent the tendency simply to copy the sample. The list on the board is then read, and the children are told to see how many words they can make from each word. The children may rule their papers in blocks, writing each word and the words made from it in separate blocks. The following list is typical of the kind of words that should be used: *fish, milk, skate, draw, laugh, paint, run, black, dress, help.*

5. Making rhyming words

Give a list of words. Have the child make new words that rhyme with the words, having all of the new words begin with the same letter. Here is an example of this exercise: The child is to write a new word that begins with *f* which rhymes with each word on the list.

a) sat   f_____
b) sit   f_____
c) sun   f_____
d) mine   f_____
e) man   f_____

SUGGESTIONS FOR FURTHER READING

Anderson, Irving H., and Dearborn, Walter F. *The Psychology of Teaching Reading.* New York: The Ronald Press, 1952. Pages 272–279.

Betts, Emmett A. *Foundations of Reading Instruction.* New York: The American Book Company, 1946. Pages 614–644.

Bond, Guy L., and Wagner, Eva B. *Teaching the Child to Read.* New York: The Macmillan Company, 1950. Pages 234–253.

Gray, William S. *On Their Own in Reading.* Chicago: Scott, Foresman and Company, 1948. Chapters 7, 8, 10, 11, and 12.

Harris, Albert J. *How to Increase Reading Ability,* Third Edition. New York: Longmans, Green and Company, Inc., 1956. Chapter 13.

McKee, Paul. *The Teaching of Reading in the Elementary School.* Boston: Houghton Mifflin Company. 1948. Pages 292–303 and 235–268.

CHAPTER 12 **Word Skills in the Intermediate Grades**

DIFFICULTIES with unfamiliar words constitute a chief handicap of poor readers. Words outside the reader's experience—unfamiliar words for which he has no meaning—cause serious difficulty in comprehension and interpretation at any level. In the intermediate grades this difficulty becomes especially acute because many words in required reading in social studies and science are completely unknown to slow or even to superior readers. Even when the meanings are known, the child may be handicapped by being unable to recognize the word in its printed form. If long pauses are required to analyze words, the flow of thought is interrupted and the comprehension is reduced. Rapid analysis of words is essential and must be followed by quick recognition. An effective word program in intermediate grades will include word-meaning study, practice in rapid word analysis, and in word recognition.

Intermediate-grade reading is not restricted to a fixed vocabulary; the child will meet many thousands of new words in his required and free reading. Success in this task requires many transfer abilities which give the child general *word power;* it cannot be met by separate teaching of every new word.

Word-meaning problems

A large share of learning in all subjects is the acquiring of the words that convey the ideas of the subject. There is considerable pressure on publishers to write materials on an easier level in social studies and science, yet growth in those subjects requires the mastery of the specialized vocabularies which enable the expression of more exact meanings. Although it might be possible to avoid exposure to unfamiliar terms in fiction, and perhaps in much of social-studies material, such a procedure would diminish the child's possibilities of future growth in reading. If growth in word meanings is considered an important part of a child's education, the teaching of unfamiliar words becomes an opportunity for enrichment rather than an obstacle to mastery of subject matter.

A selection of words appearing in seven or more commonly used textbooks in the sixth grade indicates some of the vocabulary problems encountered in teaching.

Selected list of words appearing in seven or more commonly used sixth-grade textbooks

GENERAL WORDS	SOCIAL-STUDIES WORDS	SCIENCE WORDS
abandon	abolish	aeronautics
aromatic	annihilate	automatic
audacious	authority	bacteriology
brandish	caravan	barometric
cavalcade	chamberlain	buoyant
circulate	citadel	chemical
cloven	commendation	cataract
competent	confirm	conservation
conjecture	confiscation	coupling
constructive	courier	crucible
dawdle	decade	crystalline
defiant	delegate	cylindrical
desperation	desolation	diameter
determination	document	efficiency
diligent	doublet	emboss
distinction	edifice	emerge

GENERAL WORDS	SOCIAL-STUDIES WORDS	SCIENCE WORDS
edition	emergency	endurance
eliminate	episode	engrave
enunciate	escort	evaporate
essential	exposure	excelsior
exaltation	fiord	fertility
fantastic	flourish	filament
fascinate	ford	flange
fragile	friar	forceps
fruitless	galley	gasket
genial	gauntlet	gill
gorge	glacier	globule
grievous	greensward	granular
grotesque	halyard	helium
habitual	hazard	hexagon
haven	herald	hydrogen
hilarious	hieroglyphic	imprint
illustrious	imperious	impulse
immaculate	impostor	incubator
insolent	inscription	iridescent
integrity	invade	isolate
jargon	judicious	jet
juncture	justify	laboratory
laborious	laud	larynx
lament	lease	liter
loiter	legend	lobe
ludicrous	liege	meteor
luxurious	majority	naphtha
manifest	martial	nausea
meditate	memorial	nautical
miraculous	monastery	nitrogen
narrate	nationality	nocturnal
notation	nominate	observation
oblivion	objective	oculist
obstinate	obstacle	opiate
onslaught	offensive	oxygen
optimistic	organize	palpitate
pedestrian	parchment	peat
perceive	pedigree	percentage
persevere	plague	phosphorus
placid	poacher	pinion

GENERAL WORDS	SOCIAL-STUDIES WORDS	SCIENCE WORDS
plausible	politics	piston
preface	prejudice	plastic
premium	prelate	pneumatic
profusion	prohibit	radiation
prospective	prostrate	radium
prudent	quaver	reforestation
realization	quota	reptile
reassure	rampart	resinous
reconcile	rapier	resonant
regale	ravage	rivulet
resource	recount	seedling
routine	sanctuary	sewerage
seclusion	scepter	shellac
sedate	siege	skein
sensation	skirmish	sluice
sinister	standard	soluble
spectacular	strategy	stimulate
sublime	tourney	tackle
temporary	unstable	tannic
tremulous	upheaval	tension
turbulent	vagrant	textile
unique	volunteer	unpalatable
utilize	wanton	velocity
violate	yeoman	vibrate
vivacious	yuletide	vitamin
wheedle		vulcanize

Less common meanings of familiar words may give difficulty. The child may know that a boy can run, but not that these may also run: *brooks, vines, hereditary traits, debts, luck, dramas,* or *stockings.* He may know *body* as applied to a person, but not as a group, a mass, or the consistency of a liquid. *Post* may be known as part of a fence, but not in reference to military positions or organizations, mailing a letter, putting up a notice, or making an entry in an account book. These semantic variants or multiple-meanings may lead to confusion in understanding what is read. Unusual expressions also provide trouble, such as "left no stone unturned," "faced the music," "broke the ice," "took a stand," "finger in the pie," "cut the ground from under," "tied his hands."

Locating difficult words before reading

Word meanings should generally be taught in advance of reading. Since reading is a creative process in which the reader forms images or ideas from the words of the author, the reader will do much better if meanings of words are known in advance. While it is impossible to teach all unknown words in advance of any lesson, or to anticipate the new words the child will encounter in independent reading, a burden of words too heavy for the child will cut off both comprehension and pleasure. The teacher should skim the lessons used for class instruction to locate the following: words within the child's speaking vocabulary, words with unfamiliar or new meanings, unfamiliar or unusual expressions. After a teacher knows the reading abilities of the group, such words or expressions are easy to locate.

Grouping children on the basis of vocabulary need

Since children differ greatly in vocabulary abilities, it is necessary that they be grouped for reading instruction with vocabulary needs in mind. Superior readers need not be burdened with unnecessary word-meaning practice. They may need help on a few words, but the context may provide adequate meaning or they may look up the words in the dictionary. Poor readers may have so many word difficulties in the textbooks of the grade that it would be impossible for the children to learn in a day more than half of the difficult words.

The rate of learning new meanings of words may be tested in the various reading groups by skimming a chapter to discover ten words unfamiliar to the group. The meanings of the words are taught through definition, illustration, or synonyms. Each word should be on the blackboard or on a card so that it can be referred to several times while it is being discussed. The amount of time devoted to teaching meanings should be about the same as would be spent on the word in a regular lesson. After an hour has passed, the children may be tested on the word meanings by matching the words with a list of definitions. This test will provide an estimate of the number of word meanings that may be successfully taught in a single lesson.

Another way of discovering the effectiveness of the teaching of new word meanings is to build a test over the last twenty to thirty words defined in recent lessons. If few word meanings are remembered, it will be evident that the rate of presenting word meanings is too fast.

Teaching word meanings prior to reading

When the words have been selected for presentation to the reading group, the teacher will write them on the board. Each of the words will be pronounced by the teacher and by the children. The syllable structure of the word and the accent marks may be noted, but the main emphasis should be on meaning and quick recognition. If the words are really unknown to the children, there is little point in asking them to give definitions, synonyms, opposites, or illustrations, since they will merely make random guesses. It is the teacher's task to present the meanings, synonyms, and illustrations.

In this initial presentation of the word, the teacher may call attention to prefixes, suffixes, or roots when they give definite help to the meanings, but this, too, should be subordinate to direct-meaning instruction. In addition to teaching the meaning of a particular form of the word, the teacher may call attention to its use in different parts of speech or to common combinations with prefixes and suffixes. However, this should be incidental to teaching the exact form of the word as it appears in the lesson. The essential task is to make the child ready to recognize the word and its meaning in the lesson to be studied, and the transfer skills of syllabication, accent, and derived forms should be omitted if they become cumbersome or distract from the immediate-meaning need.

If the lesson to be read contains the words *reconciled, prudent, turbulent, integrity, tension,* they may be presented on the board in syllables with accent marks and in undivided form, followed by a synonym or definition:

rec-on-ciled	reconciled	— brought together
pru-dent	prudent	— cautious, careful
tur-bu-lent	turbulent	— excited, riotous
in-teg-ri-ty	integrity	— honesty
ten-sion	tension	— strain

The teacher may say, "You will find that some people quarreled and disliked each other for a long time. Then they were reconciled; they came to be friends again. See if you can find how they were reconciled." Or, "After the uprising, the king became more prudent; he was much more cautious and careful not to annoy people. Find out how long his prudence lasted." Or, "The lesson tells about a city disturbed by a turbulent crowd. Find out what caused them to become so turbulent, so excited and disturbed, so riotous." Or, "One man in the story was known for his integrity, his honesty. People trusted him and chose him as their leader. Find out who this man was." Or, "The lesson says 'the tension was relieved'; the strain and fear were over. Find out what happened to relieve the tension."

The words may be defined in terms of known people or situations; several forms of the word may be used in illustration; other meanings may be presented if they are closely related. But the important thing is to connect the word back to the lesson. It is easy to take too much time for word-meaning practice. Therefore, it is better to have short and colorful illustrations ready rather than to engage in prolonged discussion of meanings, derivations, and variations.

Use of a glossary

The words presented in the above lesson may be left on the board for a glossary which the child may use to refresh his memory of the meaning. For those pupils who need only a glossary to understand new words, the teacher may provide such lists of words and definitions for each lesson. It is well to provide the words marked diacritically, as well as in undivided form, so that the pronunciation of the words can also be learned. The definitions should be in the same tense, number, and general form. Thus they may be substituted directly into the story.

Glossaries can be prepared in advance for several lessons, and they may be saved from year to year. They have the advantage of calling attention to words that the child might otherwise ignore. They offer much more practical help than the advice, "If you find a word you don't know, look it up in the dictionary." The delay of dictionary use interrupts the flow of thought; the dictionary often provides several meanings, only one of which is suitable to the situation; the form of the word may be different from the initial presentation in the dictionary. The well-planned glossary can assist the child much more quickly and accurately.

While dictionary use is to be encouraged, it is better for use in independent reading or for superior pupils. The school tasks of reading and study should keep attention to ideas and situations foremost, freeing the child from the disrupting effect of long pauses for study of unfamiliar words.

Adjusting to the vocabulary burden of a single textbook

When a single textbook must be used for all groups, regardless of their differences in reading ability, adjustment to the vocabulary problems may be made in the following ways:

1. *Oral presentation to very poor reading groups.*   Since it is assumed that the ideas of the lesson are important enough for the child to learn, and that reading should not be an "iron curtain" which prevents the child from learning, it is desirable to present lessons orally when higher learning will result.

The vocabulary burden may be relieved by use of synonyms or explanations when unfamiliar words arise. This oral presentation may be made by the teacher or by a superior reader selected by the group. If a pupil does the reading, it may be helpful to underline the words or phrases to be explained. If the listening group has been taught to ask for explanations when the words are difficult or the meaning of the passage obscure, the need for selecting words for definition is avoided.

2. *Oral definition of unknown words, followed by a glossary.* When a lesson contains only six or eight essential words unknown to the group, an oral presentation followed by the use of a glossary is adequate to provide word meanings.

3. *Use of a glossary only.*   If children are familiar with diacritical marks and need only the type of help provided by synonyms or definitions, a glossary with words diacritically marked will assist them.

Word skills in silent reading

The habit of ignoring difficult or unfamiliar words during silent reading is extremely common. It is probably general among adults as well as children. Almost every person has had the experience of learning the meaning of a new word and soon finding it several times in his reading. Probably the word was in previous reading material but was ignored. The prevalence of this faulty habit can be demonstrated by a simple experiment. Ask the pupils to read a chapter in any textbook they are using and write down all unfamiliar words. The best pupils will have the longest lists; the poor readers cannot find the words they do not know.

Attention to unfamiliar words is particularly important if the child is to increase his vocabulary through extensive reading. The child who ignores difficult words in silent reading fails to accumulate the many meanings of a word. Even though he is unable to pronounce all of the words encountered, the good reader generally acquires an extensive word-meaning background. Often he has an exact understanding of them from noting their many shades of meaning during extensive reading. Adults who know the exact meaning of such a word as *misled* may pronounce it as *mizzeld, misseld,* or *myzeld.*

While it is desirable to be able to pronounce correctly all words met in silent reading, this is not basic to meaning development. Most of the words presented in the elementary-school reading level, however, are of such frequency that the child should know both the meaning and pronunciation.

Several types of assignments are suitable for increasing attention to unfamiliar words in silent reading. An easy method consists of skimming the chapter for difficult words and listing them on the board or else duplicating them for individual use. Each child then reads the list and indicates the unfamiliar ones either as to pronunciation or meaning. In this way, a child often recognizes his lack of understanding of certain isolated words more readily than he would if he merely encountered the words in the context.

An alternative method is to have the child note unfamiliar words in his reading and write them on a separate sheet. He should not be penalized for the length of his list, lest he shorten the list or give himself the benefit of the doubt when he is uncertain of the meaning of the word. The penalty for unfamiliarity with words sometimes consists of the task of looking up their meanings in the dictionary.

Knowledge of word meanings is usually based on experience rather than intelligence. The task of the teacher is to study differences in word knowledge and to help the child of limited experience. The child should understand that by revealing his difficulties freely the teacher can better help him to overcome them. In the classroom there should be no penalty for ignorance unless it comes from lack of effort by the child. Concealing ignorance leads to adult habits of timidity and avoidance of situations and experiences with which the person is unfamiliar. Admitting ignorance is a step to learning. If children can be taught that unfamiliarity with words is natural but can be overcome by instruction, they will be able to aid greatly the program of silent reading.

Some teachers have each child keep a vocabulary notebook for listing new words discovered in reading. It is not necessary for the child to verify the word in the dictionary before placing it in his notebook. Recording the word calls attention to its form and enables him to notice the word and its meanings in later reading. Vocabulary notebooks should usually contain a page for each letter, with new words added under proper letters.

A child may be asked to find the first of several dictionary meanings of words in his notebook, to record the meanings of the words and also the diacritical marks that enable him to pronounce the words. Attention should be called to the large number of new words added rather than to the extent of ignorance. Thus the slow learner may discover that he is adding words rapidly and making marked growth in vocabulary. A frequency tabulation of unknown words for a class or a group may be based upon the individual vocabulary notebooks. Such a count may guide an intensive program in vocabulary instruction or in a study of common word roots.

The following three-step exercise has proved effective in increasing the ability to find unfamiliar words and to get their meanings from context. It requires the preparation and duplication of a word-definition matching test. The selection to be used is skimmed to locate difficult words. These are arranged in columns in groups of seven or eight. A total of twenty-five to thirty words should be included. Definitions should fit the meaning and should be of the same tense and number as the word defined. They should also be made up of words known to the child. A typical arrangement of an informal word-definition matching test is shown below:

a)	remove	1.	grow larger
b)	employ	2.	burst forth
c)	erupt	3.	take away
d)	weary	4.	a high place
e)	assembled	5.	came together
f)	elevation	6.	come back
g)	increase	7.	make use of
h)	transfer	8.	tired
		9.	hurt
		10.	put in another place

Even though thirty words are tested, the groups should not be longer than eight words and one or two extra definitions. Long unbroken lists of words and definitions require a much longer time for the pupil to match, without increasing the validity of the matching. When the lists are ready, the following steps may be taken:

1. The child reads the selection to make a list of all the words he does not know.

2. When his list is complete, he takes the word-definition matching test. In order to save the tests for later use, the child writes the letters for each word on a sheet of paper and places beside them the numbers for the correct definitions. His paper for the above test would begin like this:

a)	—	3
b)	—	7
c)	—	2
d)	—	8

3. When he has taken the test, the child scores his paper by hearing the teacher read the correct numbers for each word. Then he opens his book with the word-definition matching test before him. He determines the amount he can improve his score by noticing word meanings in sentence context.

A comparison of his scores on the separate parts of this testing is indicative of his needs. A short list of unfamiliar words and a long list of failures on the test indicate failure to discover new words in reading. A long list of unfamiliar words and few failures on the test demonstrate mastery of many words that seem new to him. Inability to improve his test score by rereading a chapter tells the pupil that he needs help in the use of context to discover word meanings. Marked improvement in the test score following the use of context indicates that skill in discovering word meanings is fairly well developed. These three tests provide effective practice for increasing ability to discover new words and get meaning from context.

Uses of the dictionary

The chief uses of the dictionary are for finding correct pronunciations, determining word meanings, and verifying spellings. Children differ greatly in their ability to use the dictionary. They may be assisted to more rapid and accurate use of it in some of the ways described on this page and the pages that follow.

1. Location practice

Speed in locating words may be improved by practice, without any other help. A list of ten words is usually enough for such an exercise. The child indicates location of the word by writing the first definition or by copying the guide word at the top of the page. Observation of a child locating dictionary words often reveals limited skill in using guide words and limited skill in noticing second and third letters of words which indicate whether to go forward or backward in the pages or columns.

The first lists for location drill should contain words with different initial letters and should be placed in random order. Words with the common prefixes, such as *re, in,* and *de,* should not be used; they require attention to the third, fourth. or fifth letter to locate them in the dictionary. The comparative time required to locate two ten-word lists will often be determined by several words with common prefixes in one list and few such words in the other. A second type of list should contain words with the same initial letter but different second letters. Such lists give special practice in scanning words to locate those in any letter group. A third list should be composed of words with identical first and second letters, as found in those with common prefixes.

Often observation of a child locating words will show that he is uncertain of the general position of individual letters in the alphabet. Sometimes it is helpful to divide the letters into groups of five. By learning the relative positions of the groups the child can more readily find individual letters. However, special importance should not be attached to these divisions, since the child needs to visualize clearly each letter's position in the alphabet. Exercises of this type are valuable for location practice: "What is the second letter after *h?*" "What letter comes before *j?*"

A game can be based on opening the dictionary to the proper letter. Skill in opening at the correct place may be scored by giving a mark of 5 for exactly the right place, a mark of 4 for a one-letter error, and so on. No credit is given for a location with more than a four-letter error. This game may be increased in difficulty by allowing no score for two- and three-letter errors

In another location exercise the group leader tries to open the dictionary to a specific word such as *utilize.* Reading the guide word at the top of the page, he may discover it is *window.* The children then tell him whether to turn to the front or the back of the book to find *utilize.* Words for this exercise may be chosen from the entire alphabet range.

Exercises in observing the guide words at the top of dictionary pages usually improve speed of location. At first such exercises should be confined to a single letter, accompanied by questions of this sort: "Suppose you are looking for the word *illogical,* and you open the dictionary to the guide word *imposing*. Do you turn pages toward the front or toward the back of the dictionary?" Attention should be called to the second or third letter needed for locating the word. Similar exercises are needed for words with common prefixes so that the child will learn to notice the third, fourth, or fifth letters. Several workbooks present more detailed exercises for developing skills.

2. Pronunciation practice

Often children need practice in use of diacritical marks as an aid to pronunciation. Present a list of ten unfamiliar words and ask each child to find the pronunciations and record them for later use. After the words have been found and their marks recorded, have each pupil pronounce them, and give him a score. This exercise requires knowledge of diacritical marks, syllabication, and accent marks.

At the bottom of the pages in most dictionaries are found cue words for each sound. Usually no other instruction than the use of these cue words is necessary to teach diacritical marks. However, time may be saved by giving a group exercise on the vowel sounds and the variable consonants designated by different diacritical marks. Some practice can also be provided in pronunciation of words using major and minor accent marks. Syllabication is easy for most children to understand and usually requires no special drill.

3. Practice in word meanings

Matching the story context with dictionary definitions is essential to successful discovery of word meanings. Almost every word is used in various senses, and the child may be led astray by injudicious selection of meanings. Sentences containing unfamiliar words may be taken from a book the child is to read. Then the sentences are duplicated or written on the board for dictionary drill. For each underlined word the child finds the meaning or meanings giving the most probable sense in the particular context. Full knowledge of a word's meaning develops from meeting it in many contexts rather than from direct dictionary study. Dictionary definitions are often so barren and uncertain that even teachers avoid use of new words when no other criterion for meaning is available.

4. The dictionary as a spelling aid

Use of the dictionary for verifying spellings usually requires only practice in locating words. However, if the spelling difficulty occurs in or near the initial letters, the sound of the word must be used to find possible alternatives; each of these must then be tested and the one with the correct meaning selected. Clear enunciation of vowel sounds and accurate word pronunciation are helpful in this exercise.

Whenever a child uses the dictionary to verify the spelling of a word, that word should be recorded on the child's personal spelling list. A single exposure to the word will not be sufficient to fix the word in the child's memory.

Meaning through word roots, prefixes, suffixes

There may be some benefit from teaching children to notice the general meaning of the elements that make up some words. As with most rules concerning words, however, the exceptions are so numerous and the meanings so remote or devious that children must be cautioned about expecting very great success through deriving word meanings by this method. Word meanings are determined by usage, and sometimes word elements acquire meanings quite different from their original ones. Some children seem to enjoy and profit by the study of meanings of word elements, while others find such study an added burden. It is quite possible that the success depends upon the teacher's selection and presentation of word elements.

Word roots, prefixes, and suffixes should be chosen for study when there are many English words which conform to the meanings indicated by the word element. For example, the following words formed from Latin roots might be taught together, with the meaning of the root indicated: *auditory, audience, auditorium, auditor, audiofrequency; facile, facilitate, facility, fact, faction; ignite, ignition, igneous; locate, location, locality, dislocate; script, prescription, describe, inscribe; pedal, impede, centipede, pedestrian, pedestal; port, portable, deport, report, porter, import.* Similar words formed from Greek roots are these: *biography, biology, antibiotic, biologist, autobiography; metric, meter, speedometer, thermometer, barometric, metronome; phonetics, phonics, phonograph, telephone, microphone; telegraph, telephone, telescope, telegram.*

Word roots occurring in intermediate-grade vocabulary with sufficient frequency to deserve notice are the following: *mot, mov, nat, port, jur, jus, jud, serve, act, solv, solu, tain, vent, ceive, fort, hab, ject, part, tend, val, vert, alter, cert, duc, gen, graph, labor, lect, leg, merge, mort, not, nor, pend, rect, sci, scribe, sent, set, sign, spect, stance, terr, turb, viv.*

Prefixes occurring frequently in intermediate-grade words are the following: *re, in, con, de, dis, com, un, ex, im, pro, ob, per, e, pre, en, ac, ad, em, up, be, ab, sur, ap, of, under, sub, trans, sup, a, pur, oc, for, fore, extra, af.* The teaching of prefixes is also best done through the presentation of several words in which the meaning of the prefix is self-evident. If the child misses the generalization, he will at least have added the meaning of the words.

Useful suffixes in the intermediate grades are these: *tion, ate, er, al, ic, ous, y, ious, ure, ive, ant, ent, or, ish, ment, ice, age, ize, sion, ance, ary, ful, ist, ible, able, ine, less, ly, ry, ty, ar, cy, en, fy, ial, let, eous, ion, ium, ling, ory.*

Perhaps the most useful outcome of calling attention to roots, prefixes, and suffixes is to increase the accuracy of visual perception of words. While children may profit by understanding the meaning of the more dependable roots, prefixes, and suffixes, current systematic attempts to enlarge vocabulary by such methods have not proved as profitable for most children as direct instruction in whole word meanings.

Word-analysis activities

Word-analysis activities have a high place in the intermediate-grade reading and spelling programs. When third-grade ability in reading is reached, the pupil is still a long way from the accuracy and fluency in word analysis required for sight-vocabulary growth. While word-meaning problems are recognized by all teachers in intermediate grades, actually the average reader is more greatly handicapped by his inadequacy in word-analysis skills than by word-meaning limitations. Instruction in word analysis is of even greater importance in intermediate grades than in primary grades. The carefully controlled vocabulary that appears in primary readers is largely abandoned; the intermediate-grade child encounters an endless succession of words he has not read before. If he is to be successful in reading, he must be very rapid and accurate in word analysis. One or two seconds should be sufficient for him to perceive word parts and pronounce the word.

Word study in the spelling period

Practice in word analysis is best done in a period separate from reading, preferably in the spelling period. Word analysis is more closely related to spelling than to reading. Correlations between the various word-analysis abilities and spelling are always higher than similar correlations with reading at the intermediate-grade level. Both word analysis and spelling are primarily concerned with accurate perception of the auditory and visual structure of words, although both have a relationship to word meaning. Both are affected by the deviations from a simple phonetic spelling system. The exceptions to rules and the many ways that a sound may be written cause difficulties in both.

A large share of spelling words are learned through observation of words in reading, and spelling itself is a form of word analysis. If the spelling period is considered a word-study period, with time devoted to analysis, pronunciation, writing, and meaning, both reading and spelling will benefit.

Some children and some teachers may resent the intrusion of word-analysis practice in the spelling period. Several research studies have shown that children make more progress in spelling through word-analysis practice than through daily instruction in spelling. Other studies have shown that children will make normal progress in spelling when only two periods per week are devoted to it rather than five. Certainly the close relationship between the two skills indicates that spelling can be learned in many ways other than copying and writing practice.

However, when time from the spelling period is set aside for word study, children should be told that the period is a "word-study period" that will help them both with their spelling and their reading. The time for word study may come every day as a part of the spelling period, or it may replace the spelling two or three days each week. A good practice is to test the spelling words of the week on Monday. Then allow the children to make corrections on unknown words and practice on them that day. The same thing may be done on Wednesday or Thursday, with the remainder of the spelling time devoted to word analysis. Those children who are good spellers will often master all of the words the first day.

If the teacher is afraid to depart from daily spelling practice for slow learners, the following experiment may be tried: During the first three months of the year, give the poor spellers in some classrooms word-analysis practice three days a week and spelling two days a week. In other classrooms follow the daily spelling practice with children of similar ability. At the end of the semester, test both groups on standard spelling tests and on a random sampling of the words taught during the three-months' period. It will usually be found that the children who have had the emphasis on word-analysis practice will be superior on both tests.

Each teacher should find for herself the most satisfactory adjustment of time between spelling and word-analysis practice. If it is desired, time for word study may be taken from the reading period for slow learners, but generally it is more rewarding to combine the spelling and word-analysis time. Word-recognition and word-meaning practice with the words to be found in the day's reading is a better use of the reading time devoted to word study.

Types of word-analysis practice

Most of the types of word-analysis exercises and games suggested for primary grades may be adapted for intermediate grades, the chief difference being the level of word elements to be studied. Although such practice in intermediate grades will be with syllables, roots, prefixes, suffixes, compound words, and larger word elements, some pupils will still need some work with blends and the simpler phonograms.

The following are some of the types of word-analysis practice suitable for intermediate grades:

1. *Drill on pronouncing useful words.* The pupils are given a list of words to read. Methods of choosing such words are suggested later in this chapter. Since this is oral practice, children should work in pairs or in teams of three or four, so that each child's turn will come often. Children may take turns in reading the words, with one child reading the first word, another the second, and so on, or each child may read in his turn any agreed-upon number of words. The other children will check the correctness of the reading. The length of the word list will depend partly upon the difficulty of the words and partly upon the maturity of the pupils. Lists may be as short as twenty words or as long as fifty or more. Experience will show the suitable length of list for the group.

It helps to keep attention to meaning if the words are grouped around some common topic or theme. The list may contain words that are things to eat, animals, flowers, vegetables, words telling how you feel, sports terms, automobile words, camping words, diseases, parts of the body, household furniture, things found in a kitchen, transportation words, kinds of workers, relatives, words describing motion, tools, or any of various possible groupings. Groupings of words may be suggested by the word lists to be studied. Word groupings found in a thesaurus may be useful. A single day's lesson may contain several different groupings. The fact that the word must be suitable to the group of words defined is a help in checking the accuracy of the pronunciation, and it keeps the meaning and the imagery in the words.

2. *Syllable study of words that follow regular phonics patterns.* Lists of words containing few phonic irregularities are provided for analysis practice. Words of several syllables typical of those found in more difficult words are presented as word wholes, then divided into syllables with the accented syllables marked. Since this exercise is

primarily word-structure study, it is not essential that meanings be emphasized. Coined words made up of common syllables may be used; pupils enjoy saying such nonsense words. The words are taught through small-group instruction with pupils taking turns as in the word-pronunciation study described above. A typical list might begin as follows:

radiantly	ra'di-ant-ly
voluntarily	vol'un-tar-i-ly
supplication	sup-pli-ca'tion
responsiveness	re-spon'sive-ness

The pupils first read the words with the help of the divided syllables, then cover the column of syllable division and read the undivided words. If such word lists are checked against the prefix, suffix, and word root lists on pages 265–266, words may be selected to give practice on the most essential syllables.

3. *Counting syllables in words.* Ear training does not stop in primary grades. It is helpful to ask pupils to listen for syllables in words. Prepare a list of words of three to six syllables, and have the child count the number of syllables he hears. The child prepares a record blank by numbering (or lettering, if numbers are confused with the count) twenty lines down a page. The teacher says, "Count the syllables in this first word: *intemperate.* The second word (or *B*) is *desolate.* Count the syllables. The third word is *domestication.* How many syllables?" When the child has recorded the numbers of syllables in all of the words in the list, the words are pronounced again and the papers are corrected by the pupils. Here, again, the task is word-structure analysis, and the words used need not be known to children.

4. *Identifying visual forms of sound elements in words.* Identifying visual forms of sound elements requires the preparation of a work sheet for the pupils' use. The record sheet may be prepared in either of two ways:

a) Grouping a number of words containing elements that are similar, but only one of which fits the pronunciation of the word. For example, if the word *prospecting* is to be pronounced, the pupil would find it on his record sheet that contains the following words:

inspecting   prospering   prospected   prospecting   respecting

b) Giving a list of letters, some of which are in the word and others not. For the word *prospecting*, the child would circle those sounds of that word which he finds in the following list:

br   ed   ing   pr   cl   t   sp   ly

5. *Visual analysis of flashed words.* Visual analysis also requires the preparation of a pupil's record blank, with either of the forms suggested above being suitable for the exercise. Words are printed on flash cards large enough for the children to see clearly. Each card is shown for two or three seconds, and the child circles the correct word or the letter combinations he sees in the word.

6. *Writing sounds heard in words.* The child writes the first two, three, or four letters he hears in each word pronounced by the teacher. Or he may write the whole word if all of the elements are regular in sound. Scoring must allow for acceptable variations in writing the sounds, especially of vowels.

7. *Writing from visual memory of words flashed.* Children are shown words on flash cards. After a two- or three-second exposure, the word is turned down and the child writes it from visual memory.

8. *Homophone-recognition practice.* Since the same sound may be spelled several different ways, the pupil will benefit by practice in recognizing several ways a sound may be spelled. This requires the preparation of a pupil's test sheet such as the following samples for testing the sounds *ate, eace,* and *erd.*

1. aight   ought   eight   ait   eet   ate   ach   eat
2. eece   eech   iece   ease   east   eace   eese
3. eard   aired   erd   ird   urd   ord   irred

Words containing the same sound spelled different ways may be compared by presenting them in lists: *straight, eight, strait, state, great; Greece, niece, grease, peace, geese; heard, herd, bird, absurd, stirred.* It may be confusing to some children if the teacher emphasizes too greatly the number of different ways a sound may be spelled.

However, it is desirable to call attention to these differences to demonstrate that one may not rely on spelling by ear only. Good spellers have excellent scores on tests of recognition of homophones, indicating that they have developed a "multiple-phonics" sense and have sufficient visual memory and imagery surrounding word meanings to select the right spelling of the sound in the particular case.

Rules relating to word study

It is probably not very helpful to burden the child with rules regarding pronunciation, syllable division, or spelling. Every rule has so many exceptions that the child will often be led into error by following rules that do not apply in a particular case. Many teacher's manuals for basal-reading systems provide an overabundance of rules presumed to help the child. Only those rules that appear to be very dependable should be selected. The child should be cautioned about the rules by showing him several exceptions to each. A child develops his own feeling for rules by expanding his contact with words and by increasing his perception of auditory and visual elements of words.

Sources of words for word-analysis practice

Word-analysis instruction, like spelling, may be done with word lists quite independent of the daily word needs in reading. In order to establish the pronunciation of various syllables, phonograms, homophones, or other structural elements of words, it is necessary to draw many words from outside the classroom reading of any day or week. Word analysis is a transfer skill in which power of perception of auditory and visual structure is being developed. While it is desirable to have immediate application to reading, it is often impossible to anticipate the particular word-analysis skills needed by a single pupil in a day's lesson. This is particularly true of independent reading, either for leisure reading or for individual tasks in connection with content subjects.

Although the word-analysis task is one of developing power of accurate word perception, it is helpful if the words used to develop this power are ones the child will find useful. Suggestions for selecting words for word-analysis practice are given on the next page.

1. *Words that have given trouble in recent lessons.* Word-analysis practice provides a review of previously taught words with which pupils have had trouble either in reading or understanding their meaning. The recent use of the words enables the teacher to keep meaning high by referring to the story in which the words appeared. A list may be kept of words that give the children trouble, or perhaps the teacher may skim previously taught material to discover words of this kind.

2. *Words that are to appear in future lessons.* The skimming of future lessons in various subjects will provide lists of words for word-analysis practice. If such words are difficult in meaning, the commonest definitions or synonyms may be added to the practice exercises. Grouping such words around a single topic or theme will be helpful. Spellers will also help to provide word lists.

3. *Dictionaries and word lists.* When a search is being made for polysyllabic words, or when syllable divisions and accent marks are to be indicated, one of the chief resources is the dictionary. The Thorndike-Lorge list [1] is especially helpful since the frequency of use of the word is given.

4. *Words in the child's speaking vocabulary but not in his reading vocabulary.* According to the more conservative estimates, an average child beginning fourth grade will have approximately six thousand words in his speaking vocabulary. Since fewer than two thousand words are taught in primary-grade readers, this leaves in the child's meaning vocabulary four thousand words available for word-analysis practice. Such words are especially suitable, since the child is immediately rewarded with a meaning when he has analyzed the word successfully.

While children's speaking vocabularies will vary in different communities, a good general guide for locating words known to children in the various grades is the Rinsland list.[2] This is a list of words used in the writing vocabularies of children; therefore it can be

[1] Edward L. Thorndike and Irving Lorge, *A Teacher's Word Book of 30,000 Words* (New York: Bureau of Publications, Teachers College, Columbia University, 1944).

[2] Harry Rinsland, *A Basic Vocabulary of Elementary School Children* (New York: The Macmillan Company, 1945).

assumed that the words are in the meaning vocabularies of the assigned grades. If this list is not available, many words in the selected intermediate-grade vocabulary lists in the Appendix (pages 368 to 392) may be used for word-analysis practice. Words probably known to children are those with a "B–D" (Buckingham-Dolch [3]) rating of the grade or for lower grades. These words are usually in the child's speaking vocabulary. In any of the lists, words having a "B–D" rating of 4, 3, 2, or "K–U" (International Kindergarten Union list), are suitable for building word-analysis exercises for grade 4. Grades 5 and 6 may include words with a 5 or 6 rating or lower. However, a teacher may use any words that are in the children's speaking vocabulary.

The following words are typical of those known to children at the beginning of the fourth grade. However, few of them appear in the Gates primary-grade vocabulary.[4]

List of words typical of those known to children at beginning of fourth grade

accept	birdhouse	bureau	celebrate
accident	blaze	buyer	cement
ambulance	bleed	cabbage	center
anxious	blotter	cabinet	cereal
apartment	bookcase	cafeteria	charge
arrest	border	calendar	chart
auditorium	borrow	canvas	cheap
aviator	bottle	captain	chilly
awkward	bouquet	capture	chore
bacon	bracelet	careful	chunk
badge	breathe	careless	circle
bandage	brunette	carnation	closet
barrel	bucket	carnival	clover
basement	buckle	carpenter	club
bathrobe	buffalo	carrot	collect
bathroom	bugle	carve	conductor
bayonet	bullets	catcher	control
beater	bundle	ceiling	copper

[3] B. R. Buckingham and Edward W. Dolch, *A Combined Word List* (Boston: Ginn and Company, 1936).
[4] Arthur I. Gates, *A Reading Vocabulary for the Primary Grades* (New York: Bureau of Publications, Teachers College, Columbia University, 1935).

corduroy	drench	fireworks	graham
correct	dried	flakes	grain
costume	drift	flavor	grape
cousin	drove	flicker	grapefruit
crank	dump	flip	grate
crazy	duty	football	grave
creep	eagle	forehead	gravel
cricket	earrings	forever	grease
croak	earthquake	fought	grind
croquet	edge	fountain	grip
crown	effort	frame	groceries
crumb	elbow	freckles	grove
crust	electric	freight	guarantee
crutch	elevator	friend	guests
cucumber	enemy	fringe	gymnasium
curtain	engineer	frown	gypsy
cushion	entertain	froze	habit
custard	entire	fumble	haircut
cute	eraser	fumigate	hairpin
daisy	example	furnace	halfway
damp	excellent	furniture	hall
danger	excited	future	handsome
daughter	exercise	fuzzy	hanger
daylight	exhibit	gallon	harm
deaf	express	gang	harp
decorate	eyelash	garage	harvest
deliver	eyelid	garbage	hatchet
dentist	fade	garters	haul
department	fairground	gate	healthy
depot	false	gentle	height
desert	fancy	geranium	hesitate
deserve	fasten	germs	hike
design	faucet	ginger	hinge
difficult	fault	giraffe	hint
dimple	favorite	glance	hire
dipper	feather	glide	hitch
direct	fender	glove	hoarse
discover	fertilizer	goal	hobby
ditch	figures	golf	hockey
dodge	file	government	holder
doubt	fingernails	gown	holiday
drawer	fireman	grab	hollow

homework	knot	metal	opposite
honest	label	mighty	orange
hood	labor	million	orchestra
hook	lame	miner	organ
hospital	lamp	mirror	ornaments
hump	language	mischief	outfit
husband	lasso	mister	overalls
iceberg	laundry	mittens	overcoat
icebox	lawn	moccasins	overshoes
idle	leak	modern	owner
imagine	lemon	molasses	paddle
imitate	lend	monument	pain
impatient	lever	mosquitoes	paintbox
important	liar	motion	pajamas
impossible	library	motor	pantry
injured	license	movie	pants
insects	limb	mumps	pardon
inspect	linen	murder	parents
instrument	lining	muscle	partner
invite	list	museum	passenger
iodine	load	musical	paste
island	loaf	nasturtium	patent
itch	locker	nasty	pattern
jail	lonesome	nation	pavement
janitor	lucky	native	pennant
jealous	lumber	neatness	pepper
jelly	lung	necklace	perfect
jewels	machine	necktie	perform
joint	machinery	needle	perfume
jungle	magazine	nephew	period
junior	manager	niece	phone
junk	margin	noisy	pickles
justice	marvelous	northern	pigeon
keen	mash	numb	pillar
keeper	mate	obedient	pillowcase
keg	mattress	offer	pinch
kindness	meal	officer	pirate
knee	measles	olive	pistol
knelt	medicine	onion	pitch
knife	melon	operate	plane
knit	member	operation	plank
knob	mention	operetta	planter

plaster	records	shiny	splash
platter	regular	shirt	splinter
plum	rent	shiver	split
pointer	repair	shock	sponge
poison	rifle	shout	spool
pole	rink	shove	sport
police	robbed	shower	spotted
polish	robin	shrink	spout
position	rooster	sidewalk	sprained
posters	rotten	signal	spread
posture	route	signature	sprinkle
potatoes	rubbers	silent	square
powder	ruin	silly	squash
praise	saddle	silver	squeak
prepare	safety	simple	squeal
president	sailboat	single	squeeze
pretend	salad	skill	squirt
principal	salute	skull	stack
prison	sample	slam	stage
probably	sanitary	sleeve	stain
program	satisfaction	slice	stake
promoted	sausage	slippers	starch
propeller	savage	smash	starter
property	savings	smear	starve
provide	scarce	smokestack	statue
punch	scarf	smother	steam
quaint	score	snake	steel
quarter	scout	sneak	sticky
queen	scramble	soak	stock
quilt	screw	soap	stomach
racer	seam	sore	stoop
rack	season	sour	storm
radiator	secret	spade	stout
radish	sense	spark	stove
raft	sentence	spear	strain
rainbow	separate	special	stranger
raincoat	service	speck	strap
raisin	shade	spice	stream
ranch	shark	spider	strength
rapid	sharpen	spike	stride
recess	shears	spill	strikes
recite	shelves	spin	strip

stripe	taxi	traveler	waist
stroke	team	treasure	walnut
stuck	tease	trick	wander
stump	telegraph	trim	warn
stung	tender	truth	wave
stunts	tent	tunnel	weapons
style	thaw	turnips	weave
succeed	thermometer	turpentine	wedding
success	thief	twine	weight
suffer	thimble	twinkle	western
sugar	thirsty	twist	whale
suggest	thread	typewriter	wheel
suitcase	throat	underneath	whiskers
sunk	thumb	underskirt	whittle
sunrise	thunder	underwear	wildcat
sunset	tick	uniform	wing
sunshine	tickle	untie	wipe
surround	tight	upright	wire
swarm	title	useful	wolf
sweat	toast	usual	women
sweater	toilet	usually	woodwork
swept	tomato	vacation	workers
swift	tongue	value	worst
swimmer	tonic	vanish	wound
switch	tonsils	variety	woven
sword	tool	varnish	wreath
swung	tooth	vase	wreck
syrup	toothache	vegetable	wrestle
tablecloth	toothbrush	victrola	wring
tablet	torn	view	wringer
tack	tough	vine	wrist
tackle	towel	violets	writer
tail	track	violin	yarn
tame	tractor	visitor	yawn
tangle	traffic	vote	year
tank	trailer	voyage	yeast
taught	tramp	wabble	zebra
tax	trash	waffles	zone

The words listed on the preceding pages will be of help to the teacher in building word-analysis practice lists. However, she should include other words that are known to children locally.

Spelling

When word meaning and word-analysis abilities are developed in reading, a large share of the spelling task is accomplished. The fact that spelling ability results from word instruction in reading may be demonstrated in any class by the following: Test the pupils on some of the lessons of the speller in the next higher grade. It will be discovered that average pupils will spell correctly more than half of these words that have not yet appeared in their spelling lessons. If attention to word-analysis study in reading is diminished, the adverse effect in spelling will probably be greater than in reading.

However, the ability to recognize and pronounce a word is no guarantee of the ability to spell it. Spelling requires written reproduction, a much more difficult task than recognition. Any person can recognize his friends and call them by name without hesitation; the ability to draw a recognizable sketch of any of one's friends is rare. Occasionally a child may be very skilled in word perception in reading, but he may be a very poor speller. It has been found true that poor word-analysis abilities in reading are always accompanied by poor spelling.

Analysis of spelling difficulty

The steps in the analysis of spelling difficulty are closely allied to those of studying difficulties in word perception; however, some additions peculiar to spelling abilities must be made. Spelling difficulties may be revealed by the following observations:

1. *Can the child read the words he is to spell?* There is little point in teaching a child to spell words that he cannot read unless spelling is considered a step in observation of word elements, a part of the word-analysis program.

2. *Are the meanings of the words to be spelled known to the child?* If the meanings are unknown, the child is simply spelling a nonsense word that will never appear in his composition. He will forget the spelling of such words immediately.

3. *Does the child hear sounds in spoken words?* Any of the several suggested lessons for auditory perception can determine this condition. The simplest one is to pronounce coined words made up of common word elements and see if the child can spell them by ear. The child's spelling in this case must be considered correct if any of the acceptable spellings of the sounds are used.

4. *Does the spelling difficulty rest upon inaccurate pronunciation of words?* If the child mispronounces words, the inaccurate pronunciation may appear in the spelling.

5. *Is the child's visual memory of words adequate for spelling?* Visual memory can be tested by showing the child unfamiliar words on flash cards, exposing them for two or three seconds, then having the child write them from memory. The test can be made more severe by asking the child to wait for five to ten seconds after the words have been exposed before he writes them.

6. *Can the child recognize homophones?* Good spellers have developed the ability to recognize several ways that certain sounds may be spelled; this is an ability in "multiple phonics." The suggestion for lessons in homophone recognition on pages 271–272 shows how this skill may be tested.

7. *Is the child's handwriting especially slow or poor?* If the child writes much below the normal speed for his grade, the results may show in poor spelling. Normal handwriting speeds in letters per minute for the several grades are as follows:

Grade 3—45   Grade 4—55   Grade 5—65   Grade 6—70

When certain letters are poorly formed in handwriting, the child's perception and memory of the word are diminished.

8. *Is the spelling instruction adjusted to the child's learning rate?* If more words are taught each week than the child can learn to spell, the resulting discouragement and confusion will handicap progress. Note the number of words a child spells correctly on the day following the teaching of new words.

9. *Do the words in spelling lessons transfer to written work?* Notice if misspellings appear in written work after correct spelling of these words in the spelling period. Also, it should be

observed whether the words taught in spelling appear in written work, or if the child tends to use only those words extremely easy to spell.

10. *Are there systematic errors in the child's spelling?* Tabulation and classification of spelling errors may reveal repeated errors on particular words or on special situations in words. For example, children may be found to have particular difficulty with certain vowel diagraphs or diphthongs, doubling errors, adding certain suffixes, omitting or adding letters.

Instruction in spelling

While the variations in spelling instruction will depend upon individual needs of pupils, some suggestions may be helpful in fitting the spelling program to the children:

1. *Adjusting to level and learning rate in spelling.* The use of a single book and a single rate of presentation of words for all pupils in a class cannot be justified. Rapid learners in spelling may work in pairs or small groups, completing the work of a month in a few days. This will free them for more useful educational activities. Slow learners will also work in small groups and will be given spelling lessons suitable to their level, learning rate, and perceptual-background needs.

2. *Personal spelling lists.* The use of personal lists of troublesome words is recommended. Even superior spellers should keep such lists of words they find hard to spell. These lists may be placed on a large card with spaces blocked off for each letter of the alphabet. The lists should be revised from time to time, eliminating those words that no longer give difficulty. Such lists should be available to the child at the time he is doing written work.

3. *Test-correction method for average spellers.* Most children can learn to spell through the simple method of correcting their own misspellings. The list of words is dictated by the teacher, with each word dictated, used in a sentence, then repeated. After the list has been presented, the teacher spells each word orally, and the child makes his own corrections. These words are added to the child's

personal list for study and use. The same list may be presented a second day in the same manner to show the child his growth.

4. *Flash-card method of teaching spelling to poor spellers.* The words on flash cards are pronounced by both the teacher and the child, used in a sentence, then turned down. The child writes them from memory. Learning is better if the child is asked to wait a few seconds before writing the word. After the words are taught, they may be shown on the board or on phrase cards in short sentences. The pupil is then asked to write the sentence from memory.

5. *Ear-training exercises in spelling.* The ear-training exercises recommended in word-analysis instruction should be used with those pupils whose spelling shows that they are not noticing sounds in words. Spelling by ear, however, is one of the common sources of spelling error in intermediate grades. The child must learn to rely more on the visual form of the words.

6. *Instruction in the spelling of homophones.* Calling attention to the particular spelling of sounds in certain words will help the child to select the right homophone for the word. He will notice that the *irth* sound is spelled differently in *birth, worth,* and *dearth.* Not too much stress should be placed on the spelling of these sounds apart from the words in which they appear, since overstress might result in confusion. Probably it is better to emphasize meanings, uses, and visual forms of such words, noticing the variation in spelling of sounds only as a peculiar deviation.

No amount of thinking or reasoning will help the child in selecting the right spelling in any homophone situation. The task seems to be that of enriching the imagery and meaning surrounding the word and of learning the word as a whole. The auditory pattern will give some help, indicating to the child that one of the several spellings is used.

7. *Systematic review on difficult words.* Those words that have given difficulty in spelling to a group of pupils should be recorded and reviewed from time to time. Meaning and usage should be stressed, adding imagery to the visual form of the word and increasing the chance that it will be used in the child's writing.

8. *Improving speed and quality of handwriting.* If poorly formed letters are a part of the spelling difficulty, special attention should be paid to such letters in handwriting practice. Low speed may be improved by giving tests of handwriting speed two or three times a week and recording the improvement in speed on a graph. Poorly formed letters should not be counted in the speed test. Persistence of such letters may be penalized by subtracting two letters from the speed score for each letter that is poorly formed.

9. *Improving the amount of transfer from spelling to composition.* There have been many suggestions for improving transfer from spelling to composition: having children build their own spelling lists from words they will use in a composition to be written about a particular topic; dictating stories that use the words taught in spelling; making personal spelling lists available for writing; grouping words used in such situations as personal description, describing certain sports, and so on; enriching word meanings through many uses at the time of teaching; improving statements through the addition of more precise or more descriptive words.

10. *The use of spelling rules.* Spelling rules need to be taught with caution. Rules for forming plurals, for doubling consonants, the *ie* rule, and others are taught as being only *usually* true. If in doubt, the word must be looked up in the dictionary and added to the personal list of difficult words. See page 281 for suggestions on personal spelling lists.

SUGGESTIONS FOR FURTHER READING

Betts, Emmett A. *Foundations of Reading Instruction.* New York: American Book Company, 1946. Pages 644–703.

Broom, M. E., and Others. *Effective Reading Instruction in the Elementary School.* New York: McGraw-Hill Book Company, 1942. Chapter 8 and pages 252–265.

Fitzgerald, James A. *The Teaching of Spelling.* Milwaukee: Bruce Publishing Company, 1951.

Gray, William S. *On Their Own in Reading.* Chicago: Scott, Foresman and Company, 1948. Chapters 9, 13, and 15.

Harris, Albert J. *How to Increase Reading Ability,* Third Edition.

New York: Longmans, Green and Company, Inc., 1956. Chapter 15.

Horn, Ernest. *Teaching Spelling.* Washington, D.C.: American Educational Research Association, 1954.

Horn, Thomas D., and Otto, Henry J. *Spelling Instruction.* Austin: University of Texas Press, 1954.

McKim, Margaret G. *Guiding Growth in Reading in the Modern Elementary School.* New York: The Macmillan Company, 1955. Pages 419–436.

Russell, David H. *Children Learn to Read.* Boston: Ginn and Company, 1949. Chapter 9.

13 Study Skills

SEVERAL IMPORTANT reading abilities underlie study of the content subjects. The first ability is thorough or analytical reading. In analytical reading the pupil follows the material closely in order to handle the many types of recall tasks: answering multiple-choice questions, answering detailed questions, answering general questions, following directions, giving an oral or written summary, presenting an outline, providing a complete oral or written account of what he has read. The primary task for the pupil in this type of reading is understanding and remembering what the author has presented.

The second ability is skimming or speeded reading for various purposes. This type of reading serves the following ends: locating desired information quickly; selecting material suited to a particular topic or purpose; observing the general structure of a selection; classifying or sorting materials; noticing the general tone, theme, or plot; and refreshing the pupil's memory of a selection previously read.

The third ability is elaborative thinking in relation to reading. In this type of study skill, the pupil combines his own experiences and purposes with the material read: He finds things to do about the reading, questions to ask, topics for further study; he finds illustrations, examples, applications of the points presented; he may compare or contrast the material with other presentations or other situations; he may draw inferences, interpretations, or generalizations; he may evaluate the material on various bases or he may evaluate it for various purposes.

A balanced reading program should include these three general study abilities, since each belongs in a somewhat distinct category. The thorough or analytical reading may become slow and slavish, pursuing carefully only the ideas presented by the author. It is counterbalanced by skimming reading and by elaborative thinking in relation to reading. Skimming produces the speed, but this may be at the expense of detailed comprehension and thinking about reading. These tendencies are counterbalanced by analytical reading and by thinking abilities. Elaborative thinking in relation to reading may produce both slow reading and inattention to the ideas presented by the author. The other two abilities provide practice necessary to counterbalance these faults.

The three abilities are not always clearly separate. Some tasks may require all three types of abilities or may combine any two. For highest success with some tasks, the pupil will need to skim to locate material that must be read in detail, or that must be applied to a thinking situation. Skimming may be combined with certain thinking or evaluating tasks, such as skimming to locate material useful for a particular purpose, or discovering evidence of bias or prejudice. All types of reading must be done as rapidly as the mental task required will permit.

Success of the instruction in study skills depends upon adequate motivation and graded lesson plans for each ability so that the child may progress with confidence. It also depends upon adjustment of instruction to pupil needs as revealed by observation and measurement. Adequate motivation may be achieved by setting the purpose of the assignments to tasks which seem important to pupils, by showing the child the suitability of the assignment for overcoming his difficulties and by demonstrating progress in the ability, by providing variety of assignment and accompanying activity. Gradation in difficulty of assignment may be achieved by progressing from easy to more difficult material, from shorter to longer units, from simple to more complicated assignments, and from group support to individual responsibility.

Small-group instruction with graded study guides

Studying a lesson is often a lonesome and insecure task for a child. Both the insecurity and the lonesomeness may be removed by the use of graded study guides with the pupils working in study teams of two or more. Teachers who have been using a single textbook with silent individual study followed either by pupils' answers to oral questions or by pupils' written answers to questions on the board will find a marked improvement in pupil interest and achievement when study teams replace individual study.

Three immediate results are noticed when study teams work with graded study guides: The comprehension and retention of information is greatly improved; children grow in power in attentive study and recall; the subject being studied becomes much more interesting. In the use of graded study guides, every child "recites" on every essential idea in the selection as compared to a few sentences of recitation when his turn comes. He has many times the amount of practice in recall. In some measure he is always successful in recall. When errors occur he is corrected immediately. This assurance in understanding the materials he has read leads the child to greater success either in participating in discussion or in answering "thought questions.'

Although there has been a constant concern about materials being written on "different levels" for children with different reading abilities, materials of the same reading level can be used for an entire class if the teacher provides the right amount and type of study help. It is possible that the differences among pupils in their need for study guides of different levels is greater than the differences in vocabulary load required to adjust to them.

Most textbooks have relieved the vocabulary burden very greatly, yet children still have difficulty in understanding and remembering what they read. When vocabulary load has been relieved, children may still have difficulty in attention, in seeing the relationship between ideas, in noticing the purpose or structure of a paragraph or a selection, in selecting the important ideas. and in stating those ideas in their own words. Comprehending and recalling materials they have read is much more than a matter of the right vocabulary load.

Levels of study tasks

The teacher may choose to make study easy or hard for the child; she may choose to make the task dull or interesting; she may provide much or little practice in recall; she may determine whether a subject is remembered or forgotten. The choices that she makes depend upon her skill and ingenuity in planning a number of different kinds of activities related to study for the various groups of pupils in her classroom.

When a teacher is planning the levels and types of study tasks to be used in social studies or science, she should keep in mind certain things. Here are some suggestions that will help her in her planning:

1. A series of short tasks is easier for children than a single long task.

2. Oral reading and recall are easier than silent reading and written recall.

3. Multiple-choice answers or short oral answers are easier than unaided summaries.

4. Questions prior to reading provide more help than questions after reading.

5. Immediate evaluation of results helps more than late or indefinite evaluation.

6. Working in pairs or groups is more satisfying for children than working alone.

Compare the difficulty of these two tasks set for the same lesson in social studies: (1) Children are working in teams of three, with one child serving as a teacher. The pupil teacher has a study guide consisting of a series of questions with multiple-choice answers over each paragraph. The pupil teacher reads the first question orally and gives the multiple-choice answers. The other two pupils hunt for the answer. When it is found, they give it orally. If the answer is right, the pupil teacher says, "Right. Here is the next question," and if the answer is wrong, he says, "No. Look again." (2) Children are working separately. The teacher says, "Read the lesson well enough so that you will remember it." When children have finished reading, they are told, "Now write everything you can remember about the lessson."

These two tasks differ vastly in difficulty. The first one includes the following: a series of short tasks, oral questions and oral answers, the selection of a multiple-choice answer, questions prior to reading, immediate correction of answers, pupils working in study teams. The second one includes the following much more difficult elements: a single long task, both in reading and in recall; writing rather than talking; no questions to guide the summary; the task assigned after reading; evaluation delayed and probably indefinite; each child working alone.

Almost any child could remember materials studied in the manner of the first situation; few children could score high on the second type of assignment. In between these two types of assignments there are many possibilities of lessons of increasing levels of difficulty which will help the child grow in the power of comprehension and recall and, at the same time, assure his understanding of the material read.

There is no well-established series of steps which may be followed in bringing the child from one stage to another, nor is there any method of grouping pupils for instruction which will work equally well in every situation. The teacher will find it desirable to prepare study guides that appear to be successful with the pupils, moving the pupils to more difficult tasks as a compliment to their increased powers of comprehension and recall. She can then vary the grouping as experience demonstrates to her the more effective methods of grouping.

Using study guides

Until publishers supply graded study guides to accompany textbooks, it will be necessary for the teacher to build her own. While a closely adjusted study program might require several levels of study guides for each lesson, it is usually impracticable and unnecessary to prepare more than two or three for each lesson. A single study guide may be used in several ways, depending upon the need of the group. Since study guides require time and intelligence to prepare, they should be saved for future use.

Teachers may cooperate in building study guides over different lessons and may then exchange them. The labor required of the teacher to prepare such study guides will be rewarded when she sees the growth in the study skills of the pupils and the pleasure the pupils find in their use.

The most effective time for an intensive effort to improve pupils' study abilities is in the fall. Six weeks of assistance in increasing the power to remember what has been read will prove most helpful during the remainder of the year. The study guides described on the following pages are concerned primarily with comprehension and recall rather than with the discovery of principles, the application and significance of knowledge, the use of elaborative and critical thinking, or the establishment of initiative in pursuing individual interests.

In social studies and science, where the use of study guides is most effective, the major share of the year should be spent on objectives higher than simple recall. However, thought processes rest upon understanding, and many practical tasks require the ability to tell what one has read, heard, or experienced. Moreover, it is assumed that if information is worth studying, it is worth remembering. Thus there is no need for apology for devoting time to establishing the ability to comprehend and recall, even though there are other and higher objectives in learning.

Detailed-question study guide

A study guide [1] that may be used in several ways is illustrated below:

Paragraph 1.   **Geography of Ireland.**

Which is flatter, Great Britain or Ireland?	Ireland
Which has the milder climate?	Ireland
Why is Ireland called the Emerald Isle?	Because of the thick grass
Where is the lowland region in Ireland?	Central part
What is the best known Irish River?	River Shannon

Paragraph 2.   **Relations between Ireland and England.**

Northern Ireland is a part of what nation?	United Kingdom or Great Britain
How long ago did the English invade Ireland?	Three hundred years ago
What did the English try to do?	Keep Ireland under English rule
What part of Ireland won its independence?	Southern Ireland

Paragraph 3.   **Industry in Northern Ireland.**

What part of Ireland has an industrial region?	Northern Ireland
What is the capital city of Northern Ireland?	Belfast
What things are made in Belfast?	Ships, engines, machinery
What Scottish city is opposite Belfast?	Glasgow
What are some of the products of Glasgow?	Coal and iron

Paragraph 4.   **Linen making in Belfast.**

What is the most famous product of Belfast?	Linen
What is the plant that linen comes from?	Flax
What is made of linen thread?	Cloth and laces
How good is Irish linen?	The best in the world
What city is the center of manufacture of linen?	Belfast
Where does Belfast get its flax for making linen?	Ireland and other countries

This guide provides topics for each paragraph, followed by questions in the order in which the answers appear in the paragraph.

[1] Based on the selection "Divided Ireland" in *Your World and Mine, Neighbors in the Air Age,* Ginn and Company, 1951, pages 204–206.

Answers are kept in a column at the right so that they may be folded back if desired.

Use of study guide

This study guide may be used in several ways:

1. For pupils who need much help in study (questions before reading)

   a) Use a team of three pupils, one of them a good pupil teacher. The pupil teacher says, "The first paragraph tells about the geography of Ireland. Here is the first question: Which is flatter, Great Britain or Ireland?" The two other pupils read to find the answer. If they get it right, the next question is given. They may tell the answer or read the passage which tells the answer.

   b) Use a team of two pupils of fairly equal reading ability. They fold the answers back, read the first question, look for the answer, and then agree as to the right answer. They do the same for each question in the paragraph. When they have finished all of the questions, they unfold the answers and check their correctness.

2. For pupils who need less help in study (questions after reading)

   a) Use a team of two or three pupils working together. They fold the answers back, place a covering sheet over the questions, then uncover the topic only for the first paragraph. After reading the paragraph, they uncover the questions, decide on right answers for the questions, then check their answers by unfolding the answers.

   b) This same task may be made more difficult for more advanced readers working in small groups. They may read two or three paragraphs, then uncover the questions and answer them in order. One of the pupils who has read the paragraphs may serve as questioner. He may help with the answers if he has folded the answers back, or he may have both the questions and the answers.

c) Still better readers may read the entire selection before looking at the questions. Pupils may rotate as questioners, with each asking the questions over a single paragraph.

This type of study guide should be used only at the beginning of a program for improving attention and recall. It provides a great deal of help, since it removes the necessity for organizing while reading and tests with short answers of simple fact. It may even encourage verbal replies which are not understood. Some children may need ten to twenty lessons with this type of study guide before they can progress to lessons more dependent on memory. Certainly few groups should be given very many lessons which provide such detailed questions before reading. They should progress quickly—after three to five lessons—to questions after reading a single paragraph, then to questions after two or more paragraphs.

More advanced study guides

A study guide for more advanced pupils provides only general questions to which several answers should be given. Using the same selection, the following might serve as a study guide of this type:

Paragraph 1. **What does this paragraph tell about the climate and geography of Ireland?**
Less hilly than Great Britain
Milder climate
Westerly winds bring plentiful rain
Grass grows thick and green
Ireland called the Emerald Isle because of the thick green grass
Shaped like a flat bowl
Lowland in central part, higher in north and south
River Shannon in center
Many beautiful lakes

Paragraph 2. **What does this paragraph tell about the relations between Great Britain and Ireland?**
Northern Ireland part of the United Kingdom
English and Scottish people invaded Northern Ireland
Invaded three hundred years ago
English then controlled all of Ireland
Southern Ireland won its independence

Other paragraphs are treated in a similar fashion. The amount of detail included in the answers may vary with the pleasure of the teacher.

This type of guide may also be used in several ways. It should be used only with those pupils who are fairly skilled in answering questions after reading. Children should work in pairs or in teams of three.

1. Pupils may uncover the general question for the paragraph. After reading the paragraph, one may serve as pupil teacher, asking, "What did the paragraph say about the climate and geography of Ireland?" He puts a check after each fact mentioned. Then he may ask questions about omitted items: "What do the westerly winds bring?" "What is Ireland shaped like?" "What is the name of the river?" Or he may simply read the omitted items aloud to the others.

2. The same method may be used over a selection of greater length, with all pupils in the group reading several paragraphs. They may rotate as questioners, each asking the questions over one paragraph. When several paragraphs are to be read, it would be well to put all of the questions at the top of the study guide so that they might be read without revealing the answers.

3. Superior pupils may work in pairs, each reading the entire selection, then checking each other's account of each paragraph in turn.

When this method of checking recitation is used, pupils will need some instruction about the acceptability of answers. The best rule to follow is that the "customer is always right." If a pupil insists that he has given the answer, or has said essentially the same thing, credit should be given. The important point is practice in recall rather than exact scoring of each child.

Study guides that provide steps to outlining

The ability to make an outline of materials read is usually evidence of good comprehension. Outlining does not assure unaided oral or written recall, but it does help. Practice in outlining is more useful in composition than in reading. The skills gained in observing the pattern of paragraphs and larger units of material should be helpful in the preparation of papers and talks.

Pupils may be given help in observing the patterns of paragraphs and larger units of material. They may be assisted in making outlines through the use of study guides that emphasize certain points in outlining. They may learn the first step to making headings or topics by selecting the topic or headline which best fits the paragraph. In the same selection used above, the following topics might be used for the paragraphs.

Choose the best title among the three suggested for each paragraph:

Paragraph 1.   (A)   The River Shannon
               (B)   The Climate of Ireland
               (C)   The Geography of Ireland

Paragraph 2.   (A)   English Ways of Living
               (B)   English Control of Ireland
               (C)   Ireland Wins its Independence

Other paragraphs are treated in a similar fashion.

In making the titles for the paragraphs, it is usually good practice to make the incorrect topics clearly too general or too restricted so that the children can learn how to do more exact "title fitting."

Such a study guide may be used with several "teams of three" or several pairs working at the same time. As the pupils read, they select the best title for each paragraph. Then the teacher may compare the results of the various teams and discuss the reasons for choosing a title when there is disagreement among the teams. More advanced pupils may be asked to write their own titles for each paragraph, then check against the titles given. After several groups have completed their titles and have checked them against the given titles, the teacher may discuss the variations given by the groups.

When children are adept at choosing the best title, they are ready to make titles of their own. From this, the filling in of minor topics under the heading is a relatively easy step. If the children have had practice in using study guides that require several answers to a general question, they should be able to list the details in the outlines they are preparing. While a more elaborate outline may be made, only a two-step outline is usually required for the average lesson.

The building of outlines may be done in groups, with one child serving as "secretary" and the others providing the headings and the lists of details. If children are reading from more than one source, the problem of outlining becomes more difficult since it requires the selecting of headings and rearrangement of details from several sources. Advanced pupils may be given group practice in making their own outlines from two books treating the same topic.

Outlines may be used to give the child practice in telling or writing what he has read. Children who have difficulty in giving an orderly and complete account of materials read should be allowed to use the outline as a basis for telling the story. This is especially true of oral reports from independent reading. Even experienced speakers find it necessary to use notes. The outlines may be used as a check on memory, with the child reciting without the aid of the outline, then uncovering it to see whether or not any important facts have been omitted.

Multiple recitation as a study device

If the teacher does not have time to prepare more detailed study guides for each lesson, some of the values of the study guides may be attained through group recitation. Pupils of approximately the same reading level are given an introductory talk about the significance of the lesson they are to read. Then they may be divided into teams of three for study. The following are some illustrations of uses of the method:

1. The children are asked to read the first paragraph silently. Then the teacher asks a general question which fits the paragraph: "What are some of the products of Ireland?" One child serves as secretary, writing the products suggested by the other two, or suggesting items himself but checking with the others before he writes them. When most groups have finished, one group may read their answers while others check. Additional items may come from other groups.

2. The children read the paragraph silently. They are then asked to write a title which fits the paragraph or to write a question which the paragraph answers. Or they may be asked to prepare several ques-

tions which may be asked other pupils. These are formulated by the pupils and are written by the group secretary. The teacher may then lead discussion on the titles or general questions prepared, or she may permit one group to question the others.

The chief value of the multiple-recitation method is found in wider participation in recall practice. It permits everyone to recite on the lesson, as compared to the very meager opportunity provided in the method where one pupil answers the questions while all of the rest listen. It is much more "alive" than lessons in which each pupil writes answers to questions written on the board. It is less effective in providing for differences in level of need for study aid than the proper use of study guides, but this method does add variety to the classroom.

Skimming as a study skill

In many types of study assignments partial reading, or rapid skimming, is essential. Skimming is desirable in locating specific information in a chapter, in selecting and rejecting materials for a particular purpose, in classification of short articles or extracts for filing or for use in a report, and for the purpose of noting the general organization of a selection or to refresh one's memory as to its content. Facility in these abilities is acquired by many pupils without specific instruction for developing such skills. However, many other pupils need special practice in the abilities related to partial reading, even though they already have good habits of thorough reading. In the following discussion two aspects of partial reading will be considered separately; namely, skimming to locate specific information and rapid reading to classify materials.

Steps in teaching skimming

Several steps or stages of practice are needed for the development of skills in locating information. The practice is carried on under the teacher's guidance without special emphasis on speed. After the child understands the method of locating information. later exercises are speeded by recording the number of answers the child can find in a limited time, or by recording the time required to find the answer.

The questions used for the exercises may be written on the board or duplicated on the assignment sheet for each pupil. On a sheet of paper the child indicates the page and the paragraph in which the answer is found, or the page and the first three or four words of the sentence containing the answer. If the answer is a single word or a phrase, this may be recorded instead of the page. The difficulty of the task is increased by using materials several pages in length so that rapid skimming of full pages is required, or by using material with a difficult vocabulary or with complex ideas.

Some specific facts that children might try to locate are names or dates, answers to questions phrased like the text, answers to questions containing no direct verbal cues, several answers to a single question, and information from the table of contents or the index. The following types of exercises are used for practice in locating specific information:

1. *Locating proper names or dates.* For an exercise in locating names or dates a list of four or five questions is prepared. The answers to these questions must be conspicuous in the text because of capitalization or numbering. Have the child turn to the chapter containing the answers. Let him find them as quickly as possible. Record either the time required to find the answers or the number of answers found in a limited time. Sample questions of this type are as follows:

a) What city in America makes the most automobile tires?

b) What was the first year in which more than a million automobiles were sold?

c) Which company has produced the most automobiles?

d) How many automobilies were produced in 1955?

2. *Locating answers to questions phrased like the text.* Locating answers is one of the simpler types of exercises, since the child uses the phrasing of the question as the basis for locating his answer. The exercises may be further simplified by underlining the cue phrases; later the underlining should be omitted. The exercise is made even

easier by selecting cues that are introductory phrases or sentences. Sample questions for the exercise of locating the answers to questions phrased like the text are as follows:

a) Where are furs purchased?

b) What is the average price of a single fur?

c) When is the best time of year for trapping these fur-bearing animals?

d) What is the first stage in preparing the fur for sale?

3. *Locating answers to questions containing no direct verbal cues.* For questions that do not contain direct verbal cues the pupil must seek pertinent ideas for his answer. For example, the questions suggested in the preceding paragraph contain the words of the text to be found in the answer. However, the following questions use no words of the answer, but they suggest instead only the ideas to be found:

a) At what place are the furs bought?

b) How much does the trapper receive for each fur?

c) In what season are the best furs obtained?

d) What is the beginning step in making the furs ready for the market?

4. *Locating several answers to a single question.* The following general questions are examples of the type of questions that could be used by the teacher in the exercise of locating several answers to a single question:

a) What are the reasons which Adams gave for his change in policy?

b) What five changes in the manner of living have been brought about by recent inventions?

c) What are four occupations of the inhabitants of this particular region?

5. *Locating information from the table of contents or the index.* The child is given a series of topics on which to gather information. He consults the table of contents or the index for references. He then skims the page for the sentence or paragraph containing the **answer.**

Classification of materials by means of skimming

A common task in preparing source themes is the selection of paragraphs or sentences suitable for quotation. The exercises below will teach this ability. They will also improve speed of reading and help to overcome habits of lip movements and word saying. This will be true because the reading is specific in purpose and superficial in character, a glance usually being sufficient to indicate the group or class to which the material belongs.

1. *Sorting clippings from three or four articles.* On small cards paste paragraphs from articles or stories found in discarded books or magazines. The articles should be taken from the same book or magazine so that the classification cannot be made merely by looking at the texture of the paper or the size of print. From five to ten paragraphs are taken from each article.

Place the titles of the articles side by side on the desk and ask the child to arrange the paragraphs under the proper headings as quickly as possible. Numbers or letters may be written on the backs of the cards to enable the child to check his accuracy. Record the time required to sort the paragraphs. Then shuffle the cards and give the child a second chance to demonstrate his speed in this skill.

2. *Classification of short articles from current newspapers.* Clip short articles from the sports, the financial, the society, and the general news sections of a newspaper and paste them on cards as indicated in the preceding paragraph. Shuffle the cards to obtain random order, and present them to the child with the following directions: "These stories were taken from various pages of the newspaper. Put in separate piles those from the sports page, the financial page, the society page, and the general news section." Or the child may be asked to select items of interest to an athlete, a banker, or a housekeeper. A more advanced stage of this exercise is to pass out the clippings without indicating the general classifications and to let the child devise his own classification scheme.

Other variations of this exercise are classification of articles and clippings gathered by various class members for nature study, biology, history, or any other content subject. Classification materials may be prepared and duplicated for several pupils by typing, mimeographing, or otherwise duplicating various related but randomly presented paragraphs.

3. *Determining the suitability of materials for particular purposes.* Materials for particular purposes may be clippings or paragraphs pasted on cards, or they may be stories from five or six volumes available to the child, labeled by book title, story title, and page. The child looks at the clippings or stories to determine whether they contain information on a particular topic or whether they deal with adventure, travel, humor, or historical characters and events. He may be asked to decide whether the stories are suitable for one of his age who is convalescing in a hospital, useful for class dramatization, valuable for present or future classroom use, or related to other important purposes.

Elaborative thinking in relation to reading

Unless the child is taught to react to reading in various ways, he may believe that the main purpose of reading is remembering relatively useless materials. It is the purpose of the thought and application questions which accompany reading to assist the child to acquire uses of reading in observation, thinking, and action. The ability of the child to use reading in this way seldom comes without direct teaching.

Classifications of thought processes are many and varied, usually depending mainly upon the preference of the person making the classification. It is unfortunate that we are still largely in the dark ages in relation to a better understanding of mental processes. It is equally unfortunate that there has been a diminution of interest in the "art of questioning" during the last fifty years.

Three types of thinking seem to be worth noting in connection with reading: organization and subordination of ideas; elaborating thinking, in which various associations are made to reading; and critical thinking, which is primarily a process of evaluation of a presentation on various standards or for various purposes.

The ability to organize, to group by common factors, to subordinate within groups, and to show relationships of parts to whole, appears to be a distinct mental ability which responds to specific teaching. Many of the tasks related to reading are of this type: response to word meaning by putting it in a particular classification according to any of the qualities of the object or idea represented by the word; steps to outlining suggested earlier in this chapter; speed of classification of materials.

Organization is an important ability in comprehension and recall; it is equally important in composition. Skill in organization of ideas begins in primary grades, since even the slowest learner can see the sequence of happenings in a story or can combine objects that belong together because of obvious common factors. The ability is equally important in various phases of research, whether scientific or literary, since one aid to the advancement of knowledge is the discovery of new classifications of matter or of ideas. Since so many of the reading tasks presented in previous chapters require the organization or subordination of ideas, no new suggestions for teaching this skill are presented here.

Elaborative-thinking practice in relation to reading encourages the child to tie his reading to his experiences, his memories, his observations, his actions, his purposes and plans. Elaborative thinking responds well to specific teaching. It is not highly correlated with intelligence, correlations usually running below .40. Many pupils who are not especially good readers appear to acquire elaborative thinking about reading quite easily.

Elaborative thinking is especially suitable for cooperative work of pupils in teams of three or five. Group discussion seems to stimulate elaborative thinking, and five pupils working together will usually provide a much richer list of associations than five pupils working separately. Children in such groups need not be of the same reading level, nor of the same level of intelligence. In fact, it seems better that pupils be of different levels when elaborative thinking is required.

A number of suggestions which most teachers will find helpful in teaching elaborative thinking in connection with reading are given on this page and pages 304–305.

1. *Finding topics or questions not covered by the story.* Here is a sample of an assignment in which topics or questions outside the story are suggested to the pupils: "While you read this chapter on Columbus's voyages, think of topics you would like to know more about, or questions that interest you which are not covered by this book." Pupils will need help at first in this type of task; they will be unable to think of topics and questions. Pooling the ideas of the class and the teacher will give pupils an understanding of the possibilities in this type of assignment; then study teams may discuss the selection and make their own lists. After a few class practices, pupils will learn to ask many questions and find many topics not covered by the story.

2. *Finding things to do about materials read.* Suitable activities will depend upon the story: "As you read this chapter, think of things that relate to the chapter which we could do in our classroom: making experiments, making a display, drawing pictures, giving a play, having a debate, having an exhibit. What might we do in each one?" Or, "As you read this chapter, think of things we could do to improve the appearance of our community. Jot down any ideas you have and add them to the list your team will make at the end of the lesson." Or, "As you read this story, think of interesting things that could be done about it on week ends or Saturday afternoons, in addition to the things suggested by the author."

3. *Thinking of people who have an interest in the subject being read.* In geography, children will think of people who came from or have visited the country being studied; in science and applied arts, people who have something to do with manufacture or sale of objects; in vocations and hobbies, people who are engaged in them. Discussions may include people to interview, to invite as classroom guests, to correspond with.

4. *Reading for similar experiences.* Children may be asked to think of experiences of their own or of others which are similar in

some way to the story. Similarities may be in locale, in emotional situation, in the problems involved, in people of the same age or relationship, in the same time of day or year, or any other likeness contained in the story.

5. *Finding illustrations of the author's meaning.* The assignment for finding illustrations of the author's meaning might start in this way: "This writer tries to show that good manners and courtesy make living more pleasant and also make people more successful in their work. As you read the author's illustrations, think of other illustrations that show he is correct." Or, "This writer points out that many fires are due to carelessness in the home. As you read his examples, see if you can think of other kinds of carelessness that might cause fires."

6. *Producing different endings to a story.* Here is an introductory statement for an assignment such as thinking about different endings for a story: "As you read this story, think how it would have ended if certain things had not happened. Keep the *if* in mind as you read, and think of five conditions that would have changed the ending of the story, such as: *if* the Indians had been friendly; *if* the settlers had been better prepared; *if* the reinforcements had come in time; *if* the rain had held off a little longer." Or, "When you get to the bottom of page 82, stop and think of several ways the story might end. Then read on to the end of the story and see which of your ideas is nearest right."

7. *Noting similarities and contrasts between stories or situations studied.* For a study of similarities and contrasts typical assignments are these: "As you read the story of this man's life, compare it with that of Benjamin Franklin whom we read about earlier in the year. Find ways in which they are alike and ways in which they are different." Or, "While reading this chapter on gold mining in Alaska, remember the one we read about diamond mining in Africa. Compare the methods and precautions used in gold mining and diamond mining."

8. *Drawing inferences and generalizations from reading.* Generalizations from reading may be obtained by these types of assign-

ments: "As you read this story, think of some general rules to be observed in planning a camping trip, some important 'Do's' and 'Don'ts' for campers." Or, "As you read this story, list some of the general reasons why people move from one place to another."

9. *Noting relations between the past and the present.* Relations between the past and the present may be brought out in this way: "As you read this story of colonial life, think of improvements of modern inventions; also think of colonial conditions that have not been changed by inventions." Or, "As you read this story about exploration in Africa, list the things that would not have been possible if the African trip had been made at the time of the discovery of America."

Critical thinking in relation to reading

Critical thinking in relation to reading is usually concerned with evaluation of the material for particular purposes or against various types of standards. While it is usually identified with more advanced abilities in social-studies material, especially in controversial areas, some experiences in critical thinking may be given early in the elementary school and in areas other than the social studies. Here are some suggestions:

1. *Selection of material pertinent to a topic.* "While reading this chapter on the Middle Atlantic states, think about the relative merits of city and country life. Pick out the things that make city life more interesting, and those that make country life more interesting." Or, "As you read this chapter on modern transportation, select those statements showing the increase in pleasure, freedom, and effective living that could be considered the result of improved transportation."

2. *Selection of material suitable to a particular audience or occasion.* "We in the fourth grade are going to have the kindergarten children as our guests next Thursday. They want to know what we do in the fourth grade. What things could we show or tell them that

they would find interesting?" Or, "We are to make a booklet to send to a school in Australia, and the Australian school is going to send one in exchange. Tell me what you think we should put in our booklet."

3. *Finding exceptions to the author's point of view.* "This writer believes that one should always think of others before he thinks of himself. As you read this story, see if you can think of times when it is wise to consider one's self first." Or, "This author believes that children should not be allowed to work before sixteen years of age. As you read this article, see if you can think of types of work suitable for children and helpful to them, compared to the harmful ones the author describes."

4. *Reading to distinguish sense from nonsense.* "Some of the author's suggestions in this essay are serious, while others poke fun at our ways of doing things. Pick out those suggestions that the author really does not mean." Or, "This selection says many things that could not possibly be true but are put in just for fun. Pick out the parts that you think are impossible or that probably could not happen."

5. *Making suggestions for improving a selection.* "This chapter has a great many facts but is not very exciting. As you read it, find places for examples, illustrations, pictures, explanations, diagrams, or maps that would make the story easier to understand or more interesting." Or, "As you read this story, think of other happenings that would add to the reader's interest." Or, "As you read this story, find the difficult or dull parts and see if you can tell what makes them dull. Then tell how you think these dull parts might be improved."

6. *Telling fact from opinion.* "On this article about sports, the author compares the merits of winter and summer sports. Which of the things he says could be taken as facts, and which are only opinion?" Or, "This author thinks that everyone should live on a farm for a little while. Which of his arguments do you think are most valid, and which of his arguments do you think are only his own opinion?"

7. *Finding differences in points of view.* "As you read these two stories about men working on the assembly line in factories, discover in what way they agree and how they differ. See if you can account for the difference."

Another example of calling attention to different points of view might be, "This city dweller complains about the high cost of vegetables, while this farmer worries about the low prices he gets for his products. Where do you think they agree and where do they disagree?"

8. *Noting the author's bias.* In the comparison of points of view on work on the assembly line, accounting for the difference is really a study of bias. Another example would be, "As you read this story, remember that the author lived in the South. Notice the differences between his attitude and the one a Northern writer might take toward the same topic."

9. *Reading to detect overstatements and unfounded claims.* The area that takes in overstatements and unfounded claims includes a variety of "propaganda techniques." The child encounters this type of approach in radio and television advertising: toothpastes, deodorants, soaps, desserts, cigarettes, and beer—in fact, almost anything associated with paid endorsements of professional athletes, inferred to be approved by doctors or dentists, or associated with popular or attractive people in the entertainment world. He will meet continually the technique of "proof by anecdote," in which a few examples of unacceptable behavior or practice are used to show that all members of the profession, race, or religion are assumed to follow or condone the undesirable practice. Much more of this kind of propaganda appears in adult reading than in school textbooks or children's periodicals.

Most of the critical thinking techniques are adapted to group or class discussion following reading. All oral work is more effective as the child has the chance to participate freely in a small group of his peers. While many of the assignments in critical thinking need to be presented to the entire class to show what is meant, practice in the abilities is more effective if the groups are limited to five pupils or fewer.

SUGGESTIONS FOR FURTHER READING

Bond, Guy L., and Wagner, Eva B. *Teaching the Child to Read*. New York: The Macmillan Company, 1950. Chapter 14.

Carter, Homer L. J., and McGinnis, Dorothy J. *Learning to Read*. New York: McGraw-Hill Book Company, 1953. Chapter 8.

Kottmeyer, William. *Handbook for Remedial Reading*. St. Louis: Webster Publishing Company, 1947. Pages 113–137.

McKee, Paul. *The Teaching of Reading in the Elementary School*. Boston: Houghton Mifflin Company, 1948. Chapters 12, 13, 14, 15, and 16.

Russell, David H. *Children Learn to Read*. Boston: Ginn and Company, 1949. Chapters 11 and 14.

Tinker, Miles A. *Teaching Elementary Reading*. New York: Appleton-Century-Crofts, Inc., 1952. Chapters 10 and 14.

Yoakam, Gerald A. *Basal Reading Instruction*. New York: McGraw-Hill Book Company, 1955. Chapter 12.

CHAPTER 14 **Teaching the
Uses of Reading**

THE IDEAL OF EDUCATION is to establish habits of continuous learning. The human being has a nervous system that enables him to learn throughout life. If he uses this potentiality well, every year should add to his powers of enjoyment and service. The human being is different from other animals in that he can learn through language, either spoken or written. Thus he can continually share many of the experiences of men of other generations and other places in the world. Almost every possible action, object, idea, place, plan, or problem has a literature of its own, thus making it possible for man to enrich his life continually through consultation with the writings of others.

The possibilities in reading are so vast and complex that no man may expect to utilize them completely. However, few people have learned to use reading as well as they are capable of doing. It is the task of the school to give the child early experiences in the rich possibilities of the uses of reading. Giving the child such experiences is not done incidentally or in the reading period alone; imaginative planning is required by teachers in all phases of the school program if the children are to acquire habits of initiative in the many uses of reading.

Understanding the possibilities
of reading

To understand the possibilities of reading requires a concept much broader than that of the "reading of good literature." Reading is incidental to action, and perhaps the major use of reading is to expand the choices and increase the effectiveness of action.

Reading can give the student knowledges of vocations beyond his immediate environment, and can help him discover ways of improving his services in his chosen vocation. If a vacation trip is being planned, reading will suggest places to visit, recreational and educational opportunities, as well as places to stay and places to dine. In the problems of homemaking, books and magazines offer countless ideas for meals, clothing, furnishings, and more efficient and pleasing plans and arrangements. In all of the hobby areas, reading will suggest choices in equipment and techniques, whether the field is photography, astronomy, birds, antique automobiles, gardening, magic, sports, music, fine arts, crafts, or collections. If the action contemplated includes campaigns, entertainments, organizations, surveys, or other planning ventures, reading will be an aid. If purchases are to be made—of music albums, rugs, dishes, furniture, kitchen equipment, sporting goods, automobiles, boats, shop equipment, tools— catalogues, specialty magazines, monographs, and books will assist in making decisions. The "Yellow Pages" of the telephone directory will tell possible places to make purchases. If one is interested in sports, reading about a favorite sport will provide new ideas for techniques and enjoyment.

Reading is decidedly an aid to freedom of choice in intelligent action. In teaching the uses of reading, it is most important that children have many experiences in using reading in planning and in action.

In the program of reading to broaden aesthetic interests, it is necessary to follow a concept much broader than the conventional one of music, literature, and art. Reading is a decided aid to enriching concepts of excellence and beauty. There are potentialities of excel-

lence in every person, act, idea, or object if one has adequate understanding. Far too many people miss the delights in their immediate
surroundings because their knowledge is inadequate to discover
beauty in them.

This concept of the cultural finds excellence and beauty in a well-
kept kitchen and in the Metropolitan Museum; in a well-made barn
and in the Chartres Cathedral; in the singing of children in a country school and in a performance of a great symphony; in finely
worked darning and in a Persian tapestry; in the rhythmic precision
of a skilled bricklayer and in the finest dancing; in a well-made shoe
and in an illuminated manuscript; in a prize-winning calf and in a
Rembrandt painting; in an Iowa cornfield and in the Tuileries Gardens; in conversation with a lobster fisherman and with a distinguished statesman; in observing the family life of ants and in the de-
liberation of great assemblies; in the excellent management of a
picnic and in the construction of a skyscraper; in a well-played sand-
lot baseball game and in a performance of the Metropolitan Opera
Association.

This aesthetic concept finds in every object the possibilities of
beauty; in every homely task, the possibilities of grace, rhythm, and
precision; in every person, values important to mankind. It finds
excellence quite independent of "job level" and sees worth in all
useful labor. A reading program seeking to enrich concepts of the
beautiful will need to recognize and emphasize that excellence,
beauty, and worth may be found in a million different forms and
places.

The need for an imaginative program in teaching the uses of reading is greater than ever before. Competition from television has begun to replace the former worry about comic books as an enemy of
"good reading." Television is here to stay, and with the coming of
color television and the improvement of programs, there is little
chance that the average time of three hours or more each day of television viewing will be reduced.

Neither television nor comic books need to be a threat to the vigorous use of reading if children are introduced to reading related to
purposes and action which they consider important. If reading is a

312 • IMPROVING READING INSTRUCTION

"lovely way to spend time in the realms of the imagination," or an earnest way to pursue knowledge that adults consider important, then television and comic books can offer serious competition. They make daydreaming much easier than reading, since they furnish the imagery with the plot. Television is a highly important source of interests and information of all kinds. In the long run television will stimulate reading just as the radio stimulated the sales of phonograph records.

Television programs have a weakness that reading does not have: They cannot provide immediate information needed by the child. There is no way at present to dial a television lesson on how to build a box kite, how to make peanut brittle, or how to identify a bird that has just now appeared at the feeding station. Schools, however, cannot afford to leave the use of reading to chance. There needs to be an increased attention to television programs for making reading a highly important way to increase the child's pleasure in useful action.

The use of reading cannot be taught by "hearing the reading lesson" daily in the reading corner. Nor can it be taught by the elaborate sequences of word mastery, oral and silent reading, and study skills presented in the preceding chapters of this book. It does not come from mastery of the subject matter of the curriculum. It requires a planned program of opportunities and experiences in using reading throughout all of the various school subjects and also using reading in the noncurricular activities in which the child engages.

The end sought is individual initiative in a great variety of uses of reading. The teacher may set the stage for many uses of reading, and the pupil may demonstrate high initiative in the reading tasks related to class use. However, the final success of the program of teaching the uses of reading rests upon individual enterprise in seeing the needs for reading in relation to the pupil's various interests and in taking the necessary steps to acquire and to use the pertinent reading material. The child's introduction to the many uses of reading, however, may be made in relation to various class activities and projects.

Classification of the uses of reading

The following four classifications of uses of reading are dependent upon the psychological task involved in their teaching. The first type of reading is *imaginative* reading, in which the task is getting pleasure and vicarious experience out of the imagery evoked by the words of the author. It includes fiction, poetry, drama, and humor—in which the reader is free to imagine the characters and scenes to suit himself, within the broad limits set by the writing. The second type of reading is that of *history and travel,* dealing with the information remote in time or space. Imagery is strictly controlled by the reality of the times and places mentioned, and the teaching task is that of making the situations real and relating them to the child's current purposes. The third type of reading is the *"world about you"* reading, which deals with the immediate and tangible: science, sports, arts, crafts, products, vocations, hobbies, and things available to the child's senses. Successful instruction in this type of reading requires a constant interplay of reading and the objects and activities immediately available. A fourth type of reading deals with *attitudes, ideals, and personal growth*—reading that concerns standards of conduct and personal philosophy and behavior: books on religion, conduct, ideals, manners, habits, ways of making adjustments to the problems one faces.

It is obvious that there is a considerable overlap among the various types of reading described. Fiction, poetry, drama, and humor may be related to real people, times, and places, with the imagery being restricted to the fictional elements of the writing. Part of the history and travel reading may approach the "world about you" because of objects in museums or visitors from other countries. Attitudes and ideals may be established in any of the several types of reading. However, the classifications are sufficiently discrete to permit analysis of the problems involved in teaching them.

A description and an analysis of the four types of reading will be found on the following pages. On pages 329–330 are suggestions for planning a year's use of reading program.

Teaching the uses of imaginative reading

The reading of fiction, poetry, drama, and other types of imaginative writing depends upon the child's ability to translate words into images—an ability that varies greatly among children and adults. Some people have highly vivid imagery, seeing all of the characters as clearly as though they were real or remembered persons. All of the scenes are vivid, and the reader feels that he is right there; sounds, odors, colors, temperature—all are vivid to readers with high imagery. Other readers have only hazy or blurred imagery, and read for plot or general ideas only. In reading this sentence, "The little girl sat on the steps, waiting for her father to come home," some children will describe the child's personal appearance in detail, will see the house and the surrounding environment, and will answer questions about their images as though they were seeing the situation clearly. Others will say, "I didn't see her," and they seriously doubt if the others are telling the truth about their images.

Many teachers are not aware of these differences among children in ability to create images from reading. Most teachers have high imagery and find it difficult to understand that others do not have their vivid imagery. Some readers see the characters in the books so clearly that they are troubled by the casting of characters in a motion picture of a book they have read. Some hear the voices so clearly that they know exactly the pitch, cadence, and accent being used by the characters in the book.

No two people have exactly the same imagery of the characters and scenes in a story. This is as it should be, since a part of the pleasure in imaginative reading is to create the images one desires. Although the author may give a description that seems to limit the reader, the most minute description still leaves large elements of freedom for the imaginative reader. The reader who is deficient in imagery, however, is helped little by description. He simply does not get clear impressions from the words used by the author, and the reading of fiction is very unrewarding except for plot and ideas.

Because of the difficulty of measurement which requires an intro-spective method, research in imagery has been very limited. The fol-lowing findings may be of interest: There are wide differences in the amount and clarity of imagery in reading. The relationship to intelligence test scores is low, with correlations running under .50. Imagery seems fairly universal in primary grades, but marked differ-ences appear in middle grades. Girls are generally superior to boys in the skill, but there are many exceptions. Children who are high in imagery read much more fiction than do those low in imagery. Chil-dren low in imagery appear to prefer comic books or illustrated books to a greater extent than those high in imagery.

Other findings are these: Images from reading appear to be almost as stable as memory images, not being distorted by questions asked about them. Imagery shows little relationship to rate of reading or to scores on reading achievement tests. Tests of imagery can be de-veloped which have a high reliability and appear to stand checks of validity.

All of these findings are related to imagery in reading, not general imagery. Everyone must have memory images in order to learn a language, to remember people and places, to perform tasks and fol-low directions. Some children and adults who are very skilled in other types of imagery, such as that required for construction of a machine or a house, to develop a football play, or to plan an exhibit, are quite without the ability to make images while reading a book of fiction.

The best method available to the teacher at present for discovering differences in imagery is that of asking children to report their im-agery of the stories they read. A series of such reports will discover children very low in imagery as well as those who delight in it. It is regrettable that we have no studies of how to improve imagery in reading once it is lost. If it is true that primary-grade children all have high imagery in reading or listening to stories, the fact that the ability is lost by many children by the time they reach intermediate grades is a matter of concern.

The best advice seems to be to include a number of practices in discussion about imagery evoked by stories in all of the early grades.

Possibly the imagery might be preserved by a greater amount of listening to stories, by the oral reading of plays and poetry, and by a greater emphasis on imaginative reading generally. This is one of the areas of ignorance in reading methods which needs greater attention of research and practice.

If children are deficient in imagery, it is unlikely that they will develop into extensive readers of fiction. However, they may share many of the pleasures of other types of imaginative reading.

Fiction

In the reading of fictional stories in the classroom, the primary purpose is keeping interest, enjoyment, and imagery high. Such reading should not be made a word-analysis drill or an exercise in study skills. All comment should be in relation to the story, its characters, the amusing situations, what is to happen next. The main danger in teaching is over-analysis of the story and too close checking on factual content, sequence, details. There is no need for formal book reports or for any kind of examination-taking over the story. The chief concern is to preserve the pleasure in the story, and sometimes this is best done by omitting all recitation and comment on the story.

However, most children enjoy talking about things they have read, and will pick out the things that interested them most. Usually such comment is more effective when the groups of children are small enough for spontaneous informal comment rather than when the groups are large and the children must make more formal statements.

The reading of fiction is particularly suitable for individual reading either in the classroom or at home. Once a child has a sight vocabulary that enables him to enjoy silent reading, fiction reading needs little encouragement. It is necessary, however, for the teacher to know many children's stories and to help the child discover the possibilities in the library. The extent and variety of reading will need to be observed so that the child will include the children's classics and examples of animal stories, historical fiction, children in other lands, fairy stories; in other words, a wide sampling of the possibilities of fiction.

Many children like to keep a record of their reading, but others would prefer to reflect on what they read without the burden of recording and analyzing. If the reading of every story is burdened with a laborious task, the tendency to reading is diminished. Keeping a record of reading in a personal reading notebook is usually acceptable, since children like to keep a record.

Other types of response to reading are the selection of anecdotes to be read to the group of children who are ready for the story or who have read the story, the making of suitable book jackets to illustrate the story, or the dramatization of some of the events. Children should learn how to talk about books to others who have not read the book, avoiding giving away the plot or otherwise removing suspense and interest for future readers. When all of the children in a group have read the book, the freedom of discussion is much wider.

Reading of plays

The reading of plays as a regular part of classroom instruction in oral reading has high possibilities. Some of the values in making play reading a common practice in the classroom can be described as follows:

1. Expressive oral reading is best developed through play reading, since all parts are designed to be spoken. This is not true of much of the material in basal and supplementary readers.

2. Comprehension and interpretation are assured in play reading, since every line has a point in the development of character or plot. Careless reading is largely eliminated.

3. Plays provide the audience situation, both for the audience and for the participants. Previous silent reading of the entire play does not diminish the pleasure in hearing the play read. The reason for this is that different children find values in lines not found by the silent individual reading and thus they bring this fresh interpretation in the oral presentation.

4. A second or third reading of a play is relished by children, since the possibilities of varied interpretations are many, permitting new readers to display other values in the line.

5. Plays provide excellent vocabulary enrichment. There is no need for strict vocabulary control, since each child has the opportunity to work up his part and to memorize it if necessary. This helps extend the vocabulary and frees the child from the limited vocabulary essential to the sight reading of a larger selection. However, the vocabulary of the play should be within the child's oral-language experience.

6. Children who are reading on quite different levels may be combined in play reading. Since each child works up his part, taking as much time as necessary and getting the needed help, there is no need to limit play reading to superior readers. While it might be desirable to write parts for slower pupils or to select parts with easy reading for them, this is less necessary in play reading because of the opportunity the child has for advanced study. If the play reading is extemporaneous, however, the correct adjustment of the material to the child is highly important.

7. Plays are excellent for bringing out undiscovered personality qualities in children. Timid ones often shine while being someone else in a play. Aggressive ones are helped by playing parts different from their usual character. Play reading often uncovers humor and sympathy where they are unexpected.

8. Plays are desirable for stimulating discussion of personal qualities and habits, since the characters of the play can be talked about without self-consciousness. Yet pertinent points can be made by and for the children without unacceptable moralizing.

9. Plays are especially good for maintaining imagery and for providing an imaginative reading outlet for children who are deficient in imagery. Generally, imagery is improved when the presentation is oral and when the situation is dramatized.

10. Speech habits are improved through play reading. Since interpretive reading requires a consideration for the audience, the motivation to clear and expressive speech will be much higher for the child.

It is more useful to read ten plays than to stage one play. When many plays are read, every child can experience the pleasure of par-

ticipation. The reading of plays is not burdened by borrowing prop-
erties or costumes, or by many rehearsals. When children are chosen
to read the parts, a single rehearsal is all that is necessary, although
some children who need special help may be given their parts a day
or so in advance. Usually the group of children who are to read a
play merely go to another room or into the hall, practice their parts
and help each other on interpretation; then they return to read their
parts.

It is not necessary to suspend the activities of the entire class in
order to provide an audience. The play may be read within a reading
group, with only the teacher and a few other children for the audience. The group of children themselves may be their own audience
in the reading of the play.

Play reading needs a "master of ceremonies" or narrator who reads
the necessary stage directions. These should be cut to a minimum,
with much of the stage directions being included in the lines of the
character. Children usually need little direction in the reading of
lines. Almost all children have engaged in dramatization for many
years through imaginative play. They are used to playing parts as
fathers, mothers, grandparents, babies, teachers, ministers, cowboys,
Superman, Indians, policemen, pilots, engineers; and they can im-
provise lines readily. Play reading takes advantage of this rich experience in dramatization and needs little assistance of the teacher.

Each teacher should make a collection of plays suitable for children of the age group she is working with. Most of the currently
available plays are holiday plays and health and safety plays. It is
hoped that publishers of basal readers will have the courage to offer
books of plays as a staple part of the supplementary or even the basal-
reading program.

Poetry and choral reading

Choral reading of poetry is an excellent way to give the child an
introduction to expression and the feeling of poetry. The chief requirement for choral reading is courage on the part of the teacher.
Many teachers feel that choral reading is a mystic art with established
rules known only to the initiated. Actually, any teacher of reading

who enjoys either poetry or children can use choral reading successfully.

Experience in interpretive reading and a knowledge of poetry are helpful. But the main thing is to have the courage to try it. It makes little difference whether a line is read as a "solo" or a chorus, or whether "dark voices" or "light voices" read a particular part. The teacher may use her own judgment in the interpretation of the poem into parts and in the placement of the parts being read. The interpretation of a poem may be decided by a group of children, and a child may direct the choral reading.

In selection of poems for choral reading, the poems chosen must be acceptable to children, especially to boys. Humorous poems, narrative poems, poems of adventure and action are better to begin choral-reading instruction. After children have learned to enjoy the more aggressive poems with a strong feeling, they may move to the more descriptive and delicate passages.

There has been some professional aversion to requiring the memorization of poetry. Perhaps there are sound reasons for avoiding the requirement that all children memorize the same poems. However, there can be no serious objection to encouraging children to select and memorize poems they enjoy. A teacher who helps children memorize a fund of prose and poetry selections is adding a useful resource to the child's language-arts equipment.

Humor

There should be a definite place for humor in the reading program. Humor is a highly important characteristic of the American tradition and an extremely useful part of social intercourse. It provides balance, encourages cooperation, reduces emotional pressure, relieves dullness, opens conversation. Classrooms and teachers' meetings are often burdened with overearnestness; fatigue and inattention often disappear when humor is introduced.

Humor should be a normal part of most kinds of classroom activities. If it doesn't appear normally, it should be scheduled. While the "scheduling" of humor may appear to be inconsistent with the nature of humor, it is not a bad idea to have children collect humorous anecdotes, select humorous parts of stories, or save humorous poems or short plays to be used at times when a light touch is needed. Experience may show that the teacher needs to preview the anecdotes of some of the pupils.

History and travel reading

Children in the elementary grades usually place social studies low in their list of subject preferences. One of the reasons for this is that social studies is unreal to them. Things that happened a long time ago seem of little importance except as an academic exercise. Interest in the past is not as high as interest in the present and the future, in the immediate or very near environment. Children often have very little understanding of time relationships prior to their own lives. They do not find it incongruous to believe that their teacher might have known George Washington, or that the athletic director sailed with John Paul Jones. As age increases, interest in the past will often increase. Far-off places are equally unreal. Although they may study about Italy or even some state or city in the United States, it may have no real existence for them.

Use of reality

The task in social-studies teaching is to give reality and importance to things distant in time or space. Reality may be provided through various objects such as furniture, clothing, tools, dishes, letters, and other things from other times and places. Motion pictures, film slides, photographs, and recordings may help to provide reality. Plays and spontaneous dramatization are useful.

In geography, reality is introduced through the constant use of maps, pictures, and objects. Foreign news, radio and television programs, stamp collections, and exchange of letters with children in other states or countries bring distant places closer, as do airline and steamship schedules. Such steps may add interest and reality to the study of social studies, but other means are necessary to establish the importance of social studies to the future activities of the individual child.

Reading before travel

The child may learn to use history and travel reading in his own activities by experiences that show their usefulness. Every person should learn the pleasure and necessity of reading before traveling. Field trips are essential for this purpose. If a visit to an ice-cream factory is contemplated, there are many things to learn before the trip: various types of ingredients, the testing of milk and cream, refrigeration machines and freezers, homogenization, laws regulating dairy products; sources and transportation of dairy products; marketing and distribution. The dairy industry and the manufacturers of refrigeration machinery have much helpful relevant material. When the visit is made, the pupils come as welcome and informed guests, rather than a rabble whose only interest is "when do we get the ice cream."

If a pupil is traveling with his parents during a summer holiday, or if a family is moving to another part of the country, an opportunity is provided to learn methods and sources of useful information. Imaginary trips using only textbook and standard reference materials cannot replace situations of actual travel which require the initiative and knowledge to obtain specialized current materials about travel.

Classroom visitors

Reading before meeting people so that the benefits of conversation are enriched is also a desirable part of social-studies reading. Conversation is an art which is utilized fully by few people, and it may be one of the most rewarding activities in which an individual may engage. It is an important but neglected area of language-arts instruction.

Classroom visitors who are invited because of their relationship to an area of social-studies instruction are particularly important as a means of teaching the art of conversation. Such people usually should not be invited to talk to the class. The distance between the lecturer or lantern-slide shower and the class is very great, and the resulting conversation is often stiff and stilted. It is better to invite the guest to look at and listen to the products of the children's study in relation to his interest. For example, if the class has prepared an exhibit and report on Italy, people who have lived or traveled in Italy should be invited. If wool or textiles are being studied, a person who knows wool or textile manufacture should be the guest. It is very difficult for anyone to refuse an invitation to visit school when his special interest is being presented. It is difficult for him to refuse if he is the only guest, or one of two or three invited. Invitations are more readily accepted for the person to look and listen than to speak.

But the classroom visitor who meets a class that has been studying his specialty will always speak, and he will be besieged with questions. All of the questions arising in the preparation of the exhibit, and not answered clearly by the books and materials, should be saved for the guest. Often the guest will want to return, bringing materials of his own. He knows that he will have an interested and informed audience. The use of classroom guests helps children to learn the art of conversation, and it helps them to understand that the possession of some knowledge of a person's field opens many possibilities of learning.

Pupil specialties

Pupil specialties offer good opportunities in social studies. If every child has a specialty that deals with some person, place, event, product, or period, the classroom may be very much enriched. Specialties also give the child a feeling of importance in the classroom. Too often he is merely one of a number of competitors having the same information nobody especially cares about. Specialties are highly useful for rapid learners, but they are needed equally by slow learners who often are submerged in classroom competition.

Specialties also help the child to learn the importance of individual initiative in learning, and they aid in establishing habits of the voluntary use of reading. They may replace unnecessary skills practice for the rapid learner. At the same time, they may enable him to provide enrichment to the content subjects rather than unfair competition with slower learners in textbook mastery. The specialties may be temporary, changing from time to time as the course of study moves along, or they may be more permanent.

It is not necessary to conduct "unit teaching" in order to utilize individual assignments. They may be made at any time when future topics indicate that a special report from an individual or group of children would be helpful.

Both classroom visitors and pupil specialties apply as much to other areas of reading as to social-studies reading.

"World about you" reading

One of the most rewarding uses of reading is that which relates to the pupil's immediate world. Reading will make all objects and activities full of interest and promise. This type of reading requires an abundance of many kinds of reading resources: catalogues, handbooks, brochures, manuals, pamphlets, magazines, newspapers, directions, labels, advertising materials, trade journals and publications, government bulletins, and many various types of specialized publications.

If the child is particularly interested in sports, he will discover that he may learn a great deal about tennis, football, baseball, hockey, basketball, wrestling, boxing, gymnastics, or golf through reading. The outdoor enthusiast will find books on hunting, fishing, camping, sailing, hiking, mountain climbing, forestry, wild flowers, ferns, birds, snakes, trees, geology, semiprecious stones, uranium finding, gold mining, stars, and weather. The mechanically inclined or the craftsman will find help in carpentry, wood finishing, cabinetmaking, automobiles, airplanes, diesel engines, electricity, foundry work, bridge or dam construction, railroads, highways, radio, television, fireplaces, housebuilding, bricklaying, roofing, plumbing, and painting.

Arts and crafts are represented in reading through materials on weaving, basketry, carving, painting, metalwork, paper craft, printing, photography, furniture making, upholstering, water colors, etching, jewelry making. Music has a literature of its own: composers and compositions, operas and symphonies, history of music, biographies of musicians, the development of musical instruments of many kinds, choral singing, orchestral conducting, modern music, musical journals, self-teaching books for various instruments, musical appreciation books, music magazines. The collector will find company in books, whether he is collecting stamps, coins, stones, buttons, butterflies, leaves, flowers, lace, pewter, glass, dishes, guns, books, phonograph records, or antiques.

The homemaker has a host of possibilities for use of reading: cooking and meal planning have a rich literature; the same is true of sewing, knitting, interior decoration. The person concerned about indoor recreation will find books on card games, group games, party planning, puzzles, chess, billiards, and a rich variety of commercial games. Almost anything a person may wish to do, almost any product or object, almost any vocation or hobby has a wealth of reading material around it.

Too often, these rich areas of reading are left untouched by the school curriculum and the school library. In library planning, there must be room for books on arts and crafts, sports, industrial arts, homemaking. In many schools where these subjects are taught, only a few skills are offered, and these are done through imitation of the teacher. The shop teacher, the athletic coach, the home-economics teacher, and sometimes even the science teacher may fail to start the children on the delights and possibilities of reading in their specialties.

Consumer education, although seldom taught in schools, has infinite possibilities for reading; intelligent buying requires information about the things or services being purchased. Not only is the person who buys without first discovering qualities, values, choices, unlikely to receive full value for his money; he will be unable to appreciate what he has purchased even though it does represent excellent value.

In teaching the "world about you" reading, constant interplay must be sought between reading and action. A collection of semiprecious stones offers nothing to the person ignorant of them. But a book on semiprecious stones is of little value to the person who is unable to see the stones themselves and to make field trips in search of such stones in his vicinity. A boy who reads baseball, but never plays or watches it, does not get full value from his reading. The stamp collector who only reads, never collects, might be called a "stamp dreamer," but never a collector. Reading about crafts without actually working at them also seems a weak way of enjoying reading. The reverse, however—that of pursuing action without reading—seems equally narrow in reward.

Reading about the objects and activities in the immediate world is especially suitable for pupil specialties. A search for specialized interest through the check list provided in Chapter 7 will often discover interests on which specialties can be built. The child will need help at first in obtaining books and reading materials, but after the first few are found, he will discover many other possibilities. There should be a place in the classroom program for "one-man shows" or specialty reports or displays. A specialty bulletin board or exhibit table may be assigned each week to a different child or group of children.

Reading for attitudes, ideals, and personal growth

While many types of reading may serve the purposes of molding personality, there is a place for guiding individual children into the kind of reading that specifically relates to the establishment of character values. Reading in the fields of religion, personal problems, attitudes, and conduct will be helpful to most children. Attitudes of courage, responsibility, generosity, ambition, initiative, and enterprise may assist children to establish standards of conduct for themselves.

Uses of current materials

All of the classifications of reading are represented in magazines, newspapers, trade journals, and various specialty publications. Many people are not aware of the great variety of weekly and monthly magazines of value for specialized groups of readers. In the intermediate and upper grades it is worth while to arrange a display of current magazines of all of the types that might be of interest. News dealers and librarians are often willing to assist in providing such a display of magazines.

Catalogues are a highly desirable source of information which should be called to the attention of the prospective user of reading. Every child whose parents patronize mail-order establishments will spend hours in studying the profusion of articles offered in the large catalogues. He learns of the existence and availability of many objects; he knows the many possibilities of choice, and reads descriptions of their qualities; he knows their current cost. Garden catalogues are a "must" for every gardener. Through them he begins gardening in his mind long before winter is over. Much is to be learned through specialty catalogues. The reading program should somehow provide a display of the rewards that can come from catalogue reading.

Government publications, trade publications, travel publications, timetables, "how-to-do it" periodicals, all have a place in the program of the use of reading. The lists of free and inexpensive teaching materials, as well as the specialized bulletins and charts sent out by commercial concerns, are useful in many phases of teaching. Occasionally some excessively timid educator is unwilling to use materials that contain advertising. The child has plenty of exposure to advertising on television and radio, and is not much affected by it. If the advertising material is overdone or too blatant, of course the material should not be used. But much of the material published by commercial concerns in the United States is valuable and extremely well presented.

Newspapers provide the opportunity to keep up with current happenings. A child too young to follow the adult newspapers will find his "My Weekly Reader" suited to his interests. As he gets older, he will read various sections of the regular newspaper, following sports, local news, and foreign news. Newspaper materials that relate to things studied in the classroom often give the lift of recency and reality.

Planning the use of reading program

It is obviously impossible to teach all of the uses of reading in any one year in school. However, the program may begin in first grade or even in kindergarten through having many kinds of books available for the teacher to read to the children. A child's acquaintance with bird books and flower books may begin very early; he listens to poetry and stories; he discovers that older people find many answers to questions from encyclopedias and dictionaries; he learns that cookbooks tell how to make cake and candy. In later grades he will continue to use adults to help him with references, but he will find an increasing amount of information that he may be able to obtain by himself.

Teachers vary in their interests, just as children do. A group of elementary-school teachers who are interested in giving children wider experiences may do cooperative planning in teaching different uses of reading in different grades. Teachers also gain from having specialties, and each may choose the particular specialty in the uses of reading which she can do best. The opportunities for planning are outlined in the following assignment used in a course for teachers-in-service.

Assignment: Planning a year's program in teaching the use of reading

The child does not acquire initiative in using reading for its many delights and purposes merely by covering the stories in the basal reader and doing some time-filling reading of fiction. The teacher needs to plan class activities that demonstrate to the child the riches reading has to offer.

From the lectures and from her reading the teacher should choose those topics and activities that seem to her best suited to the present needs of her pupils and to her own interests and skills in teaching. When she has decided on the topics and activities of the *use of reading* program, she should make her plans for the current semester or for the year. Some suggestions that may help teachers to plan a year's use of reading program are given below and on page 330.

1. Which of the following uses of imaginative reading will you include in your planning?

Fiction (book clubs, story hours, pupil specialties, book reports, records of extent and types of reading, library cooperation, class library, book projects, and so on).

Plays and dramatization (play reading, play writing, spontaneous dramatization, marionettes, shadow plays, radio or television performances, movies, reports on television, radio, movie shows, and the like).

Poetry and choral readings (class activities, small-group activities, recordings, responsive readings, various types of choral reading, memorization, pupil specialties, and so on).

Humor, mythology, folklore, yarns, and other kinds of imaginative reading.

2. What topics and activities in your use of reading program will you include in history and travel reading which requires making real the far away and long ago?

Trips, motion pictures, dramatization, classroom visitors, museums, collections, pictures, objects, specialties, projects, units, biography, recordings, construction, hobbies, maps, charts, graphs, drawing, art, and the like.

3. What will you do with the "world about you" uses of reading, which adds meaning and enrichment to the current activities of the child? (Various sciences, nature, weather, stars, insects, birds, animals, machines, airplanes, gardening, chemistry, manufacturing processes, all types of products and things we use, arts and crafts, fine arts and music, sports, hobbies, outdoor life, and the like.)

Projects, units, visits, exhibits, classroom visitors, pupil reports, motion pictures, visual and auditory aids, construction, collections, pupil specialities, free materials of all kinds, personal specialized library, and the like.

4. Will you include reading about personal and social problems?

Religion, courtesy, responsibility, courage, personal qualities, bibliotherapy, self-development.

5. How about the use of current materials? Magazines, newspapers, catalogues, television, radio, motion pictures, free materials, community projects, national events. What other uses of reading will you include in your planning?

In making your plans for the semester or the year keep the following things in mind:

1. That *individual initiative* in the use of reading is the end sought by the teacher of reading.

2. That high motivation of reading through class-related activities is excellent, but that the final use of reading is through the child's individual effort.

3. That a few activities, well planned and ready for use with the actual materials and much of the planning done, is better than a "firm resolve" to use a rich variety of activities in many different fields without specific plans.

4. That you should select those things best suited both to your own talents and skill in teaching and also to the current needs and interests of your class.

5. That lists of "objectives" and professional generalizations about the use of reading will not replace specific planning in teaching the uses of reading.

6. That personalized plans—"I will do the following"—is better than "the teacher should."

INSTRUCTIONAL MATERIALS IN READING

Prepared by Lorraine E. Tolman, Librarian,
Boston University School of Education

Books about books for children

Arbuthnot, May Hill. *Children and Books*. New York: Scott, Foresman and Company, 1947
May be used either as a basic text or supplementary reading by students of children's literature. Reproductions and well chosen illustrations appear throughout the book as well as study suggestions and bibliographies.

Eaton, Anne Thaxter. *Reading with Children*. New York: The Viking Press, Inc., 1943
An enjoyable discussion of children's books, covering Unicorns and Common

Creatures, Roundabout the Earth, Through Magic Doorways, Nonsense Is Fun, and many other topics. Bibliographies accompany each chapter.

Eaton, Anne Thaxter. *Treasure for the Taking*. New York: The Viking Press, Inc., 1946
An attractive bibliography with brief but complete annotations and evaluations. Beginning with picture books and easy reading, it covers many topics of interest to boys and girls, such as pets, birds and insects, folk tales and wonder stories, prehistoric times, out of doors, poetry, plays that are fun to read, and plays to act. Arranged by grade and subject levels from easy reading through high school.

Hazard, Paul. *Books, Children and Men*. Boston: The Horn Book, Inc., 1947
A penetrating analysis and criticism of children's literature the world over. Well written; enjoyable reading.

Meigs, Cornelia, and Others. *A Critical History of Children's Literature*. New York: The Macmillan Company, 1953
A comprehensive study of the entire field. The last part, written by Ruth Viguers, deals with the years from 1920 to 1950, with separate chapters on significant subject areas and types.

Smith, Lillian H. *The Unreluctant Years: A Critical Approach to Children's Literature*. Chicago: The American Library Association, 1953
A consideration of the literary aspect of children's books, with criteria for evaluating books of each type.

Magazines for children and young people
Hazen, Meribah (ed.). *Subject Index to Children's Magazines*. Madison 5, Wisconsin: 301 Palomino Lane, 1948 to present
Of particular service to elementary school people. Indexes such magazines as *Plays, Boys' Life, Nature Magazine,* and *Open Road*. Valuable for unit material on all topics.

Martin, Laura K. *Magazines for School Libraries*. New York: H. W. Wilson Company, 1950
A handy tool for use in selecting the magazines for the school library.

All-purpose tools
Children's Catalogue. Eighth Edition, revised 1951. New York: H. W. Wilson Company
A dictionary catalogue of 3400 children's books with many analytical entries. Has four parts: alphabetical listing; classified list, list by grades, directory of publishers. Information on prices, editions, publication dates, brief annotations. Kept up to date through annual supplements and revised every five years.

Educational Film Guide. New York: H. W. Wilson Company, 1936 to present
An annotated index to 16 mm. motion pictures. It contains a brief summary of each film, its length, whether sound or silent, color or black and white, grade level, price for purchase or rental, or free loan, and source where it may be obtained. Three quarterly issues with yearly cumulation in August.

Elementary Teachers' Guide to Free Curriculum Materials. Randolph, Wisconsin: Educator's Progress Service, 1954. Annual publication.

Filmstrip Guide. New York: H. W. Wilson Company, 1947 to present
Lists filmstrips released after January 1, 1947. On all subjects, sponsored, free, or purchase.

Rue, Eloise. *Subject Index to Books for Intermediate Grades.* Chicago: American Library Association, 1950
Its topical listing of chapters or sections of books makes it particularly useful in preparing supplementary reading bibliographies for units.

Rue, Eloise. *Subject Index to Books for Primary Grades.* Chicago: American Library Association, 1946
A detailed topical indexing of books, of use to preschool as well as primary teachers.

Sources of Free and Inexpensive Educational Materials. Chicago: Field Enterprises, Educational Division, 1955

Specialized indexes
Poetry, drama, and fairy tale indexes

Brewton, John E., and Brewton, Sara W. *Index to Children's Poetry.* New York: H. W. Wilson Company, 1942. First supplement, 1954
A dictionary index to 130 collections of poems for children and youth. Entries are of four types: title, subject, author, first-line. May well serve as basic poetry bibliography for librarians, teachers, parents.

Lease, Ruth, and Siks, Geraldine B. *Creative Dramatics in Home, School, and Community.* New York: Harper and Brothers, 1952

Ward, Winifred. *Playmaking with Children from Kindergarten to High School.* New York: Appleton-Century-Crofts, Inc., 1947

West, Dorothy H., and Peake, Dorothy M. *Play Index; and Index to 2616 Plays in 1138 Volumes.* New York: H. W. Wilson Company, 1953

Science indexes

Hall, Elvajean. *At Home in the Universe.* Boston: Personal Book Shop, 1954
This listing of science books includes both the natural and physical sciences, and extends in grade level from primary through junior high.

Large print indexes

Matson, Charlotte, and Larson, Lola. *Books for Tired Eyes*. Chicago: American Library Association, 1947
This catalogue is of particular value for librarians and teachers who wish to order books of large print for children of low visual acuity.

Social studies indexes

Spiesike, Alice W. *Bibliography of Textbooks in the Social Studies for Elementary and Secondary Schools,* bulletin No. 23. Washington: National Council for the Social Studies, 1949

Government bulletins

Representative Government Best Sellers. Washington, D.C.: U.S. Government Printing Office
This listing, frequently revised, along with such pertinent U.S. Government price-lists as "Forestry" or "Health" and the semi-monthly publication titled *Selected U.S. Government Publications,* may be obtained at very little expense. Will open up a wealth of valuable pamphlet material.

Choral reading

Brown, Helen A., and Heltman, Harry J. *Let's Read Together Poems: An Anthology of Verse for Choral Reading in Kindergarten and Primary Grades.* Evanston, Ill.: Row, Peterson and Company, 1949

Hemphill, Irene. *Choral Speaking and Speech Improvement.* Darien, Connecticut: Educational Publishing Corporation, 1945

Keppie, Elizabeth E. *Speech Improvement Through Choral Speaking.* Magnolia, Massachusetts: The Expression Company, 1942

Building your library

Cundiff, Ruby E. *Recommended Reference Books for the Elementary School Library.* Chicago: Wilcox and Follett Company, 1949

Hall, Elvajean. *Books to Build On.* New York: R. R. Bowker Company, 1955
Particularly valuable for schools just setting up new library collections.

Snow, Miriam B. *Basic Book Collection for Elementary Grades.* Chicago: American Library Association, 1951

SUGGESTIONS FOR FURTHER READING

Bond, Guy L., and Wagner, Eva B. *Teaching the Child to Read.* New York: The Macmillan Company, 1950. Chapters 12 and 14.

Durrell, Donald D., and Savignano, Leonard J. "Classroom Enrichment through Pupil Specialties." *Journal of Education,* Feb. 1956. Pages 1–31.

Harris, Albert J. *How to Increase Reading Ability,* Third Edition. Longmans, Green and Company, Inc., 1956. Chapter 17.

Horn, Ernest. *Methods of Instruction in the Social Studies.* New York: Charles Scribner's Sons, 1937. Chapter 5.

McKee, Paul. *The Teaching of Reading in the Elementary School.* Boston: Houghton Mifflin Company, 1948. Chapter 17.

Russell, David H. *Children Learn to Read.* Boston: Ginn and Company, 1949. Chapters 12 and 13.

Smith, Dora V. "Literature and Personal Reading," in *Reading in the Elementary School,* The Forty-Eighth Yearbook of the National Society for the Study of Education. Chicago: University of Chicago Press, 1949.

Witty, Paul A. *Reading in Modern Education.* Boston: D. C. Heath and Company, 1949. Chapter and Appendixes A and B.

Yoakam, Gerald A. *Basal Reading Instruction.* New York: McGraw-Hill Book Company, 1955. Chapters 13 and 14.

CHAPTER 15 Special Reading Services

AN INSTRUCTIONAL PROGRAM that provides fully for individual differences should make remedial-reading classes unnecessary. In such a reading program, remedial instruction is simply good first teaching in the classroom, fitting the materials to the child and providing for weaknesses as they appear. The child never repeats the work of the previous year but simply continues his progress on the level he has attained to date. Adjustments to learning rate and to individual needs are made at all levels of instruction.

Schools should not abandon the hope that remedial-reading classes and reading failures may be made unnecessary. Marked progress in reading instruction has reduced the number of children failing in primary grades. In many schools reading difficulty in the primary grades has been virtually eliminated through early and specific reading-readiness programs, followed by effective word-recognition and word-analysis instruction. Although there will always be some pupils who progress more slowly than others, it seems quite possible that schools will generally accept the proposition that any child who can learn to talk can learn to read. The intellectual task of learning to read appears to be no more difficult than learning to understand speech. The educational problem is to search for ways to provide the motivation and steps to learning that will enable children to handle visual symbols.

In-service education of teachers becomes increasingly important in a time of serious teacher shortage. Most school systems have the problem of rapidly changing staffs and the employment of teachers who are inadequately prepared. Such teachers will need guidance in analyzing difficulties, preparing and adapting methods and materials to provide for individual differences, planning effective reading programs.

The major jobs ahead in the teaching of reading are teacher education and the preparation of more effective teaching materials. While both approaches are promising, the more immediate task is that of teacher education. Even the most carefully designed basal-reading system, provided with tests for analyses of pupil need and carefully designed supplementary materials for overcoming common weaknesses, cannot be self-administering. Poor teaching can defeat the best-designed reading system; good teaching can compensate for most of the weaknesses of a poor system.

The reading consultant

For a number of years, schools most alert to reading problems have provided remedial-reading teachers to help children who had failed in reading. While remedial-reading classes have helped large numbers of children, many school people were concerned with the fact that such classes did nothing to help prevent reading failures. The regular classrooms continued to provide more children with reading difficulty than the remedial classes could accept. It was also apparent that the remedial teacher's success was attained by techniques that could be used in the regular classroom. As a result, many schools have created the position of reading consultant, whose job is to assist teachers to provide more effective reading programs.

Typical duties of the reading consultant are described in the announcement of the position in the New Britain, Connecticut, schools:

Title: Reading Consultant in the Elementary Schools.

Statement of duties: The Reading Consultant will be directly responsible to the Superintendent of Schools and work as a member of the Superintendent's staff on instruction. He (she) will be expected to cooperate closely with the Elementary Supervisor, Curriculum Coordinator, Testing Services, Health Services, and Guidance Department in the performance of the duties noted below:

1. Assist elementary teachers:

   a) Particularly with pupils in the lower third of the reading class.

   b) In the exchange of successful reading practices.

   c) In providing materials of instruction.

   d) To analyze pupil needs in reading and to make provisions for them.

   e) By acting as consultant with parents at a teacher's request.

   f) By acting as consultant with PTA groups at the principal's request.

2. Assist in the program for first-grade admission and analysis of pupil needs.

3. Advise on the prevention of reading difficulties in grade one—or assist kindergarten and first-grade teachers to provide perceptual background for reading.

4. Provide intensive analysis of children with particularly severe reading difficulties, obtaining the cooperation of other services when necessary.

5. Assist with class organization for remedial instruction, or with all-school attacks on the reading program.

6. Assist in the development of reading programs for gifted children and rapid learners in reading.

7. Provide demonstrations, discussions, materials of instruction useful in the total reading program.

8. Curriculum relationship—help with study skills and abilities in all subject areas.

9. Help with research studies related to the reading program.

10. Assist with the development of plans for increased library services and with instructional aids related to the reading program.

11. Assist with the development of a sound public relations program regarding instruction in reading; interpret the reading program to the public and parents.

12. Act in an advisory capacity with secondary instructional staff in the development of a reading program for all pupils.

Special qualifications:

1. The applicant should possess a sound philosophy of education and be thoroughly familiar with the total instructional program at the elementary level.

2. The applicant must possess those personal qualities which will gain the professional respect of members of the teaching staff as well as the general public.

3. The applicant should be a well-adjusted individual and should have demonstrated considerable ability in past teaching assignments.

4. The applicant should have the faculty of adjusting to situations caused by many and varied interruptions.

5. The applicant must, by her past training and experience, have demonstrated a thorough knowledge of the reading program—both developmental and remedial—at the elementary level.

Experience:

1. Not less than five years of successful classroom teaching experience at the primary or intermediate level.

2. Some form of experience in teacher leadership activity such as supervision, college teaching, teacher workshop leadership.

3. Work in a reading clinic or some comparable experience.

Professional preparation:

1. The applicant must be eligible for certification by the State Department of Education as a *Supervisor of Special Fields—Reading.*

2. The applicant must have the master's degree, preferably work beyond, with specialization in the reading field.

3. The applicant must have academic training in the following areas:

    a) Tests and measurements.
    b) Psychological and physical factors in reading.
    c) Child psychology.
    d) Study of school failures.
    e) Child development and guidance.
    f) Reading clinic—including modern teaching aids to reading.
    g) Courses in developmental and remedial reading.

4. Supervised training in a reading clinic.

There are several points worthy of notice in the above description of the position of reading consultant. The first is the multiplicity of duties of the position. Obviously, all of these cannot be done at once. The reading consultant will be most effective if her first year is spent in preventing reading failures in grade one. During the first two weeks of school she should provide the teachers with the reading-readiness tests presented in Chapter 3 and also assist in administration of the tests and in planning suitable instruction based on the findings. The next few weeks should be spent in helping with the reading-readiness and the beginning-reading programs: helping to provide, build, duplicate, and exchange effective instructional materials; and being on call to assist teachers who have difficult problems. Since the same materials and techniques will be needed by other children in primary grades who are reading below primer level, the services might be extended to include such children.

Preventing first-grade failures will not seem as important to many school administrators as working with older pupils who have severe difficulty. However, there is no place in which greater rewards will be obtained than in assuring reading success in the first grade. The program at this level is always effective, as will be discovered by any before-and-after test comparison. There will be very few reading difficulties among first-grade pupils when a sound program is followed, and the success carries the pupil through the primary grades. The first-grade teachers will not need such help a second year, and the attention of the reading consultant may be directed toward intermediate grades.

If the pressure for remedial instruction in upper grades is too great to resist for a year, give the reading consultant the first semester free from duties other than the first-grade program. Or if two reading consultants are available, let one concentrate on primary grades and one on intermediate grades.

The reading consultant should be in classrooms as much as possible, studying the problems of slow-learning groups through teaching them in the classroom. Her position is that of assistant to the teachers, having full-time responsibility to assist them with slow learners in reading. Her work should not be cluttered with a multiplicity of committee duties: curriculum revision, textbook selection, bulletin writing, PTA planning. Nor should it be that of endless examinaticns of children followed by report making. Equally ineffective is the giving, the scoring, and the making of charts of standard reading tests. The job is in the classrooms, not in the office, except when needed classroom materials and plans are being prepared. Her full time should be devoted to helping teachers with specific instructional problems of children who are slow learners in reading. There is no need to search for a panacea which can be sent in a bulletin from the central office. There is no such panacea.

How many teachers may be served by a single reading consultant? The answer depends upon the services needed and expected. Ten to twenty single-unit schools may be readily served by a single reading consultant if the administration is willing to wait two or three years for the program to develop while primary-grade instruction is first cared for, followed by intermediate-grade instruction. If there is a rapid replacement of teachers, the reading consultant's task is more difficult. If schools are widely separated and group meetings of teachers infrequent, more assistance is needed. The more experienced reading consultant can assist a larger number of teachers, since she will have a rich supply of helps ready for any situation. The less experienced consultant can handle fewer teachers, since much of her time must be spent in developing effective materials. Even though her training gave her an ample supply of helps, she must learn effective methods of transmitting these helps and adapting them to local conditions.

Remedial-reading classes

Although the regular classroom teacher must assume major responsibility for reading instruction suited to the needs of children, some schools have many children who are so far behind the classes that special remedial reading instruction is necessary. Such classes are held under various names, such as "the reading clinic," "the reading workshop," "the reading club," "the reading laboratory," or the "special reading class." The commonest type of remedial class brings together small groups of children for thirty to sixty minutes of reading instruction each day.

The teacher of remedial reading should have special training and special aptitude for the work. She must have the ability to get on well with other teachers, with parents, and with children. Successful classroom experience is an indispensable background for remedial teaching. The fact that pupils selected for remedial instruction are those who have failed in regular classes should indicate that an apprentice or a beginning teacher should not be chosen for remedial teaching. The psychologist without teaching experience is usually quite helpless in reading classes. She looks for emotional intangibles rather than improved teaching. It is best to choose a teacher who has been successful in teaching the basic subjects and who maintains a cordial relationship with other teachers. The ability to analyze difficulties and to provide a variety of suitable remedial approaches can be learned through university courses or through reading and observation.

Organizing the remedial groups

Generally, pupils come from grade three and above for remedial instruction. Although children in grades one and two might profit greatly by extra help, the demand for remedial work is so great that only those children very severely retarded may be selected for special reading classes. Local considerations must be taken into account in organizing the classes. In favored communities, almost every child who reads a year or more below his grade may be given remedial instruction. In less favored communities, the standard for admission may require that the child be two years or more below the reading of his class before he is given special help. In communities where no special classes are provided for the mentally handicapped, remedial reading may be offered first to those children who have higher mental abilities, then to those with lower when places are available for them.

The selection of children for remedial groups should ordinarily be done at the end of the school year so that remedial instruction may start immediately in the fall. Some remedial teachers spend so much time in giving mental tests and reading analyses every fall that remedial instruction does not begin until after school has been under way two or three months. Spring planning for fall remedial instruction permits better scheduling of remedial classes, avoiding conflicts with essential instruction in regular classrooms and resulting in better integration of the remedial program with classwork.

Some of the factors that should be taken into account in organizing remedial groups are the following:

1. Remedial groups should be kept small enough to permit close attention to pupil needs. Groups should usually be not more than five or six, although they may be larger if the pupils are very similar in reading level.

2. When possible, all members of the group should come from the same classroom so that they may help each other with extra reading practice when they return from remedial teaching. If they come from different classrooms, there should be at least two pupils from any classroom so that they may be paired for homeroom practice.

3. Children in any group should be of nearly the same age. This makes for better working relationships and more suitable choice of material for the age level.

4. Admission to remedial classes should be made by consultation of classroom teacher and remedial teacher. Neither standard test scores alone nor teacher judgment alone should be the basis for selection. The remedial class should not become a place to store "difficult" children. The main consideration should be the relative possibilities of progress in remedial classes as compared to regular classes.

5. Daily instruction in remedial reading should be provided wherever possible. A child who is severely retarded will not overcome his difficulty by two or three short periods of remedial instruction each week. Many remedial teachers are "spread too thin," dividing their time among a great many pupils in two or more schools.

6. There should be time between classes for clearing up after one group and setting the stage for the next one. One period should be reserved each day for visiting pupils and teachers in regular classrooms or for preparing instructional materials.

Coordination of remedial instruction with
regular classroom instruction

Effective remedial teaching requires that the classroom teacher and the remedial teacher share the planning for children in remedial classes. Teachers must not work at cross-purposes, with well-adjusted material in the remedial class but extremely difficult material in the regular class. Remedial reading should be thought of as a unified program for the child's school reading, not as unrelated extra help. A cooperative approach will enable the children to continue with the same material in both rooms, with the skills taught in the remedial class being put to use in the regular class.

Some of the possibilities for planning of this kind are the following:

1. The same books are used for reading instruction in both the remedial and the regular class. The remedial teacher concentrates on preparatory word-and-phrase work, review of previously taught words, word analysis, and special help on weak skills. The classroom teacher presents the stories and is especially concerned with ideas, appreciations, recall, and the application of reading skills.

2. The remedial teacher may be in charge of all phases of the child's reading normally presented in the "reading period." The classroom teacher may be concerned with reading in social studies, science, and independent reading. The remedial teacher may emphasize word-analysis instruction, using some of the words from lessons to be taught in the regular classroom. The classroom teacher may take the responsibility for word meanings and for improvement of recall.

3. When the two teachers agree upon the methods and materials to be used with the children for the following month, they may decide to divide the responsibilities differently for specified periods. Both may concentrate on the same skills, with materials being prepared and exchanged. Initial presentation of lessons may be made in one class, with the other providing practice and review.

4. Instead of working with pupils every day, the remedial teacher may occasionally spend the period in preparation of reading aids to be used in the regular classroom. This is particularly useful when children have the ability to master the regular lessons with the help of glossaries, graded study guides, and other aids to comprehension.

5. Often it will be advantageous for the remedial work to be given in the regular classroom rather than in a separate room. The remedial teacher is a "helping teacher" or an assistant to the regular teacher, sharing the responsibility for the slow learners.

6. While attendance at remedial classes should be regular, sometimes special events in the classroom must supersede remedial work. When this is necessary, the remedial teacher should be notified in advance.

The relationship between the classroom teacher and the remedial teacher may sometimes need to be clearly defined. When differences of opinion arise about what should be done, the classroom teacher's suggestions should ordinarily have priority since she has the greater responsibility for the child's education. Although the remedial teacher may have a superior knowledge of reading methods, her effectiveness will depend upon her ability to persuade rather than upon delegated authority.

The remedial-reading homeroom

Some situations may call for the child's being assigned to a remedial-reading homeroom for all of his instruction. The remedial-reading homeroom differs from the regular classroom only in selection of pupils, in precision and variety of adjustment to individual differences in language-arts instruction. The emphasis of most of the planning is on improvement of reading, spelling, and composition. Children's reading difficulties are carefully analyzed, and a greater share of the class time is spent on reading skills and interests. There is a rich variety of materials for overcoming difficulties usually encountered. Both skills and content motivation are constantly employed, and much of the activity is in pupil teams of two to five. The basic vocabulary is given emphasis through its appearance in reading, spelling, handwriting, and composition.

The remedial homeroom is more than a place of drill on reading and language skills. Guidance in independent reading is given a place of importance, and the classroom library is planned with proper regard to interests of pupils as well as to levels of difficulty. History, geography, science, art, and music may be integrated to serve the ends of growth in broad aspects of language-arts learning. Enriching activities, such as field trips, dramatization, construction, and exhibits, are a part of the classroom procedure for broadening experiences. Lantern slides, motion pictures, and other aids to motivation and development of meanings are used.

The remedial teacher must be permitted a great deal of freedom in choice of materials, methods, and curriculum content. The time allotments for the various subjects should be flexible, with much more time devoted to reading and language than is usual in the ordinary classroom. Every provision should be made for rapid growth in reading and language skills, even at the cost of dropping entirely some of the other subjects of the regular curriculum.

The supervising principal in the reading program

If the supervising principal is well informed on the specifics of reading instruction and if time is available to give the necessary attention, much of the work of the reading consultant can be performed by the supervising principal. There are many ways in which the principal can provide a lift to the reading program:

1. *Assisting in the administration of informal tests to discover reading needs of pupils.* Individual testing is particularly important for the principal since it puts him in direct touch with children. He should leave the group tests for the classroom teacher. The principal should test the slower learners so that he will be aware of the teacher's problems. Tests especially important are those determining the suitability of the books being used by children and those testing word-analysis abilities. Since the provision of textbooks is partly the responsibility of the principal, it is useful for him to know the

problems of purchasing instructional materials which adapt to different grade levels in a single classroom. Word-analysis abilities often are not well developed, especially in intermediate grades, and the principal should share in planning the attack on the problem. If word analysis is to be combined with spelling, this curricular change will need administrative approval.

2. *Providing leadership in cooperative attack on the reading program.* Since several teachers may have similar problems, the principal can facilitate the exchange of effective practices and materials. The principal will assist whenever there appears to be a need for regrouping of pupils for more effective instruction. For example, if several teachers in intermediate grades have only one or two nonreaders, these pupils may be brought together for reading instruction so that only one preparation is necessary rather than several. If the informal analyses from all classrooms are compared, it may be discovered that children from different classrooms might be served well by a temporary regrouping of pupils for intensive instruction in a particular skill. If weakness in one or two essential abilities seems to be characteristic of pupils in all grades, cooperative planning may help to improve the situation.

3. *Organizational and curricular decisions in relation to the reading program.* Although departmentalization and ability grouping have a number of disadvantages which make teachers and principals justly cautious about their use, temporary or partial use of either may sometimes be advantageous for both teacher and pupil. If one intermediate-grade teacher is particularly successful with word-analysis skills while another is not, they may find it desirable to arrange a temporary "departmentalization"—for a six-weeks' period or for three days a week—with the teachers exchanging rooms or pupils being regrouped from both rooms to receive intensive word-analysis instruction. An examination of the special abilities of teachers may often show that partial, temporary, or occasional trading of classrooms may be desirable. Teachers who are especially gifted in the teaching of poetry, science, social studies, oral reading, dramatization, composition, arithmetic, art, music, crafts, or physical education, and

the like, may serve pupils better if they occasionally appear in class-rooms other than their own.

The division between skills and content instruction, between text-book lessons and project work, often provides opportunity for curricular variation. Teachers and pupils may find it profitable to spend a few weeks or a few days a week on intensive skills instruction in the various subjects; then on other weeks or other days, devote the whole time to larger projects. It has not been demonstrated that it is necessary that every week must contain the same amount or type of instruction in every subject. If it seems too extreme to set aside whole days or whole weeks for large projects, then skills instruction may be continued for slow learners during part of each day. Although variations in scheduling may not be necessary, the possibilities should be considered if individual teachers wish to try them.

4. *Special provisions for rapid learners.* It will sometimes be evident that rapid learners are being overlooked in the instructional program of the school. The principal may encourage teachers to discover better ways to serve them. Such pupils may be permitted to complete skills work at their own rate. They may complete the work of a month, two months, a semester, or a whole year in such skills as handwriting, spelling, arithmetic. The time thus saved may be devoted to specialized work in other subjects or in desirable personal specialties. Attention should be paid to cooperative projects with less capable pupils, assisting in classroom instruction, and in other ways keeping the child a valued member of his class.

5. *The building of school libraries and expanding library services.* Few elementary schools have adequate libraries. Only the principal, working in cooperation with teachers, children, parents, and the school administration can provide the leadership necessary for building and servicing the school library. The library can often be the center of school instruction, with the librarian being the best informed person in regard to the type and quality of instruction in the various classrooms. A combination of principal-librarian has certain advantages. The library might well include teaching aids, films, recordings, and professional books for teachers.

6. *Encouraging desirable unique achievements among pupils and teachers.* Every person likes to be a part of a "distinguished" organization. There are many opportunities for a classroom or a school to emphasize special achievement in various activities related to reading. Chapter 14, on the uses of reading, should suggest many possibilities of this type: dramatizations, classroom visitors, pupil specialties, poetry and choral reading, humor, history projects, reading before travel, correspondence with children in other places, "world about you" reading, use of current materials in reading. Or the need of being unique may be served by emphasis on oral reading, on pupil instructional teams, on word-meaning development, on written and oral recall, on quality of oral reports and group projects.

The freedom to follow such classroom specialties must be earned by having a sound skills program. If parents feel that the fundamental instruction is not well done, any unique program will be criticized as distracting attention from the main problem. Unique achievements need not be publicized; it is enough that both pupils and parents feel that they are being especially well served.

7. *Encouraging teacher initiative in improving the reading program.* Attention is called to Chapter 1, in which the need for enterprise in improving reading instruction is emphasized. We tend too much to the conventional and the "standard practice" even when the result is mediocre. Each teacher should be permitted to choose her own basal-reading systems and instructional materials, try new methods of instruction, rearrange daily or weekly time schedules, make new subject combinations or other program changes, *if* she has a clear idea of the goals she is trying to reach and if her previous ventures have been sound. A regimented predictable program seems easier to administer, but it often leads to low pupil and teacher morale. Unnecessary regimentation often arises in the attempt to improve the practices of poor teachers, and it is often given the semblance of "democracy" by being derived through committee action of group vote. Freedom to improve one's service to children is highly important to superior teachers, and any incursion on that freedom should be resisted by both teacher and principal.

CHAPTER 16 **Reading Disability: Causes and Analysis**

In Chapter 1, it was noted that reading difficulties caused little concern in public schools prior to the 1920's. Most poor readers left school as early as possible; the poor readers who remained in school were generally regarded as dull. When the wider use of intelligence tests showed that many of these children were of normal intelligence, and when the depression of the 1930's and various other factors prolonged school attendance, it became essential to acknowledge the existence of the problem of reading disability and to correct it or explain it.

Unfortunately, educational techniques for prevention and correction of reading difficulties have been slow in development and acceptance. This left the field open to those people who have attempted to "explain" reading difficulties on all sorts of neurological and psychological hypotheses. Some of the "mystery" explanations for lack of reading readiness were discussed in Chapter 3.

As we progress in the educational analysis of reading difficulties, it becomes increasingly clear that most of the failures in reading rest upon difficulties and confusions in the learning process. Thus the necessity to seek elaborate psychological causes is considerably diminished.

Educational causes of reading difficulty

Many children learn to read satisfactorily through following the regular instructional procedures presented in school. Others of equal intelligence have difficulty from the very beginning and at every subsequent step. To one who has examined the difficulties of many thousands of these children and has directed the remedial instruction restoring them to normal reading, it becomes increasingly evident that learning to read is a highly complex process providing countless opportunities for confusion in learning.

Almost every one of the sixteen chapters in this volume on improving reading instruction is concerned specifically with the prevention or the correction of difficulties in the many sub-skills of reading. These sub-skills of reading may be summarized in the following way:

1. *Lack of adequate background to perform the reading task set.* The lack of background for reading is particularly evident in beginning reading where children come to first grade without the visual and auditory background to acquire a sight vocabulary. It constantly reappears in reading situations at all levels of instruction. The child may lack meaning vocabulary background for certain social-studies or science material; he may not have the word-analysis skills adequate for recognition of words whose meaning he knows; or he may be confronted with comprehension tasks for which his experience is inadequate.

2. *Failure to master the early elements on which later abilities are based.* There is a great deal of teaching that does not result in learning. Even though the child has been presented with the opportunity to acquire a sight vocabulary, to learn applied phonics, or to summarize orally materials he has read, his learning may have been fragmentary.

3. *Confusions resulting from instruction not correctly adjusted to the level and learning rate of the child.* The child in fourth grade who reads on a primer level will make little progress when he is con-

fronted with fourth-grade material; nor will second- or even first-grade material be suitable. If the pace of instruction is too fast for mastery of new skills, confusion and discouragement result for the child.

4. *The acquisition of faulty habits which impede progress.* All learning offers opportunity for errors. If a faulty technique continues, it remains a stumbling block to further progress until it is corrected. Learning to read is full of such opportunities.

Common faulty habits in children's reading are word-by-word reading, ignoring difficult words or failing to correct word errors, lip movements in silent reading, incorrect book position or poor reading posture, inattention to content, and failing to adjust speed to the reading task.

5. *Inability to acquire transfer skills—to discover the "system" and generalized abilities that apply to many situations.* A child who is unable to identify separate sounds in spoken words will be blocked in any attempt to learn to read a phonetic language. The acquisition of a high level of word analysis rests upon many transfer skills. The child's growth in meaning vocabulary through context clues rests upon a generalized habit. Abilities in recall and in thinking skills that are related to reading require the mastery of a "system" of approach.

6. *Lack of vigor in attack, resulting from continued failure and ineffective motivation.* Educational analysis seeks difficulties which may be corrected by specific teaching. It is the first and most promising approach to take in all types of learning difficulties. It gives the teacher a specific and orderly plan of remedial instruction and fixes the responsibility primarily in the school. Until the educational analysis is made and remedial instruction is provided, psychological studies of emotional problems, home factors, and personality factors are likely to be misleading. Emotional problems of children are usually the result of failure, rather than its cause. An effective remedial program which enlists the vigorous effort of the child and produces specific progress that he can see is usually the most effective psychological therapy for the child.

Physical causes of reading retardation

A number of physical conditions may be associated with slow learning in reading. Physical deficiencies include special sensory defects such as poor vision or hearing or more general bodily conditions such as low vitality due to malnutrition, low-grade infections, or internal glandular disturbances which produce inattention. Among children coming to reading clinics have been found chorea, rheumatic fever, malnutrition, anemia, low metabolism, as well as the more usual physical problems of children.

A child who fails to learn to read should have a thorough physical examination, including a careful check of vision and hearing. Defective vision or hearing might well be the sole cause of a reading difficulty. The more common eye defects among children with reading difficulty are farsightedness, astigmatism, and muscular imbalance. Nearsightedness occurs very rarely among children with reading difficulty. Other visual factors that may have some relation to reading difficulties are size of retinal fields, differences in ocular images, extreme sensitivity to light, and disease or fatigue factors which make persistent visual attention difficult. The usual school eye test—reading the Snellen Chart [1] at a distance of twenty feet—reveals only nearsightedness, the other defects of vision not being discovered by the test. An inexpensive screening test for discovering most of the visual problems has been developed by Eames.[2]

Reading disability and special mental functions

The early inability of school people to discover and correct the educational causes of reading difficulties left the field open to other approaches. A great deal of mystery was thrown about "nonreaders"

[1] A test for visual acuity, used to determine the smallest-sized letters that can be read at a standard distance.

[2] T. H. Eames, *Eames Eye Test*, Revised Edition (Yonkers, New York: World Book Company) .

and "specific reading disability" by some psychologists and psychiatrists. Neurological explanations included such items as "congenital word blindness," caused by "lesions in Broca's convolutions," and "strephosymbolia" or "lack of unilateral brain dominance." The latter condition was used to explain "reversal tendencies" in reading such as the reading of *was* as *saw*, *on* as *no*, and the confusion of *b*, *d*, *p*, and *q*. It is now recognized that these reversals are normal in all beginning reading, and are simply confusions resulting from inadequate perception.

At one time, techniques of reading analysis were filled with tests of general perceptual functions such as "visual and auditory memory span," "visual analysis and recognition," and "form-sound-meaning association." These tests included various complicated designs, nonsense syllables, and other material which had little meaning or interest for the child. The intent of such tests was to discover faulty associational tracts in the child's brain. However, it has long been recognized that such approaches are not helpful in the analysis of reading difficulty.

Emotional and personality factors

A highly popular approach to the study of reading difficulties is the search for emotional and personality factors presumed to produce a sort of mental haze that prevents normal learning. The search is largely centered in the home, with nothing left uncovered from conception onward. Everything from sibling rivalry to maladjustment in the sex life of the parents has been used to explain reading failure. The conclusion is usually that the child is confused, insecure, lacks affection or a sense of belonging. The parent either is overanxious about the child or has too little concern for the child's success; the child is suffering from inferiority feelings from any of numerous causes; or, if the child happens to be uncooperative in the schoolroom, "lack of discipline at home" usually appears in the school records.

Occasionally the reading of a child may be affected temporarily by home conditions. However, the emotions of children are usually attached to a specific situation, and the fact that a child is inattentive, discouraged, confused, or rebellious in one or more phases of his activity does not necessarily make it impossible for him to find delight in another. The only uniformly successful way to remove an emotional blocking that interferes with reading is to provide the child with a carefully graded and well-motivated reading program. It is natural for a child to have a dislike for reading after spending several years of unsuccessful attempts at learning to read. The motivation program is always of primary importance in remedial reading.

Clinical study of reading difficulties

The analysis of pupil's difficulties in reading ordinarily requires use of only the tests described in Chapters 3 and 5. Such informal tests and observation charts usually indicate the correct level on which to start remedial instruction, the specific reading abilities in which the child is weak, and the faulty habits and confusions that must be overcome in the remedial program. When informal tests and observation charts are properly used, it is usually unnecessary to refer many children to reading specialists or clinics for further analysis.

As a rule, the examination at a reading clinic or by a reading consultant differs from the informal classroom testing program only in the use of more detailed and more precise measurement and observation. In place of certain of the informal tests, individual diagnostic and achievement tests are employed. Some reading clinics use measuring instruments such as precision tachistoscopes, eye-movement cameras, stereoscopes, handedness tests, and other devices. While these instruments sometimes yield supplementary information about the child, none is particularly useful in the analysis of reading difficulty. Certain reading clinics include in their diagnostic efforts psychiatric examinations and detailed social histories. These yield interesting bits of personal history but rarely provide information of much significance to the remedial program. The analysis of reading difficulties is primarily an *educational-analysis* task, and is best done by an experienced teacher who knows the essential elements in reading instruction. The only outside assistance required for an analysis of difficulty in reading is that of thorough medical examinations, with special emphasis on sight and hearing.

The detailed analysis of reading difficulties usually includes the administration of measures of mental capacity for reading, measures of reading achievement, the observation of faulty habits in reading, and the consideration of certain items in regard to school and home background. If eye and ear examinations have not been given, tests to detect difficulties in sight and hearing should be used. The plan for analysis of reading difficulties outlined in this chapter includes only those items that are important in planning a remedial program.

Examination for physical and sensory defects

Before any intelligence or reading test is given to a child with severe reading difficulty, a careful medical examination should be made. The child may have a physical condition that seriously affects his performance on such tests. The medical examination will reveal no serious physical defects in the majority of children with reading difficulty, but in certain cases the medical findings are so important as to indicate that the educational difficulty may be only a minor manifestation of a problem essentially physical. Inattention and lack of persistence, which appear in spite of apparently good motivation, are sometimes found to be based on visual defects, hearing loss, low metabolism, or other conditions that interfere with attention. Teachers sometimes are reluctant to insist that parents spend time and money on sensory and medical examinations, since some parents feel cheated if the examinations reveal no defects. However, unless such examinations are made, the teacher can never be sure that the remedial program will be unimpeded by a physical handicap. The school nurse and school physician often give invaluable help in cases of educational failure.

The screening tests of vision, such as the *Eames Eye Test*,[3] will

[3] T. H. Eames, *Eames Eye Test*, Revised Edition (Yonkers, New York: World Book Company).

often show the presence of many of the visual defects common to reading difficulty. While some physicians frown upon the use of eye tests by teachers, the majority understand that the tests are designed to discover defects that would otherwise go undetected. A complete eye examination should be made by a competent eye specialist in all cases of reading difficulty, but if such an examination has not been made, the school screening test will be of value.

Measuring capacity for reading

The measure of mental capacity most commonly used in cases of reading difficulty is the *Revised Stanford-Binet Scale*.[4] This is an individual test requiring about an hour of testing time which should be given only by an examiner who has had formal training in its use. Any teacher of reading who expects to specialize in the correction of educational difficulties should have formal training in university courses.

Another suitable measure for discovering how well a child should be able to read is the *Durrell-Sullivan Reading Capacity Test*.[5] It is simple to give, and children always respond well to it. It measures listening comprehension through the use of picture responses, and age and grade norms are provided.

Neither the mental age from the *Stanford-Binet* nor the listening comprehension age from the *Durrell-Sullivan Reading Capacity Test* indicates a limit on the reading achievement of the child. A mental age is nothing more than an "average achievement" of the child on the materials tested. Half of all children read above their mental ages, half below. The same is true of the *Durrell-Sullivan Reading Capacity Test*, in which half of all children read above the "capacity" indicated by the test and an equal number below. There is no reason to suppose, therefore, that a child cannot make further progress when his reading grade is equal to his mental age. About four per cent of all pupils read two years or more above mental age or the "reading capacity" age.

---

[4] Lewis M. Terman and Maud A. Merrill. Published by **Houghton Mifflin Company**, **Boston, Massachusetts.**

[5] **Donald** D. Durrell and Helen B. Sullivan. Published by World Book **Company.**

The main reason for using measures of mental age or listening comprehension is to discover the amount of reading retardation below the child's "average achievement" independent of reading. Children should not be barred from remedial instruction because of mental-age findings, or because the reading achievement is at or above mental age. Nor can the rate of gain in remedial instruction be predicted from I.Q. or the difference between reading age and mental age. Gains in remedial instruction seem independent of such factors. If the child is bright enough to attend regular classes, and if his understanding of spoken language is reasonably good, he should be considered as eligible for remedial reading.

Educational analysis of reading difficulties

The method of educational analysis used in many reading clinics is the *Durrell Analysis of Reading Difficulty: New Edition.*[6] The following descriptions of materials and method are adapted from the manual of directions of that *Analysis.*

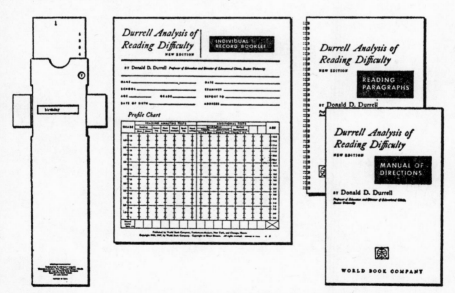

The *Durrell Analysis of Reading Difficulty* is designed for pupils from nonreaders to sixth-grade level. The child in the nonreader or

[6] Donald D. Durrell. Published by World Book Company, 1955.

preprimer level is studied through the use of tests of visual memory of word forms, auditory analysis of word elements, letter recognition on various levels, phonics, learning rate, and listening comprehension.

Tests for children from primer level through sixth grade are the following: listening comprehension, oral reading, silent reading, word recognition and word analysis, visual and auditory analysis of word elements, spelling, and handwriting. The tests are accompanied by check lists for observation of errors and faulty habits, and provision is made for recording pertinent information from sources other than the tests.

APPENDIX

A. Remedial-reading vocabulary for primary grades

The following list of 754 words was compiled for use in preparing for older children suitable remedial-reading materials with a vocabulary at the primary-grade level. It was derived by first selecting the words of highest frequency in the Faucett-Maki list. These were then checked against the International Kindergarten Union list and the Fitzgerald list in order to make sure that the words finally included are known and used by children.

The list contains 90 per cent of the words ordinarily used in the written compositions of children in the intermediate grades and is therefore also useful as a remedial-spelling list.

Complete alphabetical list of 754 words

The number before each word indicates its frequency; for example, "1" means that the word is among the most frequently used words in the list, while "7" means that it is least frequently used at this level.

1 a	7 alive	2 any	4 bad	4 being
7 able	1 all	7 anybody	5 bag	4 believe
1 about	4 almost	5 anything	4 ball	5 bell
3 above	3 alone	7 apart	7 bank	7 belong
7 absent	3 along	7 apple	5 barn	3 best
6 across	5 already	1 are	4 basket	2 better
7 act	5 also	5 arm	2 be	3 between
7 add	7 although	4 around	3 bear	1 big
6 address	4 always	2 as	7 beat	7 bill
4 afraid	3 am	3 ask	5 beautiful	3 bird
3 after	7 among	7 asleep	4 because	4 birthday
6 afternoon	7 amount	1 at	3 bed	5 bit
2 again	2 an	4 ate	3 been	3 black
3 against	1 and	2 away	3 before	5 blow
4 ago	7 angry	7 awful	6 beg	3 blue
7 ahead	4 animal		4 began	5 board
6 air	3 another	4 baby	6 begin	4 boat
7 alike	3 answer	2 back	5 behind	6 body

359

3 book	5 child	3 does	7 fed	4 glad
7 born	3 children	7 doesn't	5 feed	7 glass
3 both	7 choose	3 dog	3 feel	1 go
7 bother	7 church	7 dollar	5 feet	7 gold
7 bottom	4 city	4 done	5 fell	5 gone
7 bought	6 class	5 don't	6 felt	2 good
5 box	4 clean	3 door	4 few	3 got
2 boy	6 clear	2 down	5 field	7 grade
5 bread	7 climb	5 draw	7 fight	3 gray
6 break	3 close	5 dress	5 fill	4 great
7 bridge	7 cloth	5 drink	3 find	4 green
5 bright	7 clothes	6 drive	3 fine	7 grew
4 bring	5 coat	6 drop	7 finger	5 ground
7 broken	4 cold	7 dry	6 finish	5 grow
5 brother	7 college	7 during	4 fire	3 guess
6 brought	6 color		3 first	
3 brown	2 come	4 each	6 fit	2 had
7 brush	5 company	5 ear	5 five	3 hair
6 build	7 cook	4 early	6 fix	3 half
7 burn	7 cool	6 east	5 floor	3 hand
7 business	6 copy	3 eat	5 flower	7 handle
5 busy	5 cost	4 egg	5 fly	7 hang
2 but	2 could	6 eight	7 fold	7 happen
7 button	7 count	4 either	7 follow	4 happy
4 buy	4 country	6 else	7 food	3 hard
2 by	5 course	4 end	6 foot	7 hardly
	3 cover	4 enough	1 for	3 has
2 call	6 cross	3 even	6 forget	6 hat
2 came	5 cry	4 evening	7 forgot	1 have
1 can	7 cup	5 ever	3 found	7 haven't
7 candy	3 cut	4 every	3 four	1 he
6 can't		5 everything	7 free	3 head
5 cap	5 dance	6 except	3 friend	3 hear
3 car	5 dark	7 excuse	2 from	3 heard
6 card	2 day	5 expect	6 front	6 heart
4 care	6 dead	3 eye	7 fruit	6 heavy
4 carry	7 decide		5 full	5 held
6 case	6 deep	5 face	5 fun	2 help
3 cat	2 did	4 fair	7 funny	2 her
3 catch	6 didn't	4 fall		2 here
7 caught	6 die	6 family	5 game	5 hide
6 cause	5 different	3 far	5 garden	4 high
7 cent	6 dig	4 farm	3 gave	5 hill
7 certain	4 dinner	3 fast	2 get	2 him
3 chair	1 do	7 fat	3 girl	1 his
4 change	7 doctor	4 father	2 give	5 hit

4	hold	3	laugh	6	mine	7	office
5	hole	4	lay	5	minute	5	often
4	home	6	lead	4	miss	3	oh
3	hope	4	learn	7	mistake	2	old
7	horn	7	least	7	mix	1	on
5	horse	5	leave	5	money	3	once
5	hot	5	left	4	month	1	one
7	hour	6	leg	3	more	4	only
2	house	2	let	3	morning	3	open
2	how	3	letter	3	most	3	or
4	hundred	7	lie	3	mother	7	order
5	hungry	7	life	7	mountain	3	other
7	hunt	7	lift	5	move	6	ought
7	hurry	4	light	3	Mr.	4	our
7	hurt	2	like	5	Mrs.	1	out
		4	line	3	much	2	over
1	I	7	listen	6	music	4	own
7	idea	1	little	2	must		
3	if	3	live	1	my		
5	I'll	2	long	6	myself		
1	in	2	look				
7	inside	7	lose	3	name		
6	instead	5	lost	3	near		
7	interest	5	lot	4	need		
2	into	3	love	3	never		
7	iron	6	low	3	new		
1	is			7	news		
1	it	2	made	6	next		
2	its	6	mail	6	nice		
		2	make	3	night		
5	jump	2	man	7	nine		
2	just	2	many	2	no		
		6	mark	7	nobody		
3	keep	3	matter	5	noise		
4	kept	2	may	7	nor		
7	kick	1	me	7	north		
7	kill	2	mean	7	nose		
5	kind	7	measure	1	not		
5	knew	7	meat	6	note		
7	knock	3	meet	3	nothing		
3	know	5	men	2	now		
		7	middle	5	number		
6	lady	3	might				
4	land	6	mile	7	o'clock		
5	large	3	milk	1	of		
3	last	4	mind	3	off		

7	price
6	print
4	pull
7	push
2	put
6	quick
5	quiet
6	quite
3	rabbit
5	rain
2	ran
6	rather
4	reach
4	read
5	ready
6	real
7	really
4	reason
7	receive
3	red
4	remember
4	rest
7	rich
5	ride
4	right
5	ring
6	river
5	road
7	rock
4	roll
4	room
4	round
7	rubber
7	rule
2	run
7	sad
7	safe
2	said
7	sail
7	sale
3	same
4	sat
6	save

6	page
7	paid
7	paint
4	paper
4	part
5	party
4	pass
6	past
3	pay
7	pencil
4	people
6	person
7	pick
5	picture
5	piece
4	place
7	plan
6	plant
2	play
2	please
4	point
5	poor
7	possible
7	pound
7	pour
7	practice
3	present
4	pretty

2 saw	2 so	6 sweet	4 town	2 when
2 say	7 soft	7 swim	7 trade	2 where
3 school	6 sold		4 train	6 whether
6 sea	2 some	4 table	3 tree	1 which
7 seat	4 something	2 take	7 trip	5 while
4 second	5 sometime	4 talk	7 trouble	3 white
1 see	7 son	6 teach	4 true	2 who
3 seem	5 song	7 teeth	3 try	4 whole
5 seen	3 soon	2 tell	4 turn	7 whom
5 sell	7 sorry	4 ten	2 two	6 whose
3 send	6 sound	4 than		2 why
4 sent	6 south	2 thank	3 under	6 wide
4 set	5 speak	1 that	7 understand	1 will
6 seven	7 spend	1 the	3 until	5 win
4 several	7 spoil	3 their	1 up	5 wind
7 sew	6 spring	1 them	4 upon	5 window
5 shake	7 stamp	2 then	2 us	5 winter
5 shall	4 stand	1 there	3 use	3 wish
1 she	7 star	5 these		1 with
7 shine	4 start	1 they	3 very	3 without
6 ship	7 state	3 thing	6 visit	5 woman
5 shoe	7 station	3 think		6 wonder
7 shoot	5 stay	5 third	7 wagon	7 won't
4 short	7 steal	2 this	4 wait	5 wood
7 shot	6 step	4 those	3 walk	4 word
5 should	3 still	6 though	6 wall	3 work
4 show	7 stitch	5 thought	2 want	6 world
7 shut	5 stone	6 thousand	6 war	2 would
6 sick	3 stop	3 three	5 warm	7 wouldn't
5 side	6 store	7 threw	1 was	7 wrap
6 sign	3 story	7 through	6 wash	3 write
6 silk	7 straight	7 throw	5 watch	7 written
7 since	7 strange	7 tie	2 water	6 wrong
4 sing	4 street	4 till	3 way	6 wrote
7 sir	5 strong	2 time	1 we	
5 sister	7 struck	7 tire	6 wear	5 yard
5 sit	7 study	1 to	6 weather	3 year
4 six	3 such	4 today	4 week	4 yellow
7 size	6 suit	4 together	7 weigh	3 yes
7 skin	4 summer	5 told	2 well	6 yesterday
3 sleep	5 sun	5 tomorrow	1 went	4 yet
7 slip	7 supper	2 too	2 were	1 you
7 slow	5 suppose	3 took	6 west	3 young
5 small	3 sure	5 top	7 wet	2 your
7 smoke	5 surprise	6 touch	1 what	6 yourself
5 snow				

List by frequency-of-use levels—Level 1

a	do	in	of	the	we
about	for	is	on	them	went
all	go	it	one	there	what
and	have	little	out	they	which
are	he	me	see	to	will
at	his	my	she	up	with
big	I	not	that	was	you
can					

Level 2

again	come	him	many	said	two
an	could	house	may	saw	us
any	day	how	mean	say	want
as	did	into	must	so	water
away	down	its	no	some	well
back	from	just	now	take	were
be	get	let	old	tell	when
better	give	like	over	thank	where
boy	good	long	play	then	who
but	had	look	please	this	why
by	help	made	put	time	would
call	her	make	ran	toe	your
came	here	man	run		

Level 3

above	best	close	fine	has	matter
after	between	cover	first	head	meet
against	bird	cut	found	hear	might
alone	black	does	four	heard	milk
along	blue	dog	friend	hope	more
am	book	door	gave	if	morning
another	both	eat	girl	keep	most
answer	brown	even	got	know	mother
ask	car	eye	gray	last	Mr.
bear	cat	far	guess	laugh	much
bed	catch	fast	half	letter	name
been	chair	feel	hand	live	near
before	children	find	hard	love	never

new	other	send	their	under	wish
night	pay	sleep	thing	until	without
nothing	present	soon	think	use	work
off	rabbit	still	three	very	write
oh	red	stop	took	walk	year
once	same	such	tree	way	yes
open	school	sure	try	white	young
or	seem				

Level 4

afraid	clean	high	point	start
ago	cold	hold	pretty	street
almost	country	home	pull	summer
always	dinner	hundred	reach	table
animal	done	kept	read	talk
around	each	land	reason	ten
ate	early	late	remember	than
baby	egg	lay	rest	those
bad	either	learn	right	till
ball	end	light	roll	today
basket	enough	line	room	together
because	evening	mind	round	town
began	every	miss	sat	train
being	fair	month	second	true
believe	fall	need	sent	turn
birthday	farm	only	set	upon
boat	father	our	several	wait
bring	few	own	short	week
buy	fire	paper	show	whole
care	glad	part	sing	word
carry	great	pass	six	yellow
change	green	people	something	yet
city	happy	place	stand	

Level 5

already	barn	blow	brother	company
also	beautiful	board	busy	cost
anything	behind	box	cap	course
arm	bell	bread	child	cry
bag	bit	bright	coat	dance

dark	full	leave	ring	sun
different	fun	left	road	suppose
don't	game	lost	seen	surprise
draw	garden	lot	sell	these
dress	gone	men	shake	third
drink	ground	minute	shall	thought
ear	grow	money	shoe	through
ever	held	move	should	told
everything	hide	Mrs.	side	tomorrow
expect	hill	noise	sister	top
face	hit	number	sit	warm
feed	hole	often	small	watch
feet	horse	party	snow	while
fell	hot	picture	sometime	win
field	hungry	piece	song	wind
fill	I'll	poor	speak	window
five	jump	quiet	stay	winter
floor	kind	rain	stone	woman
flower	knew	ready	story	wood
fly	large	ride	strong	yard

Level 6

across	didn't	heavy	quick	teach
address	die	instead	quite	though
afternoon	dig	lady	rather	thousand
air	drive	lead	real	touch
beg	drop	leg	river	visit
begin	east	low	save	wall
body	eight	mail	sea	war
break	else	mark	seven	wash
brought	except	mile	ship	wear
build	family	mine	sick	weather
can't	felt	music	sign	west
card	finish	myself	silk	whether
case	fit	next	sold	whose
cause	fix	nice	sound	wide
class	foot	note	south	wonder
clear	forget	ought	spring	world
color	front	page	step	wrong
copy	hair	past	store	wrote
cross	hat	plant	suit	yesterday
dead	heart	print	sweet	yourself
deep				

Level 7

able	church	haven't	paint	soft
absent	climb	horn	pencil	son
act	cloth	hour	person	sorry
add	clothes	hunt	pick	spend
ahead	college	hurry	plan	spoil
alike	cook	hurt	possible	stamp
alive	cool	idea	pound	star
although	count	inside	pour	state
among	cup	interest	practice	station
amount	decide	iron	price	steal
angry	doctor	kick	push	stitch
anybody	doesn't	kill	really	straight
apart	dollar	knock	receive	strange
apple	dry	least	rich	struck
asleep	during	lie	rock	study
awful	excuse	life	rubber	supper
bank	fat	lift	rule	swim
beat	fed	listen	sad	teeth
belong	fight	lose	safe	threw
bill	finger	measure	sail	throw
born	fold	meat	sale	tie
bother	follow	middle	seat	tire
bottom	food	mistake	sew	trade
bought	forgot	mix	shine	trip
bridge	free	mountain	shoot	trouble
broken	fruit	news	shot	understand
brush	funny	nine	shut	wagon
burn	glass	nobody	since	weigh
business	gold	nor	sir	wet
button	grade	north	size	whom
candy	grew	nose	skin	won't
caught	handle	o'clock	slip	wouldn't
cent	hang	office	slow	wrap
certain	happen	order	smoke	written
choose	hardly	paid		

B. Durrell-Sullivan reading vocabularies for grades four, five, and six derived from word counts of books commonly used in each grade

Some of the most urgent problems among slow learners, especially in the intermediate grades, could be helped by a knowledge of the words most frequently used in books. Thorndike has shown that books recommended for a single grade level reveal a wide range of vocabulary.

The number of words to be met by the child in any of the intermediate grades is apparently almost limitless, while his power of learning words is definitely limited to a small fraction of this total. Economy in learning, then, demands that lists be drawn up of words most frequently encountered by children in reading in each of the intermediate grades. Such lists would be an aid not only in direct vocabulary instruction, but also in teaching transfer skills such as word-analysis and word-derivation methods. They would also assist in making a better correlation between the reading vocabularies and those of writing, spelling, and composition.

The books selected for the present study were reading series and social-studies books, with a few books in natural science, found to be in wide current use for each of the intermediate grades. Seventeen books were used for grade four, twenty for grade five, and nineteen for grade six. While the basal readers predominate, social-studies books were included because under present curriculum tendencies the social-studies work provides a large part of the reading program.

In counting the words, only those words were recorded which do not appear in the Gates Primary list. In the final list words are included which appeared in seven or more books at each grade level. Words appearing in the lower-grade lists are, of course, not repeated in the later lists. It seemed more desirable to use a basis of one or more appearance in each of seven books than to use a total frequency count, since a single book might use a word so frequently that it would be weighted incorrectly in the final list.

The size of a word list is, of course, determined by the criterion used for including the word in the list. For the purposes of the author it was desirable to have lists of from 500 to 700 words at each of the grade levels. The criterion of use in at least seven of the books for the grade level was the one which produced the most satisfactory word groups. This basis for selection of words yielded 691 words in the fourth-grade list, 525 words in the fifth-grade list, and 849 words in the sixth-grade list. While it would be desirable to have an increase in the number of words for each grade, rather than the marked dropping off in the number for the fifth grade, it seemed best for various reasons not to change the basis of word selection for an individual grade.

Selected vocabulary for grade four

a	T^1	$B-D^1$	balcony	10	4
abide	4a	6	balk	9	5
ablaze	17	—	banister	18	5
abode	4a	7	banquet	3b	5
absent	3a	KU	bargain	3a	4
abuse	3b	6	barren	3b	5
acre	2b	5	baste	10	3
action	2a	3	beacon	10	2
actor	5a	3	behave	4a	3
addition	2b	2	bellows	17	3
adopt	3a	—	bewilder	7	7
adore	4a	6	blade	2b	2
adventure	3b	5	blast	3a	3
advertise	5a	6	bleach	6	6
agent	4b	4	blessed	1b	KU
agree	2a	4	blinds	—	KU
airship	17	2	blinker	—	2
alien	7	6	blister	6	7
almond	7	5	blizzard	11	4
alter	3b	5	blood	1b	KU
alternate	6	6	bluff	5a	4
anger	2	4	blunt	4b	—
annoy	5b	3	bolt	3a	5
antelope	13	6	bomb	9	5
appetite	3b	4	boost	13	7
appoint	2a	5	bore	2b	3
arch	2b	6	boss	6	KU
arctic	5b	—	bound	2a	2
army	1b	2	brace	4b	2
arrest	4a	KU	bracket	9	6
artist	3b	3	bravery	5a	8
attire	4b	7	bray	9	3
attract	4a	6	breathe	2a	6
avoid	2b	4	bribe	5b	—
awe	4a	5	brief	2b	4
awl	17	6	brilliant	4a	4
			brisk	5a	—
b	T	$B-D$	broad	1b	3
bacon	4a	KU	bureau	3b	KU
badge	6	KU	bustle	7	7

---

[1] The column headed "T" shows the rating of the word in the Thorndike list; the column headed "B–D" shows the grade placement in the Buckingham-Dolch list.

c	T	B–D			
cab	6	KU	continue	1b	4
cabinet	4b	KU	contrary	3a	3
cactus	10	8	control	2b	3
calk	16	—	coral	5b	5
calm	2b	5	couch	3a	KU
cancel	8	5	council	2b	4
canoe	4b	KU	coupon	11	5
canopy	9	6	courage	2b	4
capable	3b	5	cove	9	5
carcass	8	—	cramp	8	3
cargo	4b	3	crank	8	KU
carver	13	—	crate	7	3
cash	3b	2	credit	3a	4
cashier	6	5	creep	2b	2
cast	2a	2	crest	4a	5
central	2b	3	crew	2a	5
cereal	8	2	crude	6	7
challenge	6	5	crust	4a	3
chamber	2a	4	curate	11	—
chapel	3a	6	custard	9	5
charge	1b	3			
charter	4b	5	d	T	B–D
cheat	4a	2	dagger	6	5
chef	18	KU	daily	2b	2
chest	2b	KU	dainty	4b	3
chew	6	KU	damage	3b	4
chief	1b	KU	damp	3b	2
chilly	8	4	darn	6	KU
choir	4b	5	dazzle	5a	7
chorus	7	4	deal	1b	3
chuckle	6	8	decide	1b	3
click	10	2	declare	2a	4
cling	5a	2	deface	9	7
clutch	5a	5	defeat	3b	5
coach	2b	3	defend	2a	5
coax	8	5	delight	1b	2
combine	3a	6	dent	13	2
comical	10	6	depart	2a	5
commence	3b	5	deposit	3b	4
compound	5b	2	desire	1b	4
conceal	3a	6	dessert	7	6
concert	4a	5	difficult	2a	5
congress	2b	4	dike	12	2
consume	4a	7	dilute	11	8
content	2a	4	direct	1b	3
			discuss	4a	6

disease	2b	4		expel	5b	7
dismal	4b	4		eyesight	9	5
dismiss	3b	4				
dispatch	7	6		f	*T*	*B–D*
distance	1b	4		fable	4a	2
distress	3a	4		fade(less)	2b	2
district	2b	3		failure	5a	5
ditch	3a	KU		faith	2a	3
dose	7	2		false	2b	KU
drain	2b	5		falsehood	4b	4
drift	4a	3		famous	1b	3
drill	2b	KU		faucet	10	KU
drip	4a	2		female	3a	4
drug	3b	2		fencing	—	—
dull	3a	2		fender	12	4
dumb	3a	2		ferocious	11	7
dump	8	KU		ferry	5a	KU
dusk	6	3		fever	2b	3
dwell	2b	3		fiber	19	6
dye	4a	3		fidget	14	—
				fiery	3b	6
				file	3a	2
e	*T*	*B–D*		film	5b	5
ebony	8	7		filthy	6	5
education	3a	3		flash	2a	2
elastic	5b	5		flask	9	4
elect	2a	4		flesh	2a	4
electric	3a	KU		foliage	6	6
elegant	4b	5		folk	2a	2
elevate	4b	4		fondle	16	8
else	1b	KU		foreign	2a	3
embark	7	8		forenoon	4a	3
emblem	9	4		forge	4b	5
embrace	3a	5		form	1a	2
engineer	4a	KU		fort	2b	3
enter	1b	3		fountain	2b	KU
envy	3a	6		frame	2a	2
erect	2b	4		fraud	5b	8
escape	1b	3		frightful	6	5
event	2a	4		frigid	9	4
evergreen	7	4		froth	11	—
evil	2a	4		frown	3b	2
exact	2a	4		fudge	—	5
examine	2b	4		furnace	3b	KU
example	2a	3		furnish	2a	3
exchange	2b	2		furniture	2b	KU

g	T	B–D		hatchet	5a	KU
gale	4a	2		haughty	4a	7
gallery	4a	6		haven	5b	8
gallon	5b	2		heap	2b	2
gaseous	8	6		height	1b	2
gem	2b	2		hem	4a	KU
generous	3a	5		herd	2b	2
germ	6	KU		hint	4b	3
ghost	2b	3		hitch	8	KU
glance	2b	3		hither	3a	7
gleam	4a	5		hobby	7	8
glide	3b	2		hobo	—	6
glimpse	5a	8		holiday	2b	2
globe	3a	3		holy	2a	3
gloomy	5a	4		homesick	7	5
glory	2a	3		homespun	10	8
glossy	8	5		homestead	7	8
glue	5b	KU		honest	2a	3
glutton	12	8		honor	1b	2
gnash	10	—		hoof	3a	2
governor	2a	4		hook	2b	KU
gown	2b	KU		horrible	3b	6
grab	8	KU		hostile	5b	8
grade	2b	KU		hovel	5a	5
grammar	5a	3		human	2a	4
granite	5b	4		hustle	7	6
grant	1b	3		hysterics	11	8
grasp	4a	7				
gravel	5b	4		i	T	B–D
grease	5b	2		iceberg	9	2
grief	2b	4		ideal	4a	4
groove	6	7		idiot	5a	6
group	2b	3		idle	2b	4
guest	2a	3		illness	5b	5
gypsy	8	3		immense	3b	5
				imp	11	5
h	T	B–D		import	3b	5
habit	3a	2		improve	2b	4
halibut	14	6		impure	11	8
halt	4a	2		infant	3b	5
halter	7	7		inhabit	4a	6
harbor	2b	4		injure	3a	4
hardy	4a	—		inland	5a	--
harp	4a	2		inquire	3a	5
harvest	2a	5		insect	3a	4
haste	2a	2		instant	2b	5

intend	2a	3	launch	5a	5
introduce	3a	2	laurel	4b	7
itch	6	2	lawyer	3b	3
ivory	3b	4	leak	6	2
ivy	5a	6	lecture	4b	5
			leisure	5a	6
j	T	B–D	lemon	4a	KU
jail	5b	KU	lens	10	3
jaw	3a	KU	leopard	8	4
jealous	3b	3	level	2a	4
jelly	4a	KU	library	2b	KU
jest	4b	3	lice	11	2
jet	5a	3	limb	2b	3
jewel	3a	3	linger	4a	3
jingle	8	4	links	3b	—
jitney	—	—	liquid	3b	5
job	3a	KU	litter	5b	2
jog	10	—	loan	7	3
jolly	4a	2	loosen	6	—
judge	1b	3	lounge	9	6
juice	4a	KU	lucky	4a	3
junior	5a	2			
jut	6	—	m	T	B–D
			machine	2a	KU
k	T	B–D	mackerel	11	4
keen	3b	2	magic	3a	2
kennel	8	6	magnet	7	6
kerosene	6	5	magnify	5a	6
keyboard	15	—	manage	2b	4
kidnap	12	4	manger	6	KU
kiln	13	—	maniac	15	7
kimono	12	6	manner	1b	2
kindle	4a	4	margin	5a	3
kindling	—	7	marine	6	6
kink	19	—	mattress	7	KU
knight	2a	KU	mayor	3a	4
			medicine	2b	KU
l	T	B–D	meek	4a	2
labor	1b	3	megaphone	20	7
lacy	—	—	mellow	5a	3
laden	4a	3	melon	6	3
lame	3a	2	memory	2a	4
language	2a	2	menu	13	5
lapse	7	—	mercy	2b	4
larceny	16	8	merit	3a	4
latch	5a	2	mesh	8	—

word	T	B–D	word	T	B–D
metal	2b	4	rib	3a	2
midget	20	5	rifle	5b	3
migrate	7	—	rigid	7	—
mild	2b	2	rinse	11	7
military	3a	5	risk	4a	3
millinery	10	5	rob	2b	2
mince	6	4	royal	2a	3
			ruby	5b	5
p			rude	2b	2
prairie	5b	4	ruin	2a	5
principal	2b	5	rummage	12	—
puppet	13	—	rust	3b	2
purchase	2a	5	rut	13	2
q	*T*	*B–D*	**s**	*T*	*B–D*
quarter	1b	KU	saint	2b	2
quill	9	5	salad	5b	KU
quilt	5a	KU	saliva	8	—
quotient	9	2	salmon	6	3
			sandal	7	KU
r	*T*	*B–D*	sank	4a	2
racket	12	4	satisfy	2a	4
rage	3a	2	sauce	4a	KU
railroad	2a	KU	scale	2a	2
ramble	8	—	scarce	2a	5
range	2a	4	scare	3a	KU
rank	2a	2	scarf	4a	KU
ransom	5b	5	scatter	2a	3
rapid	1b	5	scrape	3b	KU
rare	2b	3	scratch	3a	KU
rave	5a	3	screw	5a	2
razor	6	5	scrub	5a	4
read	3b	2	seal	2b	2
recent	3a	5	seldom	2b	4
recess	3b	KU	senior	6	4
record	2a	KU	sense	2a	3
recover	2b	3	sensible	4b	5
refuse	2a	4	separate	1b	3
relation	3a	4	serene	5a	3
remnant	4b	7	serious	2b	4
remove	2a	4	service	1b	2
rent	2a	2	settle	1b	2
repair	2a	3	settler	4a	5
repeat	2a	4	shallow	3b	5
report	1b	2	shame	2a	2
rescue	3b	7	shanty	18	5

shark	9	2	thrash	5a	—
shave	4b	3	threat	5a	8
shelve	4b	4	thrill	4a	2
shield	3a	4	tickle	5a	4
shovel	4b	KU	tide	2b	2
sink	2a	KU	tile	4a	2
situate	3b	5	trace	2a	KU
slice	4b	KU	trail	3b	2
snore	6	2	trash	11	2
snout	7	5	tread	2b	2
social	3b	6	trench	5a	4
spatter	10	—	trespass	6	6
special	2a	4	triangle	6	KU
sphere	3b	4	trickle	8	—
sprawl	10	6	trinket	10	5
stagger	4a	8	trumpeter	12	4
stake	3b	2	turpentine	7	KU
stale	4b	3	twine	4a	3
stall	3b	2	twist	3b	3
startle	4b	8	typewriter	5b	4
stiffen	8	—			
stingy	18	5	u	T	B–D
streak	6	7	uncertain	4b	8
stuff	2b	KU	understand	1b	3
sulky	11	8	uneasy	5a	7
			unequal	6	8
t	T	B–D	unfit	5a	4
tab	13	2	unfold	5a	8
tack	6	2	union	2a	2
talkative	15	7	unite	1b	3
tank	4b	KU	unknit	—	—
tape	6	2	unless	2a	KU
tart	6	2	unloosen	14	—
tax	2a	2	uplands	8	—
taxicab	14	7	upset	5a	2
teeming	7	—	usual	1b	4
telegraph	4a	3			
temper	3a	4	v	T	B–D
tenant	5a	5	vacation	3b	KU
tender	2a	2	vain	2a	2
terrify	6	4	value	1b	2
test	2b	2	vapor	3a	6
thicken	7	—	variety	3a	2
thief	3a	3	veil	3b	3
thimble	6	KU	vein	3a	3
thistle	4b	—	vex	3a	6

view	1b	4	weight	1b	2
vigil	7	—	wept	3b	2
villain	5a	4	wicked	2b	3
vote	2b	3	wisdom	2a	3
vowel	7	2	witty	5b	8
voyage	3a	3	wondrous	4a	7
vulgar	5b	5	wreath	3a	3
			wreck	3a	KU
w	*T*	*B–D*	wreckage	19	8
wage	2b	5	wrench	5a	4
wail	4a	2	wriggle	11	—
waist	2b	KU			
waive	14	—	y	*T*	*B–D*
waltz	15	3	yelp	8	—
wander	2a	2	yowl	—	—
warn	2b	2			
waste	1b	KU	z	*T*	*B–D*
wealthy	3b	3	zeal	3b	7
weaver	6	—	zone	3a	3

Selected vocabulary for grade five

a	T	B–D
accident	3a	2
accomplish	2a	5
accord	4a	6
accuse	3b	7
acquit	9	—
active	3a	5
actually	6	—
advise	2b	6
affair	2b	5
affectionate	5b	5
airtight	18	—
alternate	6	6
amazingly	—	—
ancestor	4a	6
anxious	2b	6
apology	7	7
approach	2a	4
armor	3a	3
arrival	3a	6
astir	14	—
astonishment	5b	—
astride	13	—
audience	4a	6
aviator	15	3

b	T	B–D
bade	3a	3
baggage	7	KU
bargain	3a	4
barrel	3a	KU
barrier	5b	7
bawl	8	KU
bayberry	20	—
bazaar	15	5
beacon	10	2
bemoan	9	—
billow	5a	7
bin	8	2
bind	2a	2
bishop	4b	5
blacksmith	3a	KU
blast	3a	2

blest	5a	2
blunt	4b	—
bluster	10	—
boast	2b	4
bodice	14	—
bolt	3a	5
boom	8	KU
borrow	3a	3
brew	6	5
brood	4a	3
bulb	5b	KU
bumper	10	7
bury	2a	4
butternut	—	6

c	T	B–D
canal	3a	5
canvas	3b	6
career	4b	6
carnation	11	KU
cathedral	4b	6
caustic	14	—
cavalier	6	7
central	2b	3
chamois	14	8
char	13	—
charcoal	8	5
charm	2a	3
christen	10	6
cipher	—	—
clad	4a	2
claim	2a	2
cleft	6	—
cliff	3a	2
clump	9	3
cluster	3b	7
cockpit	—	8
collie	17	3
combine	3a	6
comforter	5b	—
commander	4b	4
committee	3b	4
commotion	7	7

companion	2a	4		disguise	3b	5
compare	2a	4		disgust	5b	6
compass	2b	4		dispute	3a	5
complain	2b	5		distress	3a	4
comrade	4a	5		district	3b	3
confess	3a	5		disturb	3a	5
conquer	2b	5		doily	12	KU
conscience	3a	5		dome	4b	2
contain	1b	4		doubtless	4a	5
container	12	—		dragon	3b	3
contemptuous	7	—		drawbridge	13	8
control	2b	4		dreary	5b	5
conversation	3a	4		drubbing	—	—
costume	5b	4		duffer	—	—
courtier	4b	—				
crag	6	3		e	*T*	*B–D*
crisis	8	—		earthenware	9	—
croak	5a	KU		elbow	3b	2
crunch	20	3		elder	3b	—
cuckoo	4b	KU		embrace	3a	5
cultivate	5a	5		embroider	5b	5
cunning	3a	2		emerge	6	7
curiosity	5a	5		encouragement	8	7
custom	2a	4		endure	3a	5
cylinder	5b	7		energetic	8	7
				enormous	3a	5
d	*T*	*B–D*		entry	4a	6
dart	3a	2		ere	2a	3
dash	2a	2		erect	2b	4
debate	3b	4		ermine	13	6
decay	3a	2		eruption	9	6
deceive	2b	5		essential	5b	5
decorate	6	KU		estimate	4a	5
definite	6	6		event	2a	4
delicate	3a	5		exclaim	3a	4
delicious	4a	3		expensive	4a	5
depth	3a	4		explore	4b	4
descendant	7	8		extra	4a	2
deserve	2b	3		extraordinary	4b	6
despair	3a	7				
detach	9	7		f	*T*	*B–D*
dike	12	2		fame	2b	2
dipper	6	2		fertile	4a	6
disagreeable	6	4		fertilizer	6	5
disappearance	11	8		festival	4b	6
discourage	4a	5		finally	2a	—

firm	1b	3
flannel	6	5
fleece	4b	5
flint	5b	2
fluid	4b	8
footman	6	7
forehead	2b	4
forge	4b	5
fortunate	3b	5
fortune	2a	3
fragment	5b	7
friction	7	6
frisk	9	—
frock	5a	3
fuel	3b	3
furious	3b	4
furrow	5a	3
future	2a	3

g	T	B–D
gait	5b	4
gasp	6	—
gather	1b	2
gauge	2b	5
gaze	9	7
gentian	14	—
geometry	9	6
geranium	8	KU
gild	4a	—
glare	4a	3
glint	11	—
glitter	3a	6
goblin	9	5
gourd	10	—
grackle	—	—
grasp	4a	7
grateful	3a	4
gravity	7	7
graze	3b	4
gridiron	—	8
grieve	3a	5
groove	6	7
grove	2b	3
gruel	10	8
gurgle	13	7

h	T	B–D
hangar	10	—
hastily	5a	6
hasty	4b	—
haul	5a	KU
haycock	11	3
heap	2b	2
hearty	4a	3
heave	3b	—
hedgerow	11	—
helmet	4b	6
herb	4a	—
highway	4a	5
hither	3a	7
horizontal	7	7

i	T	B–D
ignition	13	7
imagination	3b	4
immediate	2a	4
immense	3b	5
immortal	3a	6
impatient	5a	6
impress	5a	6
imprison	5a	6
improve	2b	4
inhabit	4a	6
inherit	4a	6
injure	3a	4
instant	2b	5
instantly	8	—
intelligent	5b	5
invention	3b	4
investigate	6	4
irregular	4b	4
irritable	9	—
irritate	7	7
isle	3a	5

j	T	B–D
jagged	17	—
jaundice	13	—
jaunt	18	—
jiffy	16	—
joint	3a	3

jostle	7	6	morsel	6	6
judgment	2b	3	motionless	7	7
			motor	4a	KU
k	*T*	*B–D*	mournful	5b	5
keen	3b	2	mourning	5b	—
knead	8	6	mucilage	17	6
knell	4a	3	murder	3a	3
knickers	—	—	murmur	3a	2
			muskrat	12	5
l	*T*	*B–D*	muster	6	7
lance	4a	3	mystery	3a	6
lash	5a	3			
lever	9	KU	**n**	*T*	*B–D*
liberty	2a	2	nasturtium	13	KU
lilac	10	KU	native	2a	4
lime	4a	2	necessary	1b	4
linden	7	6	necessity	3a	6
linger	4a	3	nectar	13	8
link	3b	2	nimble	5b	3
liquid	3b	5	noble	2a	3
lo	4b	—	nonsense	5a	3
lodge	6	—	noose	11	3
loft	8	3	nosegay	14	—
lofty	3b	6	notch	8	6
lye	15	2	nursery	6	5
m	*T*	*B–D*	**o**	*T*	*B–D*
majesty	3b	5	oath	7	6
mansion	4a	5	obedient	5a	3
mart	9	—	obscure	5a	7
marvelous	3b	3	obtainable	10	5
meek	4a	2	occupy	2a	4
mellow	5a	3	offer	1b	4
midst	3a	3	officer	1b	3
mighty	2a	2	opportunity	2b	5
minstrel	6	6	orchard	2b	3
miraculous	8	8	ordeal	12	—
mischievous	7	5	ordinary	3a	6
mistress	2b	3			
miter	6	—	**p**	*T*	*B–D*
moat	8	3	paddle	6	KU
model	2b	5	pant	3a	2
moist	4a	3	panther	10	5
molasses	8	4	paraffin	10	8
monoplane	—	7	particular	2a	4
monster	4b	3	partridge	6	—

	T	B–D			T	B–D
patent	5a	3	ravine	11	5
patience	3a	5	realize	3b	4
pause	3b	5	rebel	3b	6
peak	4b	3	reflect	4a	7
peal	4b	2	refrain	5a	4
pelt	8	8	reliable	6	3
perspiration	11	6	relish	6	—
persuade	3b	7	remarkable	3b	5
pester	12	8	repeat	2a	4
physical	5b	5	reverence	4a	5
pioneer	5b	3	reverse	4b	6
pirate	6	3	rheumatism	7	5
piston	11	7	ridiculous	6	5
piteous	12	—	ripple	5a	2
pivot	8	—	roam	3b	2
plead	3b	5	rogue	5a	3
plentiful	5a	6	romance	6	7
plunge	3a	3	roost	11	2
population	3a	4	rosin	12	7
porcupine	9	3	royal	2a	3
porridge	10	KU	rude	2b	2
porter	4b	5	rustle	4b	6
potash	12	—			
pottery	11	2	**s**	**T**	**B–D**
practice	1b	3	sacrifice	2b	5
precious	2b	4	sausage	5b	4
preen	19	—	scandalize	12	—
presently	7	6	scenery	7	5
prim	12	8	scent	4b	5
prime	4a	4	sentinel	10	6
procession	4b	3	sexton	10	5
progress	3a	4	shark	9	2
prolong	4a	6	shift	3b	7
protest	4b	4	shilling	7	6
provide	2a	3	shiver	3b	3
provoke	3b	6	shred	8	7
public	1b	2	shriek	3b	—
purpose	1a	4	shudder	6	5
			simpleton	15	—
r	**T**	**B–D**	slack	6	3
raccoon	17	2	slight	2a	3
radiant	5a	5	smite	4b	8
radical	7	8	snare	4b	5
rage	3a	2	snip	10	3
rally	—	—	snort	7	8
raven	3b	5	snuggle	—	—

word	T	B-D	word	T	B-D
sociable	13	7	tunic	10	—
solemn	3b	5	tunnel	5b	KU
solution	5b	6	tureen	—	—
solve	3b	5	turmoil	11	
soot	9	2	turntable	—	—
spiral	9	8	turret	6	—
split	3b	2	twilight	3b	3
stadium	16	4	twine	4a	3
stain	3a	2	twitter	6	3
stall	3b	2			
statute	6	8	u	T	B-D
stock	1b	2	umpire	9	5
streak	6	7	unaccustomed	12	6
stride	4b	3	uncanny	—	—
stubborn	4a	5	uncomfortable	5b	7
student	2b	4	uncommon	6	7
stunt	9	3	unconscious	4a	6
suggestion	6	8	ungrateful	5b	8
surveyor	13	8	unoccupied	7	—
swerve	7	7			
			v	T	B-D
t	T	B-D	vacant	3b	6
tallow	8	5	valueless	16	—
telescope	8	6	vat	9	—
tenant	5a	5	vault	4a	4
terrace	6	5	venerable	7	8
territory	3a	5	venison	7	6
terror	2b	6	venture	3b	5
tether	10	—	veranda	12	7
thatch	8	7	vertical	6	7
thicket	4b	KU	viand	11	—
thoughtful	5a	4	vineyard	6	5
thrifty	6	5	violent	3b	6
throb	15	—	vision	3b	5
throng	3b	5	volcano	7	5
throttle	11	6	volume	3a	4
tranquil	6	6	vow	3a	4
transform	5a	7			
transparent	7	7	w	T	B-D
tread	2b	2	waft	6	—
treasure	2a	3	waggle	—	—
tremendous	5a	3	waistcoat	9	6
triangular	10	6	wait	1a	KU
trim	2a	KU	wander	2a	2
trout	5a	2	warrior	3a	3
trudge	7	—	wary	8	—

wayfarer	20	—		withdraw	3a	7
weapon	3a	4		wizard	5a	5
weary	2b	6		woodcraft	—	—
weird	6	—		writhe	9	—
wharves	8	—		wry	12	—
whinny	20	—				
whir	11	—		y	*T*	*B–D*
whisk	6	7		yearn	5a	6
whittle	14	—		yeast	7	2
whiz	9	5		yonder	3a	5
wicket	11	7		yule log	—	—

Selected vocabulary for grade six

a	T	B–D	b	T	B–D
abandon	4a	6	bacteriology	18	—
abbey	6	7	baffle	7	—
abbot	7	7	ballast	9	—
abolish	5b	6	bandanna	7	7
abound	5b	7	barbaric	9	—
abyss	6	4	barbecue	12	8
accentuate	13	—	barometric	—	—
acute	7	7	barrage	16	—
adaptation	8	—	basis	4b	6
admiral	5a	6	baton	19	—
admiration	4a	4	bauble	10	—
adverse	6	—	beam	2a	3
aerial	7	5	becalmed	15	—
aeronautics	—	—	belfry	12	7
agonize	12	—	besiege	5a	8
alabaster	9	8	bevy	13	—
alacrity	12	—	bewitch	7	8
allegiance	5b	5	bier	8	—
allies	—	7	bladder	8	8
alpaca	19	6	blemish	7	—
animate	6	8	blubber	11	6
annihilate	9	8	bobbin	18	7
anoint	6	—	bombardment	12	—
antics	10	6	boon	5b	—
application	3b	6	booty	7	—
apprentice	9	7	bowsprit	17	—
arcade	15	—	braggart	14	—
aromatic	8	—	bramble	6	—
array	4a	6	brandish	8	—
artificial	5a	5	brawny	14	7
astronomer	8	7	brazier	16	—
astronomy	12	5	brigade	11	6
atom	8	8	brooch	8	7
audacious	11	—	buffet	5b	KU
august	18	—	bulrush	12	8
authority	2b	6	bunting	7	8
autograph	15	6	buoyant	8	8
automatic	7	5	buzzard	11	7
avenge	5b	3			
aviation	15	6			
azure	6	7			

c	T	B–D
caisson	—	—
calculate	7	6
caliph	14	—
capsize	13	6
captor	17	6
carat	15	—
caravan	6	7
carbine	18	—
castanet	—	—
casual	6	7
cataract	6	7
cavalcade	17	—
cavernous	16	—
census	10	6
ceremony	4a	6
certificate	5b	5
chamberlain	7	—
champ	13	—
chandelier	13	6
chant	5a	—
chasm	8	7
chemical	8	6
cherish	5a	—
chink	7	3
chore	13	5
cinch	18	—
circuit	4b	6
circulate	8	—
citadel	10	—
citron	10	—
cloister	9	8
cloven	15	—
cockle	10	—
codger	—	—
coffer	9	—
collision	9	6
comet	7	5
commend	3b	—
commodore	12	8
compact	5a	5
companionable	18	—
compartment	10	8
competent	9	7
competition	6	8
confine	4a	6

	T	B–D
confirm	4a	5
confiscation	15	—
conjecture	7	7
conscious	7	—
conservation	7	8
constable	6	5
constructive	16	—
contrive	6	—
coöperation	8	7
corduroy	12	6
cornice	10	8
counselor	8	8
coupling	9	—
courier	11	7
crane	7	2
croon	14	6
crucial	16	—
crucible	13	—
cruiser	10	7
crystalline	12	—
cylindrical	13	—
cymbal	8	7

d	T	B–D
damask	11	—
damsel	5a	7
data	10	2
dawdle	15	—
dean	6	5
decade	7	6
defiant	9	8
deficiency	7	—
delegate	5b	7
derelict	—	—
design	3a	KU
desolation	5b	6
desperation	10	—
detail	4a	7
determination	7	7
devour	4a	3
dialogue	7	7
diameter	8	4
diligent	5a	4
dingy	9	—
dirigible	15	4
disappointment	4b	4

disaster	5b	4	exaltation	12	—	
disciplinarian	—	—	exceeding	5a	—	
discordant	10	—	excelsior	20	7	
disembark	13	—	exertion	8	—	
distinction	3b	—	exhaust	4a	6	
distinguish	3b	6	experiment	5a	6	
distract	5b	5	exploit	5b	—	
divan	11	—	exposure	8	8	
divert	7	7	extensive	5a	7	
divinity	6	8				

f	T	B–D
faculties	5a	—
falter	6	7
fantastic	6	7
fascinate	7	7
fatal	3b	6
fawning	7	—
fertility	17	—
filament	8	—
filigree	8	—
fiord	13	6
flagon	14	—
flange	12	—
flaunt	9	—
flintlock	—	—
flounder	7	4
flourish	3b	6
flue	12	6
flume	—	—
flurry	12	—
font	12	—
forceps	15	8
ford	4a	5
foul	3a	5
fracas	20	—
fragile	8	5
fraught	7	—
freshet	16	—
friar	5b	3
fricassee	20	—
fruitless	7	—
fusillade	—	—

document	6	5
dolphin	8	8
dormitory	12	4
doublet	11	—
dramatize	10	4
drought	8	—
dullard	—	—
dusky	6	7

e	T	B–D
edifice	5b	—
edition	6	5
editorial	8	7
efficiency	9	6
elapse	8	6
eliminate	7	6
elusive	17	—
embalm	10	—
emboss	10	—
emerald	7	5
emerge	6	7
emergency	7	5
emit	9	—
encounter	3b	7
endurance	8	7
engrave	7	6
entreaty	8	8
enunciate	16	8
episode	9	—
escort	6	8
essential	5b	5
establishment	5b	6
etch	14	3
evaporate	8	3
eventide	12	—
exalt	4b	3

g	T	B–D
gala	16	—
gallery	4a	6

	T	B–D		T	B–D
galley	8	6	hearse	16	6
garland	4a	7	heather	10	—
gasket	—	—	heave	3b	—
gaunt	6	—	hectic	14	—
gauntlet	10	8	heiress	14	6
genial	4b	8	helium	19	8
genius	3a	6	helm	5a	5
genuine	5a	5	herald	5a	7
gigantic	7	7	heredity	10	—
gill	7	2	heroic	4b	6
girder	20	7	herring	8	3
glacier	6	5	hexagon	11	8
glade	6	3	hieroglyphic	12	—
globule	12	8	hilarious	17	8
gnome	15	4	hospitality	7	7
goad	9	—	host	2b	3
gored	5b	—	hulk	9	—
gorge	6	5	hull	8	2
gouge	16	—	humane	7	3
gram	12	7	humiliate	9	8
granular	11	8	hydrogen	7	7
grapple	9	8			

i	T	B–D
greensward	14	— (left col)
grievous	5a	6
grotesque	8	—
grub	8	2
guidance	9	—
gusty	10	—

i	T	B–D
ignoramus	—	8
illustrious	5b	—
immaculate	9	7
impend	8	—
imperious	8	—
implement	5a	6
impostor	9	7
impressive	8	—
imprint	12	—
impulse	7	—
incubator	11	8
infancy	6	—
inflate	10	—
inmate	10	—
inscription	7	6
insolent	8	—
insolvent	16	—
instantaneous	14	7
instruction	3a	4
integrity	7	7
intense	6	6
invade	4a	6
invisible	4b	5

h	T	B–D
habitual	8	—
haggard	8	—
halo	15	2
halyard	—	8
hamlet	4b	5
hamper	8	5
handicap	8	4
harmonica	—	5
harpoon	17	5
hart	5a	2
haunch	10	—
haunt	3b	5
haven	5b	8
hawser	16	—
hazard	5b	8
haze	9	7

irate	—	—		larder	11	—
iridescent	20	8		larkspur	16	—
irony	12	—		larynx	13	8
irritant	9	—		lath	14	—
irritation	9	7		lattice	15	8
isolate	7	8		laud	10	—
				lavish	5b	—
j	*T*	*B–D*		lax	13	—
jag	13	—		lease	7	5
jargon	14	—		lecture	4b	5
jasper	11	—		ledge	5b	4
jaunty	11	—		lee	4b	—
jealous	3b	3		legend	5b	6
jerk	7	5		liege	18	—
jet	5a	3		lilt	16	—
jib	14	7		liter	14	7
jonquil	18	—		livelihood	8	8
journal	5b	5		livery	5b	7
jubilant	14	—		loath	8	8
jubilee	6	—		lobe	11	—
judicious	8	8		locality	7	—
juncture	15	—		locust	6	6
jury	6	5		loiter	6	7
justify	4a	6		lope	11	—
juvenile	13	7		lore	10	—
				lout	17	—
k	*T*	*B–D*		ludicrous	10	8
keel	8	7		lurch	11	—
kernel	7	6		lure	5b	7
kindred	4a	6		lurk	4a	—
kine	10	—		luscious	18	7
kingpin	—	—		lusty	5b	—
knapsack	16	3		luxurious	7	8
knave	4a	4		luxury	3a	7
knell	4a	3				
knelt	9	3		**m**	*T*	*B–D*
knoll	6	—		mackerel	11	4
knowledge	2a	3		majority	3a	6
knuckle	10	5		malice	5a	5
				mandolin	18	6
l	*T*	*B–D*		manifest	4a	7
laboratory	8	5		mantle	3b	6
laborious	10	7		martial	19	7
laggard	12	—		martyr	5a	6
lair	8	2		marvel	4a	5
lament	4a	7		massive	7	6

matron	6	7		notary	9	7
meager	7	—		notation	13	7
medical	5b	5		notorious	7	—
meditate	5b	8		noun	10	5
memorial	4a	4		novel	5a	6
menace	8	5		novelty	4b	6
mermaid	9	7		novice	8	—
meteor	6	6		nuzzle	—	—
metric	12	7		nymph	5a	—
mimic	9	7				
miraculous	8	8		o	T	B–D
monastery	9	7		oaten	15	—
monotonous	12	7		objective	14	7
monstrous	4a	5		obligation	5b	—
mortal	2b	7		oblivion	8	—
mortality	7	8		obscene	9	4
mosaic	9	6		observation	4a	6
motif	15	—		obstacle	5b	7
motive	3b	—		obstinate	5b	7
mummy	9	7		obvious	7	6
murderous	8	—		occupant	8	8
mysterious	4b	6		oculist	16	7
mythology	10	8		offensive	7	7
				onslaught	15	—
n	T	B–D		opiate	13	—
nape	15	—		opinion	2a	5
naphtha	14	8		opponent	7	7
narrate	12	7		oppose	3a	7
narrative	7	7		optimistic	17	8
nasal	9	8		oracle	5a	—
nationality	8	5		orator	6	7
naturalist	12	7		orchestra	5b	KU
nausea	15	—		orchid	11	7
nauseate	19	—		ordinary	3a	6
nautical	12	—		organist	9	5
navigate	10	5		organize	4b	5
negative	6	6		original	3a	5
niche	12	—		oust	15	—
nick	7	2		outwit	15	—
nigh	4a	3		overwhelm	5b	7
nitrogen	7	8		oxygen	6	6
nocturnal	12	—				
nominate	8	6		p	T	B–D
nomination	6	6		pacify	11	8
nondescript	16	—		pact	—	—
normal	5a	5		palate	10	8

pallet	13	—	prey	3a	7
palpitate	18	—	primitive	7	5
palsy	9	—	principle	3b	5
parachute	12	6	prior	7	7
parchment	7	6	portable	9	6
parole	19	7	portico	14	—
partial	5b	7	probe	10	—
peat	19	3	product	2b	3
pedestrian	12	7	profession	5a	6
pedigree	9	—	profusion	13	—
penal	12	8	prohibit	5a	6
pension	6	8	project	5a	8
perceive	3a	6	prominent	4a	6
percentage	9	5	promote	6	4
percolator	20	—	prophesy	5a	8
percussion	—	—	prospective	9	—
perplex	4b	7	prostrate	6	—
persevere	7	7	protest	4b	4
personal	3b	4	prow	10	6
peruse	7	—	prudent	5a	—
pessimist	16	8	publish	3a	4
pheasant	10	7	pun	13	2
phosphorus	18	—	purity	5a	4
photoplay	—	—	pursue	2b	7
pinafore	15	—	pursuit	4b	6
pinion	8	8			
pinnacle	8	5	q	*T*	*B–D*
piston	11	7	quaint	5a	2
pithy	14	—	quarry	5a	6
placid	7	—	quartet	13	4
plague	3b	7	quaver	11	—
plastic	10	—	quell	6	—
plausible	11	—	quest	5b	6
plight	5b	5	queue	—	—
pneumatic	12	—	quicken	4a	3
poacher	19	—	quince	14	7
politics	4a	7	quiver	4a	—
portal	6	5	quoit	12	—
pose	9	2	quota	14	—
precipice	7	7			
preface	8	6	r	*T*	*B–D*
prejudice	6	7	rabble	8	7
prelate	7	—	radiation	16	7
premium	7	6	radium	13	6
prescribe	4a	8	rafter	6	7
prescription	9	7	raid	8	2

rampart	9	4		scepter	4b	8
rapier	14	—		schedule	6	3
ration	7	—		scholar	4a	3
ravage	8	—		scientist	7	5
realization	9	—		scorn	3a	7
reassure	8	7		scramble	6	3
recipe	9	6		scribe	9	7
recline	7	8		scrimmage	—	—
reconcile	4a	8		scrutiny	12	—
recount	6	—		sculptor	8	7
recruit	7	7		seclusion	13	6
recur	9	—		secretary	3b	5
referee	17	7		sedate	13	7
reforestation	—	—		seedling	8	—
regale	14	—		seep	17	3
rejoice	2a	6		sensation	7	7
reluctant	7	8		sentry	12	5
repair	2a	3		serf	8	7
reptile	8	7		sewerage	19	—
reserve	3	4		sheaf	6	7
resign	3b	6		sheen	10	6
resinous	10	—		sheer	8	—
resist	4a	5		shellac	13	8
resonant	16	—		shelter	2a	3
resource	6	4		sheriff	6	4
respect	2a	4		shift	3b	7
reveal	3a	5		shoal	8	—
reverse	4b	6		shrewd	5a	7
review	2b	3		shrivel	10	—
revise	7	7		shroud	5b	—
rind	9	2		shuttle	11	8
ringlet	9	—		siege	5b	6
rivulet	7	8		signature	5b	3
rocket	9	5		silt	19	—
roller	5a	KU		simplicity	4b	3
routine	8	7		sinister	9	—
rural	3b	—		skein	10	5
				skirmish	7	—
s	*T*	*B–D*		slash	8	6
sage	4a	3		sledge	5a	4
sanctuary	5a	8		sliver	19	—
sapling	8	8		sluice	10	—
scabbard	9	—		smite	4b	8
scaffold	7	8		smooch	—	—
scandal	6	4		sober	3a	6
scanty	5b	—		solemnity	7	—

soluble	8	7		tango	—	—
spaniel	10	—		tank	4b	KU
spectacular	12	—		tanner	14	6
sphinx	11	7		tannic	19	—
spoil	2a	KU		tapestry	6	6
spout	6	2		tarry	5a	5
squeal	13	3		taunt	9	—
squid	18	—		taut	8	—
squirm	13	7		tawny	8	—
squirt	14	KU		telegraphy	4a	6
stadium	16	4		temporary	5a	8
stagnant	7	—		tense	17	7
stalwart	17	7		tension	12	8
stanch	9	8		terrace	6	5
standard	2b	2		terse	19	—
staple	7	7		test tube	—	—
stationer	16	2		tether	10	—
statuary	10	6		textile	10	6
stealthy	12	—		thorough	2b	5
stenographer	10	5		thresh	17	—
stimulate	7	7		thrifty	6	5
stockade	10	5		throttle	11	6
strategy	12	—		tinker	16	3
strode	8	6		token	4b	5
strove	5b	—		toll	7	7
strut	6	6		tourney	14	—
studio	11	6		tow	6	2
sublime	5a	7		trammel	15	—
subtle	5b	8		transit	8	4
subway	10	3		tremulous	7	—
sucker	9	KU		tropic	6	4
sunder	7	7		truce	11	7
superb	9	—		tumult	5a	7
suppliant	9	—		turbulent	7	—
surgeon	7	5		turmoil	11	8
surgery	8	8		tutor	5b	6
survive	5a	8		typist	16	6
suspense	9	8				
swath	20	—		**u**	*T*	*B–D*
sympathetic	8	8		underhanded	18	—
system	2a	4		undertake	3a	5
				unfortunate	3b	6
t	*T*	*B–D*		unique	9	7
tackle	7	6		unpalatable	—	—
tallyho	—	—		unstable	11	8
tambourine	15	KU		unstrung	—	—

	T	B–D		T	B–D
unwise	7	6	vitamin	11	8
upheaval	15	—	vivacious	14	8
upright	3a	3	vivid	5b	6
uprose	11	—	vocalize	6	—
urge	2b	6	vogue	6	—
utensil	7	5	volunteer	7	5
utilize	8	8	vulcanize	18	—
utter	2b	7			
			w	T	B–D
v	T	B–D	waddle	11	—
vagabond	8	6	wafer	8	—
vagrant	7	—	waffle	20	5
vague	6	7	wallop	18	6
valise	16	6	wallow	8	8
valor	5a	4	wane	7	3
valued	3a	—	wanton	4b	—
vaudeville	17	5	weft	—	—
vegetarian	18	—	weld	8	—
vehicle	7	5	wheedle	11	—
vellum	14	8	whit	7	4
velocity	9	8	wicker	13	5
vender	14	—	wigwag	—	—
veneer	11	8	windlass	10	—
vengeance	4a	6	wither	3b	4
ventilate	9	5	wobble	19	—
venture	3b	5			
verdant	11	—	y	T	B–D
vermin	16	7	yacht	11	5
vesper	9	7	yam	20	—
vexation	6	—	yearling	13	8
vibrant	14	—	yeomen	9	8
vicinity	6	5	yield	2a	5
victim	4a	4	yolk	10	3
violate	4b	6	youthful	4a	8
viper	7	7	yuletide	—	—
vise	14	7			

C. Word-pronunciation test for intermediate grades

The test [2] that follows was designed to measure pupil ability in word recognition and word analysis. It contains word elements typical of those in intermediate-grade reading, although some extremely difficult and infrequent words are used to provide a measure of superior pupils.

When the test is used to measure word analysis, it is scored very leniently. Any pronunciation which includes all of the sounds in correct order is accepted. Simple analysis will not always reveal correct sounds of vowels, some consonants, silent letters, syllable division, or accented syllables.

The directions for giving the test are as follows:

1. The test is duplicated in clear and legible typewriting or printing.
2. The child reads across the page, not down the columns.
3. Each word is marked as follows:
   a) Place a plus (+) after words immediately recognized and readily pronounced.
   b) Place a check (√) after words for which an acceptable pronunciation is given after a brief hesitation or analysis.
   c) Place a minus (−) after words in which sounds are omitted, incorrect, or in wrong order. Score minus any word not pronounced after seven seconds.
4. Discontinue testing when five *successive* words are failed.

The grade medians given are based on the sum of plus and check scores. The medians are tentative; approximately 200 pupils from each grade were included in the study. This test may be duplicated for school or research use but not for commercial publication. Data to supplement norms will be welcome.

Boston University word-pronunciation test — Form A

before	comfort	enclose	nation
honor	depend	reject	justice
notch	value	disturb	venture
observe	bolster	compile	inspector
abash	terrace	banish	projection
vertical	pendulum	abnormal	excess
scientist	vivid	superintendent	emerge
embankment	companion	ruminate	engage
invalid	gossamer	advertise	incomparable

[2] This test was designed as a group Ed.M. project by Mary T. Chapman, Mary J. Hernblad, Harold E. Johnson, Shirley Lai, and Florence M. Ross. The thesis is on file in the Boston University School of Education Library. Ed.M., 1955.

rudimentary
circumstance
interrogate
identical
abbreviation
unquenchable
misconception
materialize
retribution
prerogative
proportionate
impartial
audacity
resiliency
menispermaceous
balsaminaceous

dialect
denominator
predatory
congratulations
exemplary
mortality
antagonize
allegiance
exigency
embryonic
horticultural
complacency
valedictorian
presumptuous
philoprogenitiveness
vivacious

pugilist
predicament
certification
exhilarate
subsequent
gauntlet
eccentric
numismatics
thermonuclear
genial
excommunicate
lexicographical
indefatigable
infinitesimal
deteriorate
petrologically

inimical
fascination
abdicate
specify
resignation
intercolumnar
commemoration
dereliction
ingenious
endocardium
voluminosity
subterranean
peripheral
juxtaposition
actinodielectric
facultative

GRADE MEDIANS: *Grade 4—27   Grade 5—50   Grade 6—69*

Boston University word-pronunciation test — Form B

broken
normal
halter
conjure
enormous
whither
liniment
deliberate
readjust
vertebrate
precious
notation
indigent
concentric
exorbitant
unattainable
surveillance
notorious
fraudulent
vivisection
accoutrement
autointoxication
sarcophagus
ejaculatory
enigma

mountain
product
receive
motorist
justify
taut
fortunate
insolvent
garner
artificial
botanical
verdure
adhesive
jurisdiction
perspiration
gentian
refractometer
dissemination
rehabilitate
infuriate
executioner
maladroitly
iconography
thermogalvanometer
bibliophilistic

report
impend
elect
submerge
emergency
emplacement
discordant
trampoline
cavernous
soluble
nationality
fortification
reticent
preliminary
unconscious
impeccable
devaluate
unequivocal
condescension
restitution
odontornithic
adjudicate
sublapsarian
extemporaneous
similitudinize

builder
correct
agent
infuse
abide
promotion
governmental
valise
admonish
heraldic
designate
porcelain
reverberate
empirical
audible
monoplanetary
luxurious
ingenuity
emphasis
masticatory
iniquity
undenominational
predecessor
pronunciamento
ricinoleate

GRADE MEDIANS: *Grade 4—27   Grade 5—51   Grade 6—70*

INDEX

J
K
L
M